Resilient Life

For Those Past and Present who we
Continue to Collaborate with
'In Confidence'

—— Resilient Life ——

The Art of Living Dangerously

Brad Evans
and
Julian Reid

Polity

First published in 2014 by Polity Press
Reprinted 2015

Polity Press
65 Bridge Street
Cambridge CB2 1UR, UK

Polity Press
350 Main Street
Malden, MA 02148, USA

ISBN-13: 978-0-7456-7152-9
ISBN-13: 978-0-7456-7153-6(pb)

A catalogue record for this book is available from the British Library.
Typeset in 11 on 13 pt Sabon
by Toppan Best-set Premedia Limited
Printed by CPI Group (UK) Ltd, Croydon, CR0 4YY.

The publisher has used its best endeavours to ensure that the URLs for
external websites referred to in this book are correct and active at the time of
going to press. However, the publisher has no responsibility for the websites
and can make no guarantee that a site will remain live or that the content is
or will remain appropriate.

Every effort has been made to trace all copyright holders, but if any have been
inadvertently overlooked the publisher will be pleased to include any
necessary credits in any subsequent reprint or edition.

For further information on Polity, visit our website: www.politybooks.com

'Finished, it's finished, nearly finished, it must be nearly finished'

Samuel Beckett, *Endgame*

'It may be that believing in this world, this life, becomes our most difficult task, or the task of a mode of existence still to be discovered'

Deleuze and Guattari, *What Is Philosophy?*

Contents

Preface and
Acknowledgements

Michel Foucault's *Preface* to Gilles Deleuze and Felix
Guattari's *Anti-Oedipus* is a standalone work every student
of politics should read *before* they are indoctrinated by the
tyranny of positivism. Allowing us to denounce all trite
readings of his *oeuvre* as criticism for criticism's sake, this
politically charged essay provided us with clear and meticulous guidelines for a liberated existence. Capturing the
mood of the times, the target for Foucault's intervention
was not simply an increasingly dominant neoliberalism
revealing of its own novel fascistic tendencies, but the
orthodox voices on the Left whose political artistry (*ars
politica*) was more than complicit in the perpetuation of
oppression as it failed to challenge power on its own terms.
Foucault took direct aim here at what he termed the 'sad
militants' of theory who were incapable of withdrawing
their allegiance from the 'categories of the negative'. The
spirit of this critique is most relevant today. For the power
of the negative remains as dogmatic as ever – albeit
shrouded in the new guise of an authenticated vulnerability that underwrites our concerns in this text. Revising,
then, Foucault's work in light of the new cartography of
political power in the twenty-first century, we maintain

that every intellectual project of a political kind should follow a number of basic principles:

(1)   Be deeply suspicious of anything that masks itself in universal regalia. Bring into question that which is not being questioned in the *normal* state of affairs.

(2)   Move beyond any self-righteous and self-absolving assessments of the operations of power. Look to deal with power at the level of its effects and the ways in which it positively manipulates subjects to wilfully abandon their own political freedoms.

(3)   Foreground the affirmative qualities of subjectivities. Not only is this integral in the fight against fascism in all its forms. It opens a challenge to the narcissism of those who would have us surrender to the mercies of the world.

(4)   Speak with confidence about the ability to transform the world, not for the better, but for the sake of it. Without an open commitment to the people to come, the struggle is already lost.

(5)   Use provocation as a political tool. Not to evidence extremist views. But to illustrate how normalizing power truly fears anything that appears remotely exceptional. The poetic most certainly included.

(6)   Trust in the irreducible qualities of human existence. The feelings we have, the atmospheres we breathe, the aesthetics we enfold, the fables we scribe, the playful personas we construct, they are all integral to the formation of a new image of thought.

(7)   Have faith in people. Just as they will resist what they find oppressive and intolerable, so they will also find their own dignified solutions to problems in spite of our best efforts.

(8)   Do not shy away from conflict. Without conflict there is no resistance to power. And without

resistance to power there is no creation of alternative existences.

(9) Reveal fully your political orientations. Do not abstract them from the work. Such a deception is of the order for those embarrassed by the mediocrity of their power.

(10) Speak with the courage to truth that narrates a tale to affect a number of meaningful registers. No book should be read if it doesn't intellectually challenge and emotionally move us.

Just as there is no affirmation to be found in a technical pursuit of happiness, so is there nothing compelling to any political prose that does not excite our imagination to compel us to live our lives differently. Such a journey begins by challenging what seems to be reasoned, benevolent and in keeping with the logic of the times. Both of us came to the problematic of this book by adopting precisely this angle of vision. We detected before everyone else that resilience was becoming ubiquitous, and hence this is the first substantial political critique of the concept. While its traces were already well established in a number of fields, it was apparent to us that the political sciences were going to become fully complicit with its influence. While the mergers of security, development and ecology permitted the cross-fertilization of ideas on systemic resilience, thereby introducing the term into our political lexicon, soon it became a key term of art deployed by funding bodies and human resource departments that were seeking to promote both the resilience agenda and resiliently-minded academics. We were especially troubled by the pace with which this doctrine went from being an ill-defined curiosity to a universal dogmatism that was bereft of any rigorous critical reflection. Our work was to take the prevailing mantra that we 'must all learn to become more resilient' and question the ontological and epistemological assumptions out of which this dogmatism had emerged with such speed. The political stakes could not be clearer to us. More than simply asking that academics study resilience so that we could improve the lives of oppressed peoples, providing new ways to authenticate and disqualify the meaning of lives in times of unending crises, resilience presented a new form of political intervention, impacting upon all aspects of human existence and experience.

But what did it mean to be academically resilient? And what assumptions underwrite this demand such that to question it is seemingly futile? A number of these assumptions became very evident to us by simply looking at the prevailing dogma of those in the worlds of policy and notably the fields of ecology, economics and psychology which had a particular lead (not surprisingly) to political academies still mourning the demise of its sovereign stranglehold that once afforded, albeit in a deluded way, some privileged position in the world. Resilience spoke the language of insecurity as the natural order of things; it made itself morally imperative on account of its relationships to catastrophic reasoning as a logical response to unavoidable major crises; and it presented itself as a universal attribute, one that required us to learn the complex skills of adaptation and bouncebackability. None of this is controversial from the perspective of survivability, unless of course we consider the political stakes. As academics, should we, for instance, accept that our working environment is fundamentally insecure by design? Must we simply accept our vulnerable and precarious status as producers, such that education, like anything else, is prone to catastrophic failure? What does it really mean for academics in the social sciences and humanities to actively partake in a world that promotes vulnerability as the authentic basis for intellectualism? What would an intellectual commitment to survivability look like, given the continued neoliberal assault upon academia wherein success increasingly appears to be a precarious conformity to the dominant yet crises-laden mantra of the times? How did we come to think that individuals and societies must accept catastrophe as the start point for comporting themselves towards the future? And what does it mean to deny us the possibility of constructing new imaginaries and concepts for political belonging beyond the catastrophic imaginaries of late liberal rule? We have been compelled to question and rethink the meaning of our acknowledgements given this state of affairs. What does it mean, after all, to give acknowledgement to an intellectual project such that we stay true to the principles we outlined above? This book undeniably owes a tremendous personal debt to some remarkable colleagues with whom we have shared our ideas, thoughts and problems. Not that we hoped that they would respect some confidentiality pact – as if we could only impart our ideas to a select few who we believed wouldn't give the game away until it was ready for market so to speak. We have no fear for the sharing of ideas. Every one of us is a collaborator of multiple kinds. We maintain that friendships worthy of the name demand giving over the work to those who will offer a rigorous critique and infidelity to the prose. It is done so *with* confidence. And so it is to the critically minded in our midst, those who have the courage to speak truth to power that we begin our acknowledgements and offer our sincerest gratitude. Their names are sufficiently etched throughout this text for those who are intrigued to know more about our sources of inspiration to be able to recognize.

Increasingly in academia we are being forced into a confidential deception. On the one hand, there is the need to authenticate and establish ownership of the work. Such crude assessments which accompany this prove to be a mockery to the notion that genuinely original thought never appears in the most established of places. And yet, as academics, we are also forced to accept that our contributions may only resonate today for the briefest of moments. For the next crisis on the horizon, we are told, in all its catastrophic permutations, invalidates all that went before. To operate in the academy today, then, is to be as vulnerable as anybody else operating in late liberal

xiv   Preface and Acknowledgements

societies. Confidence and principles about reclaiming the
meaning of the University as such go out of the window
as we are told to accept the intellectual realities of the
times. The friendships we openly celebrate with colleagues
and students alike categorically reject this model which, at
best, continues to lead to the promotion of intellectual
mediocrity, while at worst, naturalizing new forms of insecurities by disingenuous careerists who militaristically continue to rank and profile colleagues. And so we acknowledge
intellectuals worthy of the term, who still believe that the
essential function of the University is to continue to hold
power to account. We thank those who refute the crudity
of intellectual quantification, and find motivation in the
field of critical pedagogy not simply for the sake of education as a public good in itself, but out of a love for the
impossible, the intangible, and for the poetry of imagining
and crafting lives that may be lived with dignity and
freedom. We remain inspired by those who put a lifetime
of principled effort into their works, so they may forever
outlive their own wilful capture so common in the one-
dimensional personalities of reasoned experts.

Academia is a fraught and sometimes openly hostile
place, especially for those of us who have never really been
on the 'inside' of any particular school or movement, as if
that is any reflection on an intellectual corpus which is
primarily driven to interrogate the conditions of the new.
While both of us can personally relate to encounters with
previous colleagues who appeared more like 'thought
police' as they preferred to suffocate or diminish the force
of our ideas instead of celebrating intellectual differences,
in these testing times, we have been thankful to the personal advice and institutional support offered to stay true
and principled to the work. We have also found allies with
those who we continually collaborate with *in absentia*.
Whether we return to the enriching words of Friedrich
Nietzsche, Michel Foucault, Hannah Arendt, Gilles
Deleuze and Jacques Derrida, who continue to teach us
that another political imaginary is possible, or the creative

and illuminating force that still resonates through the works of Franz Kakfa, Ingmar Bergman, Bertolt Brecht, Lewis Carroll, George Orwell, Samuel Beckett, Francis Bacon, and Philip K. Dick, our project is fully indebted to those who sided with the poetic over and above the tyrannical attempts to make our political imagination the servant of a normalizing reason. And so we acknowledge here the real revolutionary figures – the poetic subjects of our historical present, who continue to shape our existence in the most creative, compelling and affirmative ways.

The real wonder of any book is the way in which it potentially forces pasts, presents and futures to collide. It is made up of all our past experiences, many of which may seem insignificant or fleeting at the time, and yet may end up profoundly influencing our contemporary sense and perception of 'the world' which is always, ultimately, 'our world'. We sometimes forget to acknowledge these chance encounters, brief moments of disruption, which nevertheless constitute the complex archive of our minds and its connections to the material and immaterial facets of existence. Further to this, there is always the prospect it will resonate beyond the *body of the text*. If the work works at all, it must perform and function in ways that the authors could not have envisaged during its production. While this inevitably leaves us open to malicious and arbitrary readings by those who fail to properly engage with the integrity of the prose, hopefully it will also bring about transformations in the thought processes of its readership, not to establish a gospel or creed, but to inspire the creation of new subjectivities that continue to condemn the abuses of power and the greying of existence by those who demand that we surrender ourselves to the mercies of the world. Nietzsche once gave to us his arrows so that unknown thinkers could pick them up and fire in new directions. And so we acknowledge and welcome those encounters with academics, students and poets yet to have happened, with a certitude that they will continue to transform our lives, in hope of a new time to come, and against political imaginaries that continue to construct a fascistic earth.

That said, there are some debts to be paid and acknowledgements to be made to those who have truly helped us along the way of the writing of this text. We both wish to thank the organizers of the Resilience Workshop at the University of Copenhagen, Denmark, for a truly mind-blowing experience that affirmed to us with renewed vigour and intellectual purpose why this project was important, if not untimely in terms of its reception in a policy-dominated field. We also extend our most sincere appreciation to Louise Knight and all the Polity team for their continued professionalism, integrity and commitment to critical pedagogy. They remain a shining light in a world of publishing increasingly driven by the power of conformity and the seduction of mediocrity.

Brad Evans would like to thank Tom Osborne for his continued support and guidance while Head of School and his colleagues within the Global Insecurities centre at the University of Bristol, who foster a truly collegial and welcoming environment. A special mention goes to Henry A. Giroux, Mark Duffield, Michael Shapiro, Saskia Sassen, Sam Weber, Simon Critchley, Gregg Lambert, Keith Tester, Terrell Carver, Raymond Bush and Michael Dillon for their continued guidance and inspiration. Friendship is extended to Nadine Boljkovac for her compassion and poetic commentary on a variety of issues. Brad would also like to thank all the members of The Society for the Study of Bio-Political Futures. He remains honoured and privileged to be part of such a vibrant and generous collective of pioneering scholars. Students past and present forever remain a source of inspiration. Long may you continue to remain suspicious of the prevailing dogma and deception of those who only reason to teach mediocrity on account of their intellectual limitations! He remains blessed by the timelessness of personal bonds of friendship and the care of his wonderful family. None of this, however, would be possible were it not for the continued love and support of

Christine, and the presence of his beautiful daughter Amelie who is growing into the most delightful, intelligent and endearing little girl.

Julian Reid thanks his friends at the University of Nottingham Malaysia, Mika Aaltola at the Finnish Institute for International Affairs, friends at the University of Lapland, and Dan and Nandita Mellamphy at the University of Western Ontario, Canada, for invitations to keynote events, where many of the ideas developed in this book were first tried out. He also thanks participants at the IPSA Conference at the University of Madrid, Spain, the Western Political Science Association Annual Meeting in Portland, Oregon, the Association of American Geographers Annual Meetings in New York and Seattle, United States, the International Studies Association North East Annual Conference in Providence, United States, the Global Studies Conference, Rio de Janeiro, Brazil, the State and State-Building: Theory and Practice in Retrospect Conference, Belgrade, Serbia, the National Security and Strategic Contexts Conference, National Institute for Advanced Study, Bangalore, India, the International Studies Association Convention in New Orleans, United States, all of which were also useful events. In addition, the Violence and the Environment Workshop, at Coimbra University, Portugal, the Climate Change, Migration and the Border Research Conversation, University of Durham, Durham, UK, the Critical Approaches to Climate-Induced Migration Workshop, University of Hamburg, Hamburg, Germany, the Political Violence after the Death of God Workshop, University of Leeds, Leeds, UK, the International Development-Security Network Workshop, Swedish Institute of International Affairs, Stockholm, Sweden, the Politics Beyond the Biopolitical Subject Workshop, Griffith University, Australia, the Biopolitics of the Commons Colloquium, Diego Portales University, Santiago, Chile, the Calotte Academy, Inari, Finland, the Politics of the Brain Workshop, Westminster University, London, UK, the Reading Michel Foucault in the Postcolonial Present

xviii   Preface and Acknowledgements

Symposium, University of Bologna, Bologna, Italy, the Development and Colonialism Workshop, University of Vienna, Vienna, Austria, the Vulnerability Symposium, University of Otago, Dunedin, New Zealand, the Biopolitics of Development Workshop, Swabhumi, Calcutta, India, the Climate Change and Human Security Workshop, Arcticum, University of Lapland, Finland were all useful.

Thanks to Gideon Baker, Andrew Baldwin, Oliver Belcher, David Chandler, Sandro Mezzadra, Johanna Oksala, Mustapha Pasha, Manas Ray, Ranabir Samaddar, Giorgio Shani, Annika Skoglund, Jens Sorensen, Monica Tennberg, Ben Trott, Miguel Vatter and Geoffrey Whitehall, for their hospitality and invitations. He also wishes to thank Michael Dillon for the invitation to perform 'An Open Letter to Immanuel Kant' at Sehir University, Turkey as well as Marten Spangberg for the invitation to perform 'Curious Orange, Paranoid' at MDT Stockholm, Sweden, both of which performances fuelled the imaginary of this book immensely. Thanks to my students on the Biopolitics of Development and Security course taught at the University of Lapland as well as Istanbul Technical University, Istanbul, and the students on the Master's programme in Global Biopolitics at the University of Lapland. Thanks also to the Finnish Academy, the European Union and the University of Lapland for the generous funding of the research that has made his contribution to this book possible. Most of all he thanks Sandra Lolax for being the post-biopolitical subject which she is. A total inspiration.

Brad Evans and Julian Reid, 2013

– 1 –
Anthropocene

All Too Human

Friedrich Nietzsche once insisted that the surest sign of living was to forever be in danger.[1] Only now are we beginning to appreciate the political significance and consequences of this claim. As liberal regimes move beyond the security imperative so foundational to modern politics for over two centuries, along with the bounded sense of community this engendered, the dream of lasting security is being seconded by a catastrophic imaginary that promotes insecurity by design.[2] There is a long tradition of scholarly criticism of the concept of security as a political construct. Moving beyond the illusion of political neutrality, numerous authors have illustrated how security has been central to the technologies of subjectification through which liberal regimes have governed historically. But we are now in a new and distinctly different political era, defined by the emergence of a different kind of liberalism, less easy to recognize through the critical lenses of the past. As the belief in the possibility of security, once integral to the rise of the modern state and international system of states gives way to a new belief in the positivity of danger, new technologies for rule and subjectification are appearing, themselves based upon a suspicion of security, but which are no less problematic in their guiding assumptions, rationales and implications. The very concept of security itself is being shod by liberalism as it embraces not simply forms of endangerment, but a new ideal of *resilience*. Resilience is currently propounded by liberal agencies and institutions as the fundamental property which peoples and individuals worldwide must possess in order to demonstrate their capacities to live with danger. This book is the first substantial study of the significance and implications of this shift within liberalism, whereby it has seemingly embraced the Nietzschean imperative to 'live dangerously'.

Our aim, especially, is to politicize this shift by interrogating its implications for political subjectivity. What kinds of subjects do demands for resilience produce? To what kind of work is the resilient subject tasked? And what forms of life does resilience authenticate and disqualify? Answering these questions requires us to confront the ways in which resilience is aimed explicitly at encouraging subjects to live by maxims which are insecure by design. Our critique of resilience thus begins from the premise that liberalism is aimed today not at solving or preventing the manifestation of dangers and threats to security, but at making us forego the very idea and possibility of security, through the embrace of the necessity of our exposure to dangers of all kinds as a means by which to live well.

It is a fact, of course, that the future of the human species is deeply uncertain. We know ourselves to be the biggest threat to our own existence. That the earth would positively flourish were human life to be removed from it is a realization we are now forced to confront. And yet the human, it seems, has never been more important and powerful. Humans are today recognized to profoundly shape their living environment, for better or worse, more than any other species. Scientists tell us that this is not simply tied to the emergence of a new-found political sensibility or intellectual awakening. We are entering the *Anthropocene* – a distinct geological epoch that is defined by the scale of human activity. Etymologically conceived by the ecologist Eugene Stoermer, the Anthropocene was popularized by the Nobel Prize-winning chemist Paul Crutzen. For Crutzen, it is undeniable that the human species is the principal source of impact on its own lived environment. As he explains in a co-authored article with Christian Schwagerl, 'For millennia, humans have behaved as rebels against a superpower we call "Nature". In the 20th century, however, new technologies, fossil fuels, and a fast-growing population resulted in a "Great Acceleration" of our own powers. Albeit clumsily, we are taking control of Nature's realm, from climate to DNA.'[3] Not only does this imply that 'humans are becoming the dominant force for change on Earth'. It finally affirms the 'long-held religious and philosophical idea' of 'humans as the masters of planet Earth'. Hence, as the human, natural and moral spheres merge, and indeed, forcefully collide, into a consolidating framework for understanding the human's position in the world, new ethical sensibilities and modes of governance are critically sought.

The Anthropocence represents a significant departure from the homely comforts of the Holocene that was defined more by geological settlement. This is what some authors have termed the Holocene's 'stability domain'.[4] As we move into the new epoch – what we may begin to define as the 'destabilized realism of planetary endangerment' – there is no going 'back to safety' as if that ever was the lived reality of yesteryear.' Instability and insecurity are the new normal as we become increasingly attuned to living in complex and dynamic systems which offer no prospect of control. Our entire sense of what the 'life-world system' entails is invariably being transformed. As Slavoj Žižek writes:

> For the first time in history, we, humans, collectively constitute ourselves and are aware of it, so that we are

responsible for ourselves: the mode of survivability depends upon the maturity of our collective reason. The scientists who talk about the Anthropocene, however, are saying something quite the contrary. They argue that because humans constitute a particular kind of species they can, in the process of dominating other species, acquire the status of a geological force. Humans, in other words, have become a natural condition, at least today.[6]

Although humans have long since reasoned themselves to be at the centre of the universe, never before have we assumed the role of the principle architect. This comes with a formidable burden. Since this foregrounds a political imaginary of threat to create a global sense of community out of the prospect of its own planetary endangerment, humanity is bound to a formative logic that is lethally supplemented by its potential ruination. Insecurity underwrites its very existence. This gives sure impetus to a new 'responsibility of vulnerability' which stakes the future survivability of the human species on the successes/failures of its political strategies. As the Intergovernmental Panel on Climate Change's *Managing the Risks to Extreme Events and Disasters to Advance Climate Change Adaptation* (2012) report explains: 'Climate extremes, exposure, and vulnerability are influenced by a wide range of factors, including anthropogenic climate change, natural climate variability, and socioeconomic development. Disaster risk management and adaptation to climate change focus on reducing exposure and vulnerability and increasing resilience to the potential adverse impacts of climate extremes, even though risks cannot fully be eliminated'.[7] Becoming resilient, then, requires more than simply taking care of our individual precariousness. It is a planetary obligation as all forms of local instability become global cause for concern.

Vulnerability is defined as 'the propensity or predisposition to be adversely affected'.[8] This includes 'the characteristics of a person or group and their situation that influences their capacity to anticipate, cope with, resist, and recover from the adverse effects of physical events'. The notion of propensity is significant here, as it highlights a progressive (yet somewhat schizophrenic) orientation that looks *towards* the extreme ends of potential survivability. And the notion of predisposition is significant here as it suggests some *already existing* data (the guiding political presumptions) about the vulnerability of the subject. This brings together the uncertain with the certain as we encounter 'subject-centred events' in which (a) the event in all its catastrophic permutations cannot be known in advance and (b) assumptions about the subject's capacities to deal with the occurrence foster behavioural claims to empirical truth. Disaster management as such does not simply entail an ecological mode of thought, but an anthropology that, fully committed to anthropocentric reason, situates the vulnerable subject within a political drama of catastrophe which renders it the author of its own planetary endangerment. Echoing Žižek once again:

> With the idea of humans as species, the universality of humankind falls back into the particularity of an animal species: phenomena like global warming make us aware that, with all the universality of our theoretical and practical activity, we are at a certain basic level just another living species on the planet Earth. Our survival depends on certain natural parameters which we automatically take for granted. The lesson of global warming is that the freedom of humankind was only possible against the background of stable natural parameters of life on earth . . . The limitations of our freedom that become palpable with global warming is the paradoxical outcome of the very exponential growth of our freedom and power, that is, of our growing ability to transform nature around us, up to and including destabilizing the very framework for life. 'Nature' thereby literally becomes a socio-historical category.[9]

While there are a number of ways to reduce vulnerabilities, including reduced exposure, transfer and sharing of risks, preparation and transformation, resilience is key to this new ethics of responsibility defined as 'the ability of a system and its component parts to anticipate, absorb, accommodate, or recover from the effects of a potentially hazardous event in a timely and efficient manner, including through ensuring the preservation, restoration, or improvement of its essential basic structures and functions'.[10] What is truly significant here is the effective blending of the terms resilience and resistance: 'This shifting emphasis to risk reduction can be seen in the increasing importance placed on developing resistance to the potential impacts of physical events at various social or territorial scales, and in different temporal dimensions (such as those required for corrective or prospective risk management), and to increasing the resilience of affected communities. Resistance refers to the ability to avoid suffering significant adverse effects'.[11] So resistance is not a political claim that demands any form of affirmative thinking; it is a purely reactionary impulse premised upon some survivability instinct that deems the nature of the political itself to be already settled. As the subject is tasked to bounce back from the experience of catastrophe unscathed, what we encounter is a full-scale logistical enterprise wherein the human form is reduced to the barest levels of meaning. Not bare life as commonly understood in the Agambenesque sense, by which subjects are denied sovereign protection via their juridical inclusion.[12] More bare living in an organically connected sense, premised upon life's wilful *exposure* to that which makes us vulnerable.

The conflation of resistance and resilience signals the absence of any self-confidence in the liberal subject's disposition towards the world. No longer positively assured, or for that matter unrepentant in its hegemonic (sometimes portrayed as universal) vision, everywhere it appears to be under siege. Resistance is, after all, a pedagogy of relative subjugation. Much of this undoubtedly owes to the exposed relations between liberalism and its violence, which highlighted the lethality of its attempts at imposing freedoms elsewhere. What subjugates here, however, is no simple dialectical binary by which liberalism has been displaced by some greater hegemonic force. There has been no singular replacing of one system with another. Liberal societies instead are besieged by their own narcissistic impulses, which, having failed to realize the limits to their rule, has led them to a wilful abandonment of their foundational truths claims, such that their very own normative bases for rule are now riddled with self-doubt. We may argue that such universal claims to power were always a deceit, as economic rationalities continually trumped the order of the political. The imaginary has, however, radically transformed. Rather than openly declaring some vision of the future that overcomes the plagues of suffering engulfing the human species, what we encounter is a veritable landscape of projected images that is littered with corpses of our catastrophes to come.

Anthropocentric thought speaks to the emergence of global challenges. That is to say, it seeks to make sense of our radically interconnected life world system and the types of planetary threats this connectivity produces; threats which respect no geographical boundaries or disciplinary conceits. What marks a significant departure here is the debt now attributed to humanity as both a problem to itself as well as to the biosphere. The increasing political prominence given to global challenges has not only altered perceptions of national security. It is driving increased collaboration between the physical, natural and social sciences, such that previous distinctions between the natural and social worlds have been largely erased. Human life is no longer understood as distinct from any other life form. Neither can it think itself greater or lesser than the complex structuring of the universe most broadly conceived. Human problems are biospherical problems and vice versa. We only have to evidence the gradual merger between underdevelopment, security and the environment to evidence this shift towards full spectral thinking.[13] No longer is poverty, for instance, seen to be locally dangerous as it promises to exacerbate the causes of conflict. Environmental catastrophe has been added to the toxifying mix to heighten localized tensions, further decimate economies, which in turn may have unforeseen global impacts as they spill over sovereign divides. We have, then, all become part of an interconnected catastrophic topography of endangerment of which the likes of Carl Schmitt could have had no inkling, let alone credible foresight of or solution to.

There is a sophisticated life-politics at work here that disguises detailed assumptions about the *quality of lives*. Life, quantitatively speaking, has never been more human in terms of its number. At the time of the Christ event, the world population has been put at 200 million. Now there are some 6.1 billion of us by conservative estimates, with the expectation that this will grow towards a 'threshold peak' of some 9.2 billion by 2075.[14] This represents an increase of over 50 per cent in the human stock. How this species chooses to live undoubtedly leaves a particular planetary footprint. Some time between 2008 and 2010, a profound historical moment occurred when more of us began living in urban locations, i.e. rapidly changing environments as opposed to rural environments. This represents a challenging shift in migratory flows that is projected to rise to 70 per cent by 2050. In 1800, only 3 per cent of the world's population lived in city spaces. That figure now tops 3 billion city dwellers. More than having a profound impact upon dominant modes of production, as the consumerist logic of markets triumphs over localized self-sufficiencies, it radically alters the dominant matrix for political rule as neat demarcations that once held over sovereign dominions give way to forms of networked power that are globally distributed and complex in design. This has a number of important implications. Most notably, how our sense of endangerment has been transformed as that which is deemed problematic mimics the system both as an extreme and yet internal manifestation of its prevailing rationalities.

This forces us to confront like never before the finitude of our existence. Central are concerns with 'liveable thresholds' and 'planetary boundaries'. It is widely accepted within the natural sciences that human societies must change course and steer away from critical tipping points in the Earth system that might lead to rapid and irreversible change.[15] But what does the nature of this 'change' actually look like? It certainly doesn't imply the abandonment of liberal regimes of power. Neither does it entail bringing into question the rule of markets as a principal driver for human interactions and social affairs. Change means the adaptation of *certain* behaviours by *particular* populations so that the fundamental tenets of liberalism to survive in the face of rapid global change can go unquestioned. Much has been made of the need for the new emerging powers in global affairs to have a step-change in direction, and to try not to repeat the failures of the already enriched. Less is said about the ways in which catastrophic imaginaries author new forms of planetary stewardship which, ironically, tend to apply to native populations in resource-rich areas, who have contributed the least to environmental degradation. And yet, as planetary stewardship translates into the need for better neoliberal governance,[16] particularly on account of the fact that the market is still seen to be the surest way to refashion personal behaviours, what many radicals deem to be the problem is repackaged as the only credible solution.

Boundaries and thresholds are crucial to the catastrophic imaginary of contemporary liberal rule. Or at least it is the open horizon of possibility that promises a boundary-shattering event which now defines. While a number of increasingly irrelevant scholars within the political academy still fail to question problems beyond the sovereign conceit – in spite of the fact that all liberal governments now insist that the problems they face cannot be seen outside of a global frame – certain thanks are owed to a number of embedded scholars who, tied to leading policy think-tanks, offer a more honest assessment of liberal power, along with providing some remarkable aesthetical productions which are essential to the formation of resilient imaginaries.[17] The Stockholm Centre for Resilience, for instance, argues that the boundary 'refers to a specific point related to a global-scale environmental process beyond which humanity should not go'.[18] Crucially, for the Centre, although they accept that 'the position of the boundary is a normative judgement, informed by science but largely based on human perceptions of risk', the fact remains that there are certain parameters to human survivability. In a joint article by 28 leading authors with wider organizational affiliations, the idea that the earth system radicalizes our understanding of 'planetary boundaries' is forcefully articulated.[19] As the authors explain:

> The planetary boundaries approach rests on three branches of scientific inquiry. The first addresses the scale of human action in relation to the capacity of the Earth to sustain it, a significant feature of the ecological economics research agenda, drawing on work on the essential role of the life-support environment for human well-being and biophysical constraints for the expansion of the economic subsystem. The second is the work on understanding essential Earth System processes, including human actions, brought together in the evolution of global change research toward Earth System science and in the development of sustainability science. The third is the framework of resilience and its links to complex dynamics and self-regulation of living systems, emphasizing multiple basins of attraction and thresholds effects.

Such boundary setting directly relates the ideas of sustainability to the question of finitude. This is what the Stockholm Centre refers to as the 'steering away from catastrophic thresholds'.[20] This question of finitude has become so entrenched that some have even wondered what the world would be like 'without us'. As Alan Weisman popularized, 'A generation ago, human's eluded nuclear annihilation; with luck we'll continue to dodge that and other mass terrors. But now we often find ourselves asking whether inadvertently we've poisoned or parboiled the planet, ourselves included'.[21] For Weisman, since what is particularly compelling about the possibility of human extinction is the *return to Eden* for the rest of the biosphere, we are compelled to seriously ponder whether or not life on earth would positively thrive in our absence. Whatever our impressions of Weisman's worst case scenario experiment (from the human perspective); it is revealing that the manuscript is seldom stocked under *fiction*. Weisman's futurology in fact encapsulates Anthropocentic concerns: Will we eventually become the source of our very own undoing? In other words, what Weisman maps out in the starkest of terms is the widespread realization that everything on this planet has a finite lifespan – the human race most certainly included.

We have, then, become the directors and leading actors in a tragic production that forces us to confront a fate worse than death, i.e. our collective suicide. This logically inverts Shakespeare's depiction of the world as stage. No longer do we give to ourselves a bit part. Neither can we separate the question of agency (worldly actor) from the performing environment (the stage). While the possibility of extinction remains a principal cause for concern, there is no ending to our strange and eventful history. Simply a partaking in a historical unfolding which offers no exit as a matter of political foreclosure! As a result, upon entering the Anthropocence, it is no longer possible, unless one wishes to be associated with the so-called 'climate deniers' (a term in itself whose moral absolutism leaves no room for anything outside of its catastrophism), to dispute the veracity of the claims that all natural disasters can be linked in one way or another to human activity. Every single natural disaster must be understood within an anthropocentric frame. Whether proven or not, each catastrophe connects to the existence of humans in the world, and the way this species has chosen to live continues to scar, minute by minute, its increasingly

exhausting support systems. This is no doubt prophesying
– albeit masquerading under the aegis of indisputable scientific verification. The future as a terrain of catastrophe
is a vision *we must all believe in*. A rising tide of a fate
that is already, it seems, largely sealed, and through which
we truly lament our very existence. The inertia is palpable,
as doing our bit never seems to be enough. Take a ride
on a pushbike, become a vegetarian, fatalistically rejoice
in the volcanic eruptions that disrupt the flow of air
traffic for the briefest of moments, all the while feel
guilt for the violence we have already done to the Earth
and it is now doing unto us in return. This is the level
at which our political imaginaries now operate and find
solace.

There is also much to be gleaned here from another
genre no less informative to the history of our present –
Greek Tragedy. Sophocles *Oedipus Rex*[22] has classically
dominated our understanding of politics, especially the
structured, patriarchical and masculine forms of domina-
tion his embodiment allows us to think about as it extends
into the forms of oppression manifest in the modern nation
state. And yet, we have suggested, if there is an Oedipal
Leviathan to speak of in contemporary times, it openly
declares itself to be a false prophet, for the sovereign can
no longer provide the security upon which its foundational
truths came to rest. Without, then, a lead performer, what
once appeared to be the undisputed figure for political
embodiment has been displaced by the *Terror of Antigone*
who embodies the vulnerability of our times. Such is the
self-inflicted nature of the violence we are fated to endure
as a result of the novel lethality our freedoms now depend
upon. And such is the condition of the resilient subject, for
in its attempt to deal with the question of finitude, it
appeals to personal vulnerability as a matter of ontological
fact and the collective as a form of unavoidable endangerment. Humanity as a whole therefore exhibits what we
term a 'lethal conditioning' – a state of investiture that
makes it incumbent upon the subject to embrace resilience

or be subjected to a fate which, left underexposed, will prove more devastating still.

The question of finitude is personally and intellectually daunting. How may we begin to come to terms with our own passing into the absolute unknown? None of this is incidental. In fact, it brings us back to the original problematic of philosophy as we confront what it means to die? How is it possible to learn to live with death? Cornel West offers a compelling explanation.[23] 'You know', West responds, 'Plato says philosophy's a meditation on and a preparation for death. By death what he means is not an event, but a death in life because there's no rebirth, there's no change, there's no transformation without death, and therefore the question becomes: How do you learn how to die?' To philosophize is the practice of learning to die whilst living. As West further explains, 'You can't talk about truth without talking about learning how to die because it's precisely by learning how to die, examining yourself and transforming your old self into a better self, that you actually live more intensely and critically and abundantly'. That is to say, it is only by 'learning how to die', by willing the 'messianic moment' (to borrow from Walter Benjamin) in which death is read more as a condition of affirmation, that it becomes possible to change the present condition and create a new self by 'turning your world upside down'.

Resilience cheats us of this affirmative task of learning how to die. It exposes life to lethal principles so that it may live a *non-death*. Our wounds now exist before us. There is an important caveat to be addressed here. Some may counter that our societies are actually bombarded with various spectacles of violence that actually speak directly to the problem of finitude. While this is partly true, such finite moments only headline in extremity. That is to say, we learn to mourn those deaths which reaffirm the dangerous threshold of existence. Think here of 9/11, tsunamis, catastrophic accidents, incurable virulent diseases and so on. Then compare to the daily plight of suffering

that is largely ignored or not considered newsworthy
enough to draw our attentions. Indeed, as Zygmunt
Bauman explains, while liberal societies have become fas-
cinated with the spectacle of violence (especially as enter-
tainment), for the most part, death as an experience for
philosophical reflection has become a private affair hidden
from the public gaze.[24] For instance, while headstones of
the recently deceased seldom write of a person simply
having died a 'natural death' (there is always something
responsible), to think about the question of death as an
ontological condition for subsequent re-birth is relegated
to the world of religious superstition/pathology or some
dangerous attempts to counter liberal reason with the violence of self-immolation. Any rigorous critique of resilience must therefore deal with the conflict between the
lethality of freedom and the philosophical question of
death, for it is here we may expose deeply embedded ontological and metaphysical claims about what it means to
live a meaningful life beyond the biophysical.

Sublime Habitus

To suggest that the human and natural worlds are now
strategically indifferent represents a remarkable shift in our
thinking. Since antiquity we have been made aware of the
power of nature. From Pompeii, tales of a submerged city
of Atlantis, to the Plagues of Egypt, it was always accepted
that life could be annihilated by the natural world of which
it was part. The devastation wrought on Lisbon during the
three disasters of 1755, however, forced a significant
rupture in our attitudes to the catastrophic. Whereas previous catastrophic events were associated with some Godly
vengeance and fury, as the devastation wrought upon the
population of this great European city appeared horrifyingly arbitrary, it was no longer possible to believe in
some punishing or retributive divinity. This was simply
'nature at work'. Although this event forced a significant

separation in our understanding of evil as we began to philosophize differently between heavenly and earthly variants,[25] it also proposed a profound transformation of our understanding of social habitus. If nature was a problem to human existence, the natural world needed to be tamed at all costs. Hence, following Lisbon, it was thought politically and philosophically astute to think that humans had a role to play in matters of security. Urbanization from that moment became the prominent vision for Utopia, as the force of nature demanded a foundational response.

During this period another major philosophical rupture occurred, which, although appearing separate at the time, now appears significantly imbricated as we witness its effective dissolution. In his study of aesthetics, Immanuel Kant set out to provide meaningful distinctions between the beautiful and the sublime. While Kant amongst others had already written on the sublime prior to Lisbon, these events forced him to elevate the concept in his corpus to offer deeply moral and philosophical purchase. This was essential if we were to come to terms with the enormity of an event that seemed to defy intelligibility. Importantly, for Kant, whilst the sublime doesn't need to be frightening per se, the awesome power it promises demands a certain account of terror. What is more, as he explained in *The Critique of Judgment*, in which the idea of the sublime is afforded mathematical and dynamic qualities, the concept evidences a formlessness that is infinitely possible and boundless. If beauty, in other words, is a reflection of the aesthetic qualities of formed objects, the sublime exhibits a certain non-locatable quality that registers the name on account of its power to destroy fixed references. Hence, for Walter Benjamin, the Kantian sublime and its attempts to philosophically comprehend the magnitude of devastating events such as the Lisbon earthquake and tsunami, introduced the study of catastrophic phenomena that paved the way for the field of seismology.[26]

Kant's neat separation has evaporated as the beautiful and the sublime have merged to the effacement of clear

lines of distinction. To be resilient is to insist upon the
necessity of vigilance in relation with one's surrounding.
This effectively creates micro-vigilantes of all of us as we
are tasked to police our locales in a manner which comple-
ments the outsourcing logic of neoliberal governance. Such
care for the self evidences a collapse of the private into the
public, the militaristic into the civic, and the inanimate
into the animate, as insecurities are amplified by multiple
anxieties of the everyday. What is more, since discourses
on resilience encourage us to fear what we produce and
consume as danger is endemically conceived, epiphenom-
enal endangerment is a thing of the past. Endangerment
now comes from a perverse combination of elements that
make up our life-world systems. There is a tragic paradox
at work here. The greater our productive achievements,
the more the potential for destruction is amplified. Resilience then teaches us to live in a terrifying yet normal state
of affairs that suspends us in petrified awe. It blurs the
beautiful with the sublime such that every aesthetic moment
reveals a potential for something potent to emerge from
the objective surroundings. Upon disfiguring the formations of society, the inanimate thus resonates on the affective scale as something that must be seen to be altogether
terrifying, thereby viscerally turning what was once simply
urbane into the profane. So we become enlightened by the
realization of our infinite endangerment.

   A notable casualty of this is the utopian ideal. The idea
of Utopia has often been tied to modes of representation
as the future becomes an open site for projected fantasies
of worlds yet realized. Although it has never been a static
concept, overshadowed in many periods by more compelling dystopian supplements that seemed to be more in
keeping with our profound suspicions about ourselves, the
fact that we no longer even entertain the prospect of some
utopian ideal is reflective of the politics of our times. As
Fredric Jameson has written 'the waning of the utopian
idea is a fundamental historical and political symptom,
which deserves diagnosis in its own right – if not some

new and more effective therapy'.[27] Central to Jameson's
concerns has been the weakening of any sense of history,
along with the collapse of the political imaginary that
refuses to envisage anything other than the bleak current
state of political affairs. Utopia thus conceived has a distinct revolutionary capacity by allowing us to suspend
normality for a moment, take 'mental liberties' (which are
invariably particularistic and not universalistic), thereby
transgressing the present, and to believe in possible futures
to come. Despite our concerns with the totalizing metaphysics of utopianism in historical practice, Jameson does
offer a compelling diagnosis of the catastrophic imaginary
of contemporary liberal rule:

> [T]he notion of the market as an untrammelled natural
> growth has returned with a vengeance into political think-
> ing, while Left ecology desperately tries to assess the pos-
> sibilities of a productive collaboration between political
> agency and the earth . . . Ecology seems to count ever more
> feebly on its power – unless it be in the form of the apoca-
> lyptic and of catastrophe, global warming or the develop-
> ment of new viruses . . . The science-fictional figure for
> such change is the situation in which a prisoner, or some
> potential rescue victim, is warned that salvation will be
> possible only at the price of allowing the entire personality
> – the past and its memories, all the multiple influences and
> events that have combined to form this current personality
> in the present – to be wiped away without a trace: a con-
> sciousness alone remains, after this operation, but by what
> effort of the reason or imagination can it still be called 'the
> same' consciousness? The fear with which this prospect
> immediately fills us is then to all intents and purposes the
> same as the fear of death.[28]

Post-utopianism takes on a number of distinct features
in which idealized lifestyles are no longer presented as a
common good but a matter of *exclusivity*. If there is any
resonance to idealism, it is not premised on 'inclusion' but
the need to be able to 'opt out' of the social landscape.

Not only do we evidence this in the various newspaper supplements which offer temporary refuge from the maddening crowds within some idyllic and depopulated retreat (which in themselves, as we have come to learn, are also vulnerable in their exposure to the elements); the marked separation of gated lives have increasingly become the new norm for human habitation as the logic of risk calls forth the creation of local protectorates. Gated communities offer a particularly telling insight into the politics of resilience. Borrowing from Foucault, we may argue that the gated community is in fact a novel expression of a security apparatus that seeks to *distribute* risk throughout a networked system. The gated individual outsources the need to be resilient to elements throughout the gated commune, ranging from barbed fences, physical walls, surveillance technologies, disaster-proofed architectures and insurance premiums to armed guards patrolling the parameters. This is a far cry from Thomas More's vision of Utopia as a site of human togetherness and shared access to resources. Indeed, once we broach the problem of gated life biopolitically, the method of containment (whether included or excluded) which begins with the human subject, it soon becomes apparent how resilience is tied to a neoliberal ideology that clouds racial, cultural and gendered discriminations by the smokescreen of objective risk assessments. And yet, as we shall later discover, the tragic irony of resilience is that it renders problematic precisely those populations which are 'at risk' in order to permit their veritable containment and separation from those for whom resilience is seldom entertained.

Once the built environment becomes part of political deliberations, infrastructure becomes 'critical' to the understanding of living systems. The idea of Critical Infrastructure is now central to discourses and practices of securitization, especially in global cities. As Martin Coward has written, 'One might (thus) say that a reciprocal dynamic of urban securitisation is underway in which the security agenda is urbanised and urbanity is – insofar as it induces insecurity and vulnerability – securitised'.[29] While it is well established that the urban setting has always been vulnerable to a strategic attack (most horrifyingly in the cases of Hiroshima and Nagasaki which put into question urbanism like never before), the idea that the violence must be tested *before* the event (such that its conditions of possible decay and its notable weaknesses must be imagined and acted upon in advance) is a novel departure that points to the onset of pre-emptive governance more generally. 'As a consequence', Coward explains, 'cities are securitised in response to actual or imagined threats that are perceived to derive from such forms of war and the distinctive way they exploit or endanger the urban fabric'. Crucially, for Stephen Graham, this temporal shift in our understanding of urban performance, which looks directly towards the future of cityscapes before attacks upon their material fabric has come about, inaugurates a new material sensibility that is 'disrupted by design'.[30]

Architects in the United States have been at the forefront of re-thinking urban design. *The National Plan for Research and Development in Support of Critical Infrastructure Protection* (2004) set the scene, suggesting it was important to conceive of physical systems that 'must become reliable, autonomic (self-repairing and self-sustaining), resilient, and survivable in order to continue to operate in diminished capacity rather than failing in crisis conditions'.[31] Infrastructure was therefore to be imbued with a particular agency that literally breathes life into what was once deemed inanimate. This demands a more holistic assessment that merges the human, the built environment, and the virtual to the otherwise natural and unregulated Critical Infrastructures which are 'not just buildings and structures' but 'include people and physical and cyber systems that work together in processes that are highly interdependent'.[32] In this regard, 'the defence of critical infrastructure is not about the mundane protection of human beings from the risk of violent death at the hands of other human beings, but about a more profound defence of the combined physical and technological infrastructures which liberal regimes have come to understand as necessary for their vitality and security in recent years'.[33] The security, however, remains a deceit that conceals the most insecure of rationalities. Since the built environment is indistinguishable from catastrophic potentiality, instead of promising to make us safe, we have learned that all our castles are made from sand. Our understanding of the biopolitical is invariably transformed as we move from the attempts to secure populations to the embrace of contingency and all its pathological iterations:

> Taking its analytic cue from complexity science and ecology rather than statistics and demography, a neoliberal biopolitics is more concerned to promote life that is resilient, able to exist on the edge of survivability, and adapted to uncertainty and surprise; a life that has abandoned trying to know the future and its associated prudentialism. Instead of providing a modernist *freedom from* the social pathologies of everyday life through, for example, normative regimes of inter-generational social insurance, resilience is more attuned to a neoliberal ethos allowing a *freedom to* embrace contingency as the essence of foresight and enterprise . . . Resilience speaks to capitalism's constant transgression of limits, its inability to leave anything alone for long and the permanent revolution it effects in social and institutional life. Life is speciated according to the usefulness, irrelevance or threat it represents for the infrastructural and biospheric systems necessary for capitalism's widening cycles of reproduction, consumption and accumulation.[34]

A Fallible Existence

Political events such as 9/11 and 7/7, along with natural disasters more commonly, suggest that catastrophe has no consideration for subjectivity. Whether the victim is rich or poor, Western or non-Western, religious or not, threats

which define the twenty-first-century security terrain offer
no refuge whatsoever for the status of the subject. When
everything is the source of endangerment, everyone is
endangered. We may reason this to be an inevitable
outcome of the liberal disavowal of anything external to
its inclusive political imaginary. As the politics of the
exception, i.e. something that points not only to juridical
excessiveness but also to all radically anteriority, is condemned as a de facto point of principle, so it transpires
that nothing is exempt – without exception. In other
words, since liberal rule cannot entertain anything exceptional (juridical or otherwise), it necessarily follows that
the anterior appears to be more than a novel curiosity.
That which remains unknown must become known or else
we remain slaves to chance. Here we encounter both an
irresolvable dilemma and the real condition of possibility.
Since knowledge upon this terrain actually appears altogether fleeting, the principle of the unknown must remain
infinitely inaccessible. To abandon the dream of final security implies giving up on the dream of perfect knowledge.
While liberal communities are therefore insecure by design,
epistemologically they are premised upon the realization
of imperfect knowledge. Indeed, liberal systems of rule
depend upon such imperfections in order to justify continuous engagement to permit continual re-entry into the
manipulation of the souls of the living.
    Imperfect knowledge is the starting point for resilient
strategies which are far from universal in application.
Vulnerability is not a universal experience. Neither do our
coping mechanisms conform to some timeless laws of
nature. Both are highly contingent in terms of the experi-
encing subject as it appears in space and time. This is
strategically embraced. Indeed, since imperfect knowledge
is deemed integral to the understanding of infinite endangerment, it conditions the possibility for a system of rule
which produces insecurity by design. While imperfection
is presented here as a universal character trait – nobody is
perfect the Kantian inspired liberal often recites – it remains

the case that some are deemed to be more imperfect in knowledge than others on account of their lesser liberal dispositions. Such an assay is the political move made by resilient discourses and practices *before* the technical solutions are mobilized. Meaningfulness of life is qualified along various progressive/regressive schematics such that questions of vulnerability can be presented as verifiable scientific truths. The more progressively endowed, the less vulnerability the imperfect subject experiences. The less vulnerability, the less there is a need to think and act resiliently as the subject is already progressively countering. Not only is this logic a particular mask of mastery for liberal power as it encourages a technical framing of the problem in order to screen political complicity. Without any appreciation of process of biopolitical authentication that gives sure moral testimony to a life that is well lived, the problem of resilience is absolved of any political ascriptions as technocratic solutions come to the fore.

Collective Amnesia

Postmodernism is often poorly understood. It does not refer to a particular moment in time that allows us to map out a temporal shift from a *pre* to *post facto* of modernity. Neither does it refer to modes of production wherein the term gains material purchase through the shift from industrialization to immaterial forms of labour and outputs. Postmodernism is a way of thinking and relating to the world. It has no temporality as such. Neither does it have a distinct materiality as such. Bringing into question prevailing dogmas, reified assumptions, along with uncompromising holistic claims to truth, it is unashamedly concerned with opening up the fields of possibility by revealing what is already there. There is, however, an important caveat that must be addressed here. While we may argue that postmodernism has been aligned with the creation of new concepts – 'the event of thinking', there is

nothing to suggest that what is offered will not be dangerous or appropriated such that what appears to be affirmative subsequently ends up turning towards more reactive
and suffocating means. Indeed, moving beyond postmodernist dogmatism, which can be as equally stifling as political realism and liberalist alternatives, there is nothing
whatsoever to suggest that our allegiance must be given to
a concept or idea simply because its stakes offer to strike
against a particular meta-narrative.

Deleuze was fully aware of the potential for well-
intentioned concepts to be maliciously appropriated by
imperial forces. Nietzsche, in particular, he believed, was
subjected to these misadventures more than any other. For
Deleuze, the misappropriation of Nietzsche's concepts
extended well beyond the crude falsifications of 'those
abusive relatives that figure in the procession of cursed
thinkers'.[35] More maliciously, they suffered from the
'bad readings or displacements' which were derived from
'arbitrary selections' of his works. Never in the history of
thought has there been such a fallacious assassination of
the messenger.

Nietzsche for his part was fully aware of his own
untimeliness. 'I know my fate', he once famously stated,[36]
Deleuze's work in equal measure has been subjected to the
same arbitrary selections and utilized to rationalize the
most abhorrent acts of violence. It has already been noted
how a number of his concepts have been used to help
theorize the catastrophic imaginary of twenty-first-century
forms of security governance. Intentionally or not, the
problems Deleuze raised are being directly associated with
a security dilemma like no other before witnessed on earth.
Despite this, however, we are yet to truly realize the political significance of their works. If we have heeded their
messages to have become 'post-modern' along with the
disavowal of structures and limits, this hasn't been done
with any degree of confidence. That is why, for Peter
Sloterdijk, Nietzsche remains the prophet of the human yet
to come.[37]

One of the more preposterous and dangerous postmodernist interventions is the demand for a politics of forgetting. We are no doubt aware that truths about the past can be manipulated to colonize the present. To suggest, however, that we can simply forget some life-changing event is absurd. How may we even begin to think about eradicating from memory the violence of Hiroshima or 9/11? Any such suggestions are not only neurologically questionable; they are ethically compromised as they take us into the most pernicious abstraction. If the past troubles, it is because the multiplicity of experience is glossed over, not the experience itself. Indeed, as we shall explain, what remains fundamental to the art of living an affirmative life is the ability to have a distinct confidence in truth. Such an exercise positively embraces what Foucault termed the history of our present. It pays meticulous attention to the historical moment so that the contested nature of experience can be excavated from the ashes of catastrophe that otherwise impose singular reasoning. Not only does conducting any history of the present prove altogether impossible once forgetting is entertained. More contemporaneously, it plays directly into the logic of neoliberal rule in which future-orientated strategies of resilience depend upon forms of collective amnesia.

Resilience has a distinct relationship to the historical as it invokes memories of past traumas. The historical record, however, is only concerned here with the singular truth of an event as some shared experience of suffering and eventual resurrection. Out of this narrative comes an explanation of events as something inherently violent such that the precariousness and vulnerability of human existence is reaffirmed, along with the need to instigate a new angle of vision in which the particular historical rupture serves to condition the possibility for more generalizable rule. Here, then, previous forms of human tragedy find strategic alignment as the need to make us all aware of the sheer contingency of living inscribes a base level imperative as a matter of biophysical survivability and a metaphysical imperative as a matter of community under siege. The past therefore impresses upon the present to provide a moral reasoning to future governmental activities as carried out in the name of a collective, which is defined on account of its radical endangerment. Politically qualified life begins with the tragedy of its existence – the topos of the encounter – which stems from the arbitrary and inescapable violence of the world. The only response in such a predicament is to be better conditioned through some form of exposure to the fact that living is thoroughly dangerous. As Juliette Kayyem, policy adviser on homeland security to the Obama administration and Harvard academic puts it, what we choose to remember should be guided by 'less anger' (especially about distribution of finite resources which ordinarily makes us more secure through entitlement) and more through a 'quiet acceptance' of our insecurities:

> One day it will be acceptable, politically and publicly, to argue that while homeland security is about ensuring that fewer bad things happen, the real test is that when they inevitably do, they aren't as bad as they would have been absent the effort. Only our public and political response to another major terrorist attack will test whether there is room for both ideologies to thrive in a nation that was, any way you look at it, *built to be vulnerable*.[38]

But what remnants actually pass over into the present as collective memory? For sure, we don't encounter in this space of recollection the contested nature of the historical event. Neither do we often encounter any personal testimony that brings into question the truth about the shared sense of suffering and grief. We only have to look here to Thomas Hoepker's photo of people in Brooklyn relaxing against the backdrop of the violence of September 11 to evidence this point. While this image was eventually published on the fifth anniversary of 9/11, as Hoepker stated, its initial publication was held back due to its 'ambiguous and confusing' composition. It was too sensitive to deal with politically. Moving beyond any judgemental posturing towards the individuals or for that matter sweeping generalizations about cultural insensitivities of an entire nation that somehow appears emotionally bankrupt, Hoepker's photograph represents the contested reality of the historical moment in its most unstaged and raw form. Like the falling man before, it unsettles the preferred aesthetic dialectic of initial tragedy and civic heroism. Instead, it depicts a perfectly normal state of affairs that was permitted by a certain *distancing* from the action. Indeed, as the composition emphasizes, proximity alone offers no such guarantees as to some shared sense of vulnerability or experience. All events are experienced differently. Many were far more deeply traumatized viewing the unfolding of events thousands of miles away than the subjects in Hoepker's frame.

And yet, it remains the case that since resilience offers a reflection on societies that is altogether unproblematic, many assumptions about society and its relationship to catastrophic events are purged of their complex memories. It has already been noted that resilience became the defining motif of the tenth anniversary of 9/11. From art exhibitions to magazine covers, it became the rhetorical device to indicate how the United States survived in the face of adversity. It also pointed to a new political moment in which the trauma of the event shifted from discourses of retribution to a more sombre evaluation of the fragility of life. This was not presented as something to be despaired. Optimism was to be found precisely in the ability to emerge from the ashes of the catastrophic more appreciative of what it meant to live a finite existence. To be optimistic meant having a more intimate appreciation of the lethality of 9/11, for only then could the trauma of the day be turned around to positively re-enforce the moral surety of the liberal will to rule and the ways of life the system produces. President Barack Obama's commemorative speech at Ground Zero spoke volumes in this regard:

These past ten years tell a story of resilience. The Pentagon is repaired, and filled with patriots working in common purpose. Shanksville is the scene of friendships forged between residents of that town, and families who lost loved ones there. New York remains a vibrant capital of the arts and industry, fashion and commerce. Where the World Trade Center once stood, the sun glistens off a new tower that reaches toward the sky. Our people still work in skyscrapers. Our stadiums are filled with fans, and our parks full of children playing ball. Our airports hum with travel, and our buses and subways take millions where they need to go. Families sit down to Sunday dinner, and students prepare for school. This land pulses with the optimism of those who set out for distant shores, and the courage of those who died for human freedom.[39]

Obama's understanding is that the past only offers a certain amount of guidance. One thing the future does promise, he expects, is another catastrophe in some yet to be deciphered guise. While the past therefore remains imperfect as it was impossible to predict with absolute certainty what came to pass, the future in equal measure remains purely contingent. As finite beings with finite qualities in a world of infinite possibility, we are, then, it seems, somewhat incapable of 'handling the truth'. Indeed, it seems that liberal politicians no longer reason truth to be 'out there' as if to be captured and settled once and for all. Abandoning the search for fixed essences, truth has become what we make it, as we fashion our lives and produce the meaning of our freedoms and liberties as consumable products like any other. There is an important caveat to address here. The liberal fashioning of the truth as conceived in terms of its emergence in the face of vulnerability is not a courage to speak truth *to* power so that we think differently about the political. It is an allegiance to the truth *of* power, such that we maintain some allegiance to the truth about the value of political subjects already conceived. In this regard, commonality exists between the knowledge of the resilient subject and that of speculative philosophy. Rather than seeking a definitive political rupture with the present, the political subject is tasked to show *fidelity* to the truth – as witnessed in the living out of emerging events – which conforms to some nomologically reducible logic of worlds. What is wagered, in other words, is the truth-event of the vulnerable subject, whose very claim to truth arises during the catastrophic moment as a sort of hyper-negative and posthumous told you so:

> For a truth to affirm its newness, there must be a *supplement*. This supplement is committed to chance. It is unpredictable, incalculable. It is beyond what is. I call it an event. A truth thus appears, in its newness, because an evental supplement interrupts repetition . . . An event is linked to the notion of the *undecidable*. Take this statement: 'The event belongs to the situation.' If it is possible to decide, using the rules of established knowledge, whether this statement is true or false, then the so-called event is not an event. Its occurrence would be calculable within the situation. Nothing would permit us to say: here begins a truth. On the basis of the undecidability of an event's belonging to a situation a *wager* has to be made. This is why a truth begins with an *axiom of truth*. It begins with a groundless decision – the decision to say that the event has taken place.[40]

There is no truth, then, other than the truth of the emergent will to know the conditions of our vulnerability. The past is of no relevance here other than as a contingent moment in time whose passage leaves no contemporary truthfulness from the perspective of the newly emergent truth-event. But what is actually being wagered here? It is not the incalculability of the situation. Neither is it the question of belonging to the situation in all its complexity. It is the ability to excavate something of a pure and unquestionable truth that renders the undecidable decidable, the rupture normalized, the uncertain certain, so that it becomes possible to recover a political truth out of the catastrophic break. To suggest that there are no established rules, then, is the precise point. Vulnerability and insecurity make all claims to established order altogether redundant for there is no truth other than that which has just come to pass and soon to be forgotten. Collective amnesia thus becomes a default setting for a system of rule that is less about secure principles than it is about axiomatic propositions which, although fleeting, provide the most unquestionable assumptions about the subject's ontological status (vulnerability), its epistemic reasoning (radical uncertainty), and its purely contingent centre of gravity (catastrophic events).

Whose Survivability?

The question of survivability has always been central to biopolitical concerns. How might we live beyond the contemporary limits of our existence? – a question often posed by bio-strategic conscious agencies of governance. If biopolitics is therefore a key term of art for describing the progressive operations of power which, seeking to strategically battle with the forces that threaten our finite existence, renders the modern periodic as such, resilience is a term of art for biopolitical intervention that takes the infinitely possible to become the strategic point of entry for the conceptualization of threats to biospheric life broadly conceived. Strategies of resilience, in other words, are less about highlighting local claims to knowledge or autonomous capabilities to deal with problems on their own terms; instead, they evidence how liberal power is confronting the realities of its self-imposed foreclosure such that it requires new reasons to govern life despite the irresolvability of its ambitions. As liberalism now faces the reality of its finitude, haunted in fact by the very logic of infinite potentiality that its contemporary bio-philosophy of life equally promotes, the turn to resilience becomes inevitable. This brings us to a pivotal moment in the history of liberalism as universal aspirations are all but abandoned, along with any natural claims to promote all life as a self-endowed subject with inalienable rights. With the outside displaced by a radically interconnected terrain of endemic crises, survivability truly is the name of the political game.

Resilience, however, is more than a call to increase our vigilance and preparedness against impending attacks. It encourages actors to learn from catastrophes so that societies can become more responsive to a fate which is worse and still simmering on the horizon. It promotes adaptability so that life may go on living despite the fact that elements of our living systems may be irreparably destroyed. And it creates shared knowledge that will continually reshape the forms of communities and affirm those core values which are deemed absolutely 'vital' to our ways of living. With this in mind, it is perhaps no accident that the concept of resilience emanates from ecology. Such thinking foregrounds 'buffer capacities' of living systems; their ability to 'absorb perturbations' or the 'magnitude of disturbance that can be absorbed before a living system changes its structure by changing the variables and processes that control behaviour'.[41] Living systems are said by ecologists to develop not on account of their ability to secure themselves prophylactically from threats, but through their adaptation to them. They evolve in spite of and because of systemic shocks that register from the minor to the catastrophic. Exposure to threats is a constitutive process in the development of living systems, and thus the problem for them is never simply how to secure themselves but how to adapt to them. Such capacities for adaptation to threats are precisely what ecologists argue determines the 'resilience' of any living system.

Melinda Cooper and Jeremy Walker have provided an important contribution to our understanding of the genealogies of resilience. Drawing upon the number of ways complexity thinking has been shaped, they have exposed the intricate connections between ecological and economical modes of thinking. As they suggest, 'Since the nineties, global financial institutions such as the International Monetary Fund, the World Bank, and the Bank for International Settlements, have increasingly incorporated strategies of 'resilience' into their logistics of crisis management, financial (de)regulation and development economics'.[42] Much of this applicability is owed to the intellectual contributions of the great Austrian economic theorist Friedrich Von Hayek who understood that shocks to economic systems were caused by factors beyond our control, hence our thinking about such systems required systems of governance that were premised upon insecure foundations. Hence, while ecology promises to universalize and moralize resilient strategies through the creation of all inclusive catastrophic imaginaries, it is also intuitively in keeping with neoliberalism and its systems of rule:

[A]s institutions begin to recognize the looming socio-economic effects of climate change, we have seen a rapid uptake of the adaptive model of resource-management offered by resilience science. This has occurred in tandem with calls for the 'securitization of the biosphere': the privatisation and trading of the flow of 'ecosystem services' maintained by intact ecosystems, in recognition that rainforests and watersheds are critical 'natural infrastructure assets' that must be priced in financial markets in order that corporations can 'capture the value' of biodiversity conservation. In this way, neoliberal environmentalism addresses the depletion of ecosystems as a global security problem, the only solution to which is the securitisation and financialisation of the biosphere'.[43]

Resilience from this perspective is not simply a call to ignite some base level human instinct for survival, even though, as we shall discover, the reduction of life to this base level is a natural outcome. It is an ideological project that is informed by political and economic rationalities which offer very particular accounts of life as an ontological problem, i.e. a problem which emanates from the potentiality of life as ontologically conceived, along with the types of epistemic communities which scientifically verify the need to become resilient as a *fait accompli*. Resilience, in other words, is a key strategy in the creation of contemporary regimes of power that hallmark vast inequalities in all human classifications. Little wonder that resilience is most concerned with those deemed most vulnerable. For it is precisely the insecuritization of the most at risk which politically threatens the security and comforts of those who are sufficiently protected and excluded from the all too real effects of risk-based societies. The following introduction from a joint report on 'The Roots of Resilience' co-sponsored by the United Nations Development Programme, United Nations Environment Programme, the World Bank and the World Resources Institute speaks volumes on the political implications:

> Resilience is the capacity to adapt and to thrive in the face of challenge. This report contends that when the poor successfully (and sustainably) scale-up ecosystem-based enterprises, their resilience can increase in three dimensions. They can become more economically resilient – better able to face economic risks. They – and their communities – can become more socially resilient – better able to work together for mutual benefit. And the ecosystems they live in can become more biologically resilient – more productive and stable'.[44]

This invariably bring us to sustainable development, which started out by preaching that the economic development of societies must be regulated so that it contributes not just to the security of states and their human populations, but also so that it increases the resilience of all living systems. This shifted the object of concern from that of human life to that of the biosphere, incorporating every known species, as well as habitats of all kinds, vulnerable to the destructions wrought by economic development. Life, not economy, it said, must provide the rationalities according to which peoples are entitled to increase their prosperity. The emergence of such a doctrine had significant implications for the ways in which not only the problem but also the very nature of security was conceived in developmental circles. Once the referent object of development became the life of the biosphere rather than simply states and their human populations, so the account of security to which development is allied was required to transform. Security, with its connotations of state and governmental reason, territoriality, military capacities, economic prosperity, human resources and population assets became less fashionable and gradually gave way to the new concept and value of 'resilience'. Resilience is a useful concept, the proponents of sustainable development argued, precisely because it is not a capacity of states, nor merely of human populations and their various political, social and economic practices, but a capacity of life itself.

Since resilience emerged within the doctrine of sustainable development as a way of positing a different kind of policy problematic from those formulated in the security doctrines of neoliberal states and their more conventional development agencies, it would privilege the life of the biosphere in all its dimensions over and against the human focus that shaped the 'development–security nexus'. If one aspect of the subordination of rationalities of economy to rationalities of life in developmental discourse has been the shift from doctrines of economic development to sustainable development, a correlate shift has also been that from security to resilience. Development thus understood was less about closing the life-chance divide between the rich and the impoverished than it was about localized strategies for self-help. We teach how to fish in spite of the polluted waters. As Mark Duffield writes, 'development is not a modernising strategy for economic catch-up. It is more a means of improving the resilience of self-reliant life through new forms of social organisation'.[45] With the moral case for intervention taken as given, sustainable development sought to 'contain the circulatory effects on non-insured surplus life by putting the onus on potential migrants to adjust their expectations while improving their resilience and self-reliance *in situ*'.[46] Resilience, then, politically emerges as part of a containment strategy for dealing with the globally impoverished in the environment, it was declared, of their natural belonging.

By the time of the 2002 World Summit on Sustainable Development in Johannesburg – a summit that is widely recognized as the coming of age party of 'sustainable development' – the importance of resilience as a political strategy was cemented. A major report prepared on behalf of the Environmental Advisory Council to the Swedish Government as input to the process of the World Summit described how resilience is a property associated not just with the diversity 'of species', but also 'of human opportunity', and especially 'of economic options – that maintain and encourage both adaptation and learning' among human populations.[47] In an adroit reformulation of the problematic, neoliberal economic development, in which the function of markets as generators of economic diversity is basic, became itself a core constituent of the resilience which sustainable development had to be aimed at increasing. Thus was it that, post-Johannesburg, the correlation of sustainable development with resilience started to produce explicitly neoliberal prescriptions for institutional reform and a peculiar shift that abandoned any sense of egalitarianism yet wrapping itself more fully in humanitarian dressage. 'Ecological ignorance' began to be conceptualized as a threat, not just to the resilience of the biosphere, but to humanity. Resilience began to be conceived not simply as an inherent property of the biosphere, in need of protection from the economic development of humanity, but a property within human populations that now needed promoting through the increase of their 'economic options'. Remarkably, then, the biosphere itself began to be conceived not as an extra-economic domain, distinct from and vulnerable to the economic practices of human populations, but an economy of 'services' which 'humanity receives'.[48] The environment, in other words, starts to become properly bio-politicized and bio-capitalized as a moral source for human welfare and setting the conditions for emancipation. There is a double and correlated shift at work here in the elaboration of the sustainable development–resilience nexus post-Johannesburg. In one move, 'resilience' has shifted from being a property of the biosphere to being a property of humanity, while in a second move 'service' has shifted from being an element of economy to being a capacity of the biosphere. Crucified on the cross that this double shift carves are 'the poor'. For they are the segment of population of which resilience is now demanded and simultaneously the population said to threaten the degradation of 'ecosystem services'. Increasing the 'resiliency' of the poor has become a defining goal, for example, of the United Nations Environment Programme (UNEP) in the years post-Johannesburg.[49] Alleviating threats to the biosphere requires improving the resilience of the poor, especially, because it is precisely the poor that are most 'ecologically ignorant' and thus most prone to using 'ecosystem services' in non-sustainable ways. Thus ensuring the resilience of the biosphere requires making the poor into more resilient kinds of subjects, and making the poor into more resilient subjects requires relieving them of their ecological ignorance. The means to that removal is assumed to reside in building neoliberal frameworks of economy, governance and subjectivity. Developing the resilience of the poor is said to require, for example, a social context of 'flexible and open institutions and multi-level governance systems'.[50] 'The absence of markets and price signals' in ecological services is a major threat to resilience, UNEP argues, because it means that 'changes in their conditions have gone unnoticed'.[51]

Property rights regimes prove particularly telling here as they have to be extended to incorporate ecosystem services so that markets can function in them.[52] 'Markets', it is argued, 'have proven to be among the most resilient institutions, being able to recover quickly and to function

in the absence of government'.[53] When and where the
market fails to recover, development policies for increasing
resilience have to be aimed at 'ensuring access to markets'.[54]
Ensuring the resilience of the poor also requires the building of neoliberal systems of governance which will monitor
their use of ecological services to ensure they are sustain-
ably managed.[55] In order to be the agents of their own
change, the poor have to be subjectivized so that they are
'able to make sustainable management decisions that
respect natural resources and enable the achievement of a
sustainable income stream'.[56] 'Over-harvesting, over-use,
misuse or excessive conversion of ecosystems into human
or artificial systems damages the regulation service which
in turn reduces the flow of the provisioning service provided by ecosystems'.[57] Within 'the poor' itself, women are
the principal target population. 'I will transform my life-
style in the way I farm and think' has become the mantra
that poor women farmers in the Caribbean region are
demanded, for example, to repeat like Orwellian farm
animals in order to receive European Union funding.[58] So
not only does resilience have a relationship to poverty. It
reveals both cultural and gendered concerns that work to
divide life into various taxonomical groupings of distinct
vulnerability, thereby permitting strategic engagement
with lives which are qualified as scientifically divisible.

The double shift identified above is integral, we will
argue, to the strategy by which neoliberalism has absorbed
the critique of sustainable development and naturalized
profound differences in the qualities of lives by appropriat-
ing the terms of vulnerability. Whereas resilience was originally conceived by proponents of sustainable development
as a property that distinguishes the extra-economic 'life-
support systems' which humans require to live well, it has
become reconceived post-Johannesburg as a property
which humanity intrinsically possesses, is capable of developing further, and which it can never have too much of.
As a property of human populations it is dependent, moreover, on their interpellation within markets, their diversity

as economic subjects, and their subjection to systems of governance, able to ensure that they continue to use natural resources in sustainable ways. A doctrine, which started out as a critique of neoliberal policy prescriptions for development, ends up legitimating a neoliberal model of development based upon the constitution of markets and the interpellation of subjects within markets. The resilient subject is therefore the surest embodiment of neoliberal thinking as it conforms to its guiding principles without questioning the political stakes of vulnerability. In doing so, what revolutionary impetus may exist is countered by a sophisticated form of lethality that the subject is tasked to bring onto themselves. It is for these reasons, we shall conclude, resilience must be understood nihilistically. Nihilism is not only a debasement of the self. It encourages the subject to accept a political will to nothingness. By actively encouraging a self-inflicting lethal exposure, it turns political ambitions into a neutralizing embrace.

− 2 −

Insecure by Design

The Life of Late Liberalism

Over the course of modernity, the ways in which the Western philosophical imagination understands the human has undergone dramatic shifts. From its Cartesian investment in an understanding of the human as that divinely endowed animal which, with the exercise of its unique capacity for reason, could one day achieve security from nature, to the contemporary diagnosis of the sickness of reason, the 'illusion' of security, and the vulnerability of the human to the catastrophic capacities of the biosphere on which it depends, the philosophical imaginary of Western modernity has changed significantly. Liberalism has not been an exception to or victim of this shift. It has in fact been constitutive. Liberalism originated as a challenge to the Cartesian modern by foregrounding the biological life of the human subject. As Michel Foucault explained in numerous analyses, the birth and development of liberalism were inseparable from the birth and development of the age of biopolitics. Taking life as the principal referent for political strategies has always been the singularity setting it apart. Liberalism, in other words, has always been allied with the life sciences as the human increasingly appeared central to a progressive will to rule. Tasked, then, with the problem of how to govern in accordance with the needs and interests of the human defined in terms of its species existence, political theory, political science and international relations are not the principal sites of knowledge to have contributed to teaching liberal regimes how to rule biopolitically. Understood as a science of life, it is the life sciences, broadly conceived, that have taught liberalism most about how to deal with the problem of humane governance.

The search to understand the conditions for species development and security has been most earnestly conducted in the life sciences from the late seventeenth century onwards. Such enquiry led to the possibility of being able to distinguish between forms of productive life and those inimical to life; processes and organisms which threatened life, rendered life vulnerable and insecure, warring against life and the realization of its potential. Here, liberal actors would learn how to pursue and realize the full emancipatory possibilities of species existence, and the material prospering of species life. This was not in any way divorced from the great political and philosophical canon of early liberal thought. On the contrary, the impact of these same life sciences can, for example, be traced directly in the thinking of liberal philosophers throughout the (pre)industrialized settings of the eighteenth, nineteenth and twentieth centuries, onto the more complex narratives of the human as a site of continual adaptation and productive change as it now commonly appears in the twenty-first century.

Life always troubled the foundational investments of the Cartesian subject because it could never actually be secured. This aporia was fully appreciated by Kant, who, instigating the Cartesian revolution in thought, supplemented his universal aspiration by a fallen account of freedom into which life was deemed forever guilty of its own unmaking. Life, Kant understood, despite its best efforts, was to remain incapable of achieving the lofty universal heights it set to achieve. And, as a result, his vision of a perpetual peace was always fated to end in the graveyard. For, by definition, life, biologically understood, is a phenomenon of vulnerability. To live is to be a thing that can and must die; a thing which can only ever struggle to survive in competition with other living systems for the finite time of which it is capable of lasting. At best, then, prospering resiliently, amid its vulnerabilities to decay, life may adapt innovatively to the environmental conditions it is exposed to and simultaneously is dependent on only for a brief moment in time. Conceiving the human this way has meant that liberalism has always been committed, unwittingly at least, to divesting the human of any belief in its abilities to transcend the mere biological fact of being and achieve security. That is why for liberalism the question of sovereignty has always been deeply problematic. And that is why for liberalism a new biopolitical account of security had to be put forward – one which beneath the surface of its discursive reckoning is fundamentally insecure by design.

This is precisely the point that Foucault makes concerning the origins of the liberal subject.[1] The liberal subject 'is a subject who is not so much defined by his freedom, or by the opposition of soul and body'.[2] It is grounded irreducibly in the subject's preference for whatever brings it pleasure in denial of pain and the potential for suffering. Hence, what is irreducible to the liberal subject is its search for resilience to whatever may be found to threaten or reduce its capacity to live in an unending condition of relative durability to pain and suffering. Moving, however, beyond any further excavation of the biopolitical origins of the liberal subject, we are now more interested in how this biologized notion of the subject is shaping the practices of liberalism contemporarily, and how that is being played out in contemporary power relations and strategies of liberal governance as framed through the discourses and practices of resilience. When we examine the effects of the growth in influence of liberalism over the post-Cold War period, what we see are precisely those theories and practices of governance that have been shaped around the perceived needs to develop an ever wider range of biologically determined capacities in and among the subjects of governance. This forces us to confront the ways in which discourses of resilience and adaptation have arisen in response to the growing recognition of the human's supposed vulnerability to the world in which it lives and depends on for survival. That such ways of thinking about what it is to be human have become so popular to the point of becoming hegemonic, avoiding in the process any critical engagement on account of its effective normalization within imaginaries of threat, is not incidental to the story of liberalism's ascendancy in the post-Cold War world. It has been one of its principle intellectual drivers as the perceived vulnerability of the subject provides new conditions of possibility for intervening upon the souls of the living, along with morally authoring the violence of neoliberal rule on a planetary scale.

Indeed, as we will show, the contemporary concern of global governmental policies and practices with the promotion of resilience is an expression of the changing cartography of liberal power as it seeks to influence planetary life. Rather than enabling the development of peoples and individuals so that they can aspire to secure themselves from whatever they find threatening and dangerous in worldly living, the liberal discourse of resilience functions to convince peoples and individuals of the risks and dangers of the belief in the possibility of security. This is an extension of the classical trope of liberal thinking, reaching back to the origins of liberal tradition which has always taken insecurity as the condition of possibility for political rule. To be resilient, the subject must disavow any belief in the possibility to secure itself and accept instead an understanding of life as a permanent process of continual adaptation to threats and dangers which are said to be outside its control. It is all about 'thriving' in times of unending chaos without losing the faculty of neoliberal reason. As such the resilient subject must permanently struggle to accommodate itself to the world.[3] The resilient subject is not a political subject who on its own terms conceives of changing the world, its structure and conditions of possibility. The resilient subject is required to accept the dangerousness of the world it lives in as a condition for partaking of that world and accept the necessity of the injunction to change itself in correspondence with threats now presupposed as endemic and unavoidable. As Zygmunt Bauman writes:

> Fear is arguably the most sinister of demons nesting in the open societies of our times. But it is the insecurity of the present and the uncertainty about the future that hatch and breed the most awesome and least bearable of our fears. That insecurity and that uncertainty, in their turn, are born of a sense of impotence; we seem to no longer be in control, whether singly, severally or collectively – and to make things still worse we lack the tools that would allow politics to be lifted to the level where power has already settled . . .[4]

Building resilient subjects involves the deliberate disabling of the political habits, tendencies and capacities of peoples and replacing them with adaptive ones. Resilient subjects, in other words, have accepted the imperative not to resist or secure themselves from the dangers they face. Nor are they capable of viewing the world beyond the catastrophic. Instead, they adapt to their enabling conditions via the embrace of a neoliberal rationality that fosters a belief in the necessity of risk as a private good. As Lenztos and Rose suggest, resilience is all about the active promotion of a life which accepts insecurity with vulnerable surety:

> resilience implies a systematic, widespread, organizational, structural and personal strengthening of subjective and material arrangements so as to be better able to anticipate

and tolerate disturbances in complex worlds without collapse, to withstand shocks, and to rebuild as necessary . . . a logic of resiliency would aspire to create a subjective and systematic state to enable each and all to live freely and with confidence in a world of potential risks.[5]

In drawing out the theoretical assumptions behind the promotion of resilience and its implications for issues of political subjectivity, it is clear that we need to establish a biopolitical framework of analysis through which discourses of resilience, adaptation and vulnerability can be denaturalized and challenged. In contestation of this discursive framing of the human, we will go on to argue for a reconstituted understanding of the human as a fundamentally political subject; one empowered by its hubristic belief in an ability to secure itself from those elements of the world it encounters as hostile to its world, rather than being cast in a permanent condition of resilient adaptation to a biologized understanding of the nature of the world as such. Understanding how the hubris of the human has been weeded out by liberal governance requires examining the biopolitics of the neoliberal framing of the subject; the reduction of the human to the biological properties and capacities it shares with all other forms of species life and consequent constitution of a form of biohuman subjectivity. Life, we maintain, cannot simply be reduced to the level of a natural force such that any affirmative desire to find meaning beyond the biological has no political resonance.

When Foucault originally examined the biopolitics of liberalism, he was looking at regimes of power that thrived on their abilities to secure human populations from whatever was found to be threatening and dangerous. The entrenchment of liberalism in those very rationalities which claimed to protect life itself by 'making life live' through various progressive registers has only become deeper over the course of liberal modernity. As a result, the pathologization of subjects defined by their supposed antipathy to life has only become more vicious as liberalism has matured.

Whilst this violence has been well documented, there is, however, something more at stake here with the advent of the Anthropocene. For when we examine more rigorously neoliberal regimes of power today, we find that the terms of their legitimacy have changed in accordance with a much altered account of the life whose existence is now said to be endangered. That is to say, the legitimacy of neoliberal regimes, contrasted with the classical forms of liberal regime which Foucault examined, depends on claims as to their abilities to protect the life not of human populations as such, but that of the biosphere. Neoliberalism, it seems, has broken from earlier liberalisms, then, in that it correlates claims for its legitimacy not simply with practices for the development of the species life of humanity, as Foucault directed us to recognize, but with biospherical life.

These emerging correlations between security governance, development and biospherical life increasingly compromise the foundation of earlier biopolitics that simply took the life of populations to be its object. We cannot understand how liberalism functions, then, especially how it has gained a global position of political hegemony, without addressing how the category of life has been systematically organized and radically transformed, leading to the correlation of its various practices of governance with the securitization of planetary life and everything in-between. Hence, the contemporary shift in the organization of life at a social level, along with the fundamental transformation of the human to the posthuman subject, would seem to be profoundly important for anyone concerned with dealing with the raw reality of neoliberal power and the search to think beyond liberalism and political realism in the twenty-first century.

Evacuating the Social

The social state has been under attack for over three decades. While the ideas of the Austrian school of economic thought marked out a new moral agenda for neoliberal power as the market became a political force for freedom and emancipation, the absorption of these ideas into the field of security governance has displaced the delivery of social services away from sovereign states to fragmented forms of welfare provision. This shift towards what has been termed 'rule by experts' has produced novel alliances between the public and the private such that ideas of social responsibility and care have increasingly conformed to neoliberal principles, modes of operation, along with marketized delivery. Key here has been the insistence that neoliberalism offers the best way to incentivize populations which, in the process, results in the most efficient and effective allocation of scarce resources. This is more than some well-rehearsed economic argument. It gets us right to the heart of contemporary discourses on security, power, organization, political authenticity, along with the biopolitically driven contours of the human species. For it is here we encounter the subject of vulnerability which appears to be both an unending problem to be solved and a condition of possibility for modes of living once denied by the regimentation of social states. Vulnerability, in other words, is integral to management and regulation of neoliberal subjects who are encouraged to partake in a world that subscribes to a belief that everything is fleeting. As Bauman writes on the seemingly terminal fate of the social:

> Like everything else in such a liquid world, all wisdom and know-how is bound to age quickly, and quickly suck dry and use up the advantages it once offered; so there is a refusal to accept established knowledge, an unwillingness to go by precedents, and a gnawing suspicion as to the value of the received lore of experience in the search for effectiveness and productivity. Managers would rather 'scan the network of possibilities', free to pause for a while whenever opportunity seems to be knocking at the door, and free to move again once opportunity starts knocking

elsewhere. They are eager to play the uncertain game; they seek *chaos* rather than *order*.[6]

Henry Giroux calls this condition the 'twilight of the social'. As he explains, 'Social progress has ceded the historical stage to individual actions, values, tastes and personal success, just as any notion of the common and public good that once defined the meaning of progress is rendered as pathology, the vestige of a kind of socialist nightmare that squelches any possibility of individual freedom and responsibility'.[7] Recounting Walter Benjamin's comments on Paul Klee's *Angelus Novus*, Giroux stakes out here the shift from utopianism to the embrace of the catastrophic and its penchant towards the violence of the encounter. With the idea of social responsibility replaced by a neoliberalized care for the self, Benjamin's 'Angel of History' 'has been blinded and can no longer see the destruction beneath its feet or the clouds paralyzing its wings. It is now stuck in a storm without a past and lacking any consideration of the future'.[8] Giroux thus affirms our earlier suspicions about memory and the utopic vision. What we now encounter here is *difference without repetition*. Historical memory speaks nothing to the future. Nothing is repeated as far as catastrophic events are concerned. What takes its place is an imaginary of threat which, in the context of condemning certain epistemic communities for always and already being out of date as they always and already appear out of sync with our emergent times, leads to the evacuation of the political agora. As Bauman further explains:

> Left increasingly to their own resources and acumen, individuals are expected to devise individual solutions to socially generated problems, and to do it individually, using their individual skills and individually possessed assets . . . If it is not mitigated by institutional intervention, this 'individualisation by decree' renders the differentiation and polarisation of individual chances inescapable; indeed,

it makes the polarisation of prospects and chances into a self-propelling and self-accelerating process.[9]

Despite Friederich Von Hayek's protestations, neoliberalism has never been about giving everything over to the market. There is no such thing as a 'free market' in the strictest sense of the term. It remains deeply concerned with the conduct of conduct of individuals and populations to further the creation of desiring subjects. Bauman's idea here, of 'individualisation by decree', captures brilliantly how resilience is a form of neoliberal *interventionism* which, speaking in a governing tone, nevertheless segregates life on account of its vulnerable qualities as a self-propelling tendency and emancipatory orientation. The connections here to contemporary austerity measures are particularly striking. Such calls have nothing to say about political processes or opening new sites for emancipation. The political is in fact pathologized as an unnecessary impediment to the austere vision. What is demanded is a new sense of social responsibility that places the burden of the crises directly onto the shoulders of the globally impoverished, thereby rendering social safety nets as part of the wider systemic problem. This demands novel forms of interventionism based upon the premise that being resilient is to accept responsibility for one's individual position in a complex social fabric that is insecure by design. Austerity thus conceived is not simply a constraint. It is further revealing of a shift in attitudes towards insecurity such that societies must not give up hope (let alone adopt a radically new political agenda) despite the virulent turbulence. As Mark Neocleous puts it:

> This increased prominence of 'resilience' during the rise of neoliberalism is significant. Although this connection might seem odd, given that more than anything resilience assumes a massive state role in planning for the future, the point of this future is that it is unknown and uncertain . . . But the term has been expanded to straddle the private as well as the public, the personal as well as the political, the

subjective as well as the objective, and so systemic, organizational, and political resilience is connected to personal resilience in such a way that contemporary political subjectivity now has to be thought through 'the power of resilience'. Thus one finds texts about resilience as a personal attribute in which citizen-subjects are trained to 'achieve balance, confidence and personal strength', or, in the subtitle of another, 'find inner strength and overcome life's hurdles', or better still, just 'bounce back' from whatever life throws at us.[10]

We must insist that the constitution of inner strength requires certain forms of intervention. And that intervention is always the political expressed as force. Such force may resonate solely within expressive realms of ideas or translate into the expressive realm of action. Since intervention always requires acting upon life to change a particular predisposition, it always evidences certain violence. To intervene is to violate the body of the living in one way or another. That which is currently given to form needs to be exorcized to permit the future recovery of the souls of the living. Resilience follows such exorcism in unforgiving and unapologetic ways. It does not accept life in its current formations. It demands open access to the soul of the living on account of the fact that continual manipulation is the only guarantee of survivability. Strategically promoting continual adaptation and change in the subject's ontological and epistemological status, i.e. the subject can always be made more progressively secure (a formulation in itself which recognizes no point of terminus), the interventionary premise of thinking about life beyond life nevertheless still operates within a politically allegiant framework. That is to say, resilience fosters an exposure to the catastrophic or what we have elected to term the 'lethal principle' so that life may carry on living with more resolute purpose. Such is the conviction that a belief is fostered that the best way to deal with endangerment is to internalize its very occurrence within the vital networks for existence. Only then do we become more than our current selves. As we shall now discover, this has had a profound impact upon the nature of the subject, as the networked self is ensnared within both technical and natural frames that promote a certain type of intellectualism.

The Posthuman

So what becomes of the subject when traditional ideas of social belonging are displaced by the networked language of connectivity? And how does this connect to biopolitical moves away from the problem of populations to all life itself? We have come a long way since Foucault's provocation that until the modern period 'the subject' didn't exist in the sense that it wasn't compelled to live in a productive and socially minded way. Life in this respect had to be *invented* as a *problem* which required scientific verification to the fact of its existence, along with the wider development of regimes of truth which *projected* the subject beyond its current condition. The modern subject needed to be continually reworked for modernity itself to have any lasting meaning and positive purchase over the lives of those in whose name it operated. Humanism thus appeared as mediation on this projection of life wherein a certain commitment to the subject could be established in support for its capacity for self-ruination. What was humanism after all if not a discourse on the failures and limitations of the subject to achieve a more divine and eternal status? How, then, might we ask, would Foucault have revised his thesis on the 'invention of man' once we accept profound ontological and epistemological shifts in the 'fundamental arrangements of knowledge'?[11] Could we 'wager', as Foucault inquired, that 'man would be erased, like a face drawn in the sand by the edge of the sea'?

Let's consider for a moment the underside of liberal theories of international relations which address the implications of the global interconnectivity wrought by the information revolution. Social, political and governmental transformations are presumed to have followed on from the utilization of the new extents and qualities of connectivity produced by this techno-scientific revolution. From this, a new kind of people is said to have emerged; the Connected.[12] The Connected represents no less than 'the transformation of sociability' itself.[13] It is more social than any other historical social formation. For never has there been a people, we are told, more social, with more friends and contacts, or more socially and politically active, than the Connected. Facebook is its niche space of habitat. The Connected are also more skilled than any other historical social formation. For never have there been a people who are more competent analytically, emotionally and imaginatively.[14] Learning is its way of life. The Connected, then, are a people, we are told, more informed. They are exponentially richer in information than any other historical social formation. Networking is its source of power. But this is not simply a sociological phenomenon demanding new mapping practices from ethnographers. The 'skills revolution' formative of the Connected has initiated what one leading liberal in International Relations hails as no less than 'a major transformation of the global structures that govern world affairs'. A transformation in governmental vision and practice has followed as old ideals of government are outdated by new concepts of global liberal governance that aspire to generate order 'from below', through the networking practices, information sharing and learning activities of the Connected, obviating the need for recourse to the institutions and practices of state sovereignty.

The Connected here initially figures as a techno-scientific ensemble that is assumed to constitute the social basis for a new self-organizing system of international relations, gradually transforming existing institutions and practices of state sovereignty into something more benign and beneficent to human life on a global scale. Life in the process becomes a nodal point of interconnectivity, forever (dis) engaging with all the elements which constitute its active living space. But from where does this evolutionary account of the nature and power of connectivity, and its fortunate coincidence with information technologies, derive? And what impact does this have on the subject as a political problem? To understand why proponents of global liberal governance such as James Rosenau[15] valorize this shift requires understanding the development of the theory of connectivity and its importance for research into learning and the discovery of the functions of information which have gradually transformed the ways in which the life sciences understand the conditions for human evolution and survivability. This requires us to engage with the vexed and convoluted processes of epistemic transfer via which theorizations of connectivity have impacted on the social and natural sciences, not excluding International Relations.

Since the 1940s, and the advent of cybernetics in particular, it has been reasoned that of all known species humans are superiorly endowed with the capacity to learn. 'The human species', the founder of cybernetics, Norbert Wiener, argued, 'is strong only insofar as it takes advantage of the innate adaptive, learning faculties that its physiological structure makes possible'.[16] The interior complexity of the human, the immense interconnectivity of its body, enabling an unrivalled corporeal capacity for the circulation of information, in turn is said to have constituted the conditions in which it is able forge connections with members of its own species as well as with other species, and learn, specifically through the exchange of information with them and the environments in which they co-evolve. We are then best equipped to adapt in the great struggle for life that shapes existence in the biosphere. Wiener's gambit was, as is now well recorded, that if humans could create a machine distinguished with a physiological structure as connected as they themselves possessed, they could create a machine endowed with those powers of learning which made them superior.[17] The digital machine was the first of these experiments at self-replicating superiority. A machine consisting in a 'sequence of switching devices in which the opening of a later switch depends on the action of precise combinations of earlier switches leading into it, which open at the same time', and which thus corresponded in function to the physiological 'transmission of impulses across layers of syntactic connections' through which messages of information traverse human bodies and via which the human learns.[18]

Wiener's achievement in constructing the first digital device should not be diminished. This was a new form of techno-scientific know-how, based on remarkable insights into the centrality of information and connectivity for the processes of learning through which living systems, the human chief among them, adapt and evolve biologically. It was a know-how that proved to be of significance because of the technological spin-offs it spawned, for the military capacities of the allied powers to win the war against fascism in Europe and beyond.[19] It was also a know-how which has made possible the immense further discoveries and advances in science and technology that have impacted so widely on the organization of liberal democracies in the decades since the Second World War, as well as empowered the liberal way of war which has enabled the global hegemony of liberal democratic states worldwide since the end of the Cold War. Such technologies, however, had inevitable consequences. As life became information, so we witnessed a dramatic revision in what it was to be human as well as what it was, more broadly, to be a living thing.[20] And given, especially, the now widespread manifestation and exploitation of the ability to create machines said to display the same forms of intelligence possessed by humans as well as all other living systems, it was a knowledge which effectively collapsed earlier conceptual distinctions between the human, the living and its technological systems.[21] A *posthuman* knowledge, which undercut modernist understandings of the specificity of the human as a biological entity alone, its claims to distinction from other species, as well as the political categories on which human specificity was previously constructed in the sciences and beyond. As Anthony Miccoli writes, 'the posthuman becomes a means to substantiate and anthropomorphize the technical other into something that can be embraced (and embrace back) in light of the "building out" of skill which characterizes technological development'.[22]

It is precisely this revised and radically posthuman ontology that we encounter at work in liberal theories of International Relations championing the emancipatory potentials of the Connected. Rosenau's work is a case in point. But while following cybernetic narratives by arguing for an understanding of the Connected as the culmination of a 'continuous process of evolution',[23] Rosenau also cautions his readership as to its non-teleological character. The emergence of the Connected, he warns, 'does not just suddenly happen. Circumstances have to be suitable, people have to be amenable to collective decisions being made, tendencies towards organization have to develop, habits of cooperation have to evolve, and a readiness not to impede the processes of emergence and evolution has to persist'.[24] This is an important qualification. Alerting us to the political dimensions of connectivity, here we are forced to accept its fundamentally non-neutral and ambivalent qualities. The amenability of people, the development of tendencies, the production of habits, the removal of impositions, the persistence of evolutionary processes already in train; all of these, we are told quite explicitly, are prerequisite conditions for the emergence of the Connected. What these qualifiers openly tell us, of course, is that the advance of the Connected does not depend, simply, on the unfolding of inherently natural processes of evolutionary improvement, but on the establishment of strategic conditions in which the Connected can be constituted. If the Connected exists, its emergence has to be explained politically, not simply with reference to forces of nature or biological evolution.

So what are those conditions through which the Connected may be authenticated? As Foucault taught us, the

liberal project is distinguished by its faith in the ability to
correlate the political development of humanity with
knowledge of its biological properties and capacities. Ever
since its inception in the early modern era, its success has
depended on strategies to promote those tendencies and
habits within governed populations which accord with the
'biological destiny of the species', and that has required
the deployment of all manner of 'technologies of security'.[25] Since the eighteenth century, for example, the 'technologies of security' deployed by liberal regimes have been
concerned with promoting biopolitical tendencies and
habits of 'circulations' within a given population base.[26]
Today they are also concerned with promoting tendencies
and habits of connectivity. Indeed, we may argue that there
is no circulation, authentically conceived, without connectivity of a sort. The information technologies that
enable us to connect more and better, be they mobile
phones, laptop computers, or iPods, are, in this sense, far
from neutral in operation. They are all enfolded within
desiring frames which, rather than being used by humans
to increase natural propensities, are deployed by liberal
regimes of power to constitute humans with specific
tendencies and habits. We only need to turn to Martin
Heidegger here to appreciate that technology is never
merely an instrument that humans use for its own autonomous enjoyment; it is a way of enframing the human as a
thing which both uses and can be utilized, specifically
made as a thing that in its utilizing practices is useful for
securing a technologized order of things.[27]

Connectivity repeats the same manoeuvre. For here a
subject appears who in order to realize its capacities for
connectivity has to be taught how to be connective. As
Rosenau's qualifications makes clear, the Connected does
not merely use information technologies; it requires pre-
coded or scripted technologies to constitute the connective
habits and tendencies which will subject it to the lore of
connectivity from which information technologies derive
their utility. For the Connected to emerge, subjects must

be amenable to connectivity as such. Where they are not, or when they contest connectivity, they will require transforming, and if not transformable then removing; if necessary with violence, force and war.[28] Either way, disconnected and autonomous peoples must be made into connected and dependent ones. Not only does this demand continual intervention for every connection may hold the potential to disconnect at any given moment. The very act of disconnection at the point of the disconnect forces us to confront what Miccoli calls our *posthuman suffering* through which 'human agency is brought into question when we experience technological failures that are less about the technology per se than our ability to opt into the connected realm of experience. We subconsciously (and traumatically) cede power to our technological artefacts, and are further traumatised when those artefacts fail'.[29]

Let's look at this from a different perspective. Different formations of disconnectivity demand different strategies and modes of engagement. There is the Disconnected one can transform through establishing and promoting connectivity itself. Knock a hole in the wall of a slum, install a computer kiosk within it, allow the children of that slum to use it freely, and so the theory goes, you transform the Disconnected into the Connected, without recourse to physical force, law or military violence.[30] But there is also the Disconnected which refuses the connection and by dint of which refusal demands either violent transformation or annihilation. Thomas P.M. Barnett, adviser in the US to the Office of the Secretary of Defence (OSD), and a leading advocate of the liberal way of war, describes how there exists today a global divide between a 'functioning core' of connected peoples and a 'non-integrating gap' of disconnected ones.[31] However, the disconnection which Barnett describes is not merely a technological problem, nor can it be measured along an axis determined by analytical, emotional or imaginational variables. People who are disconnected from the 'rules' (or to use network language the 'codes'), which define the organization of life within the liberal core, by virtue of that failure, 'demand attention from U.S. military forces'.[32] As Barnett argues, 'disconnectedness defines dangers. If you're looking for instability and threats to the functioning of the international system and the global economy, you're looking at this Non-integrating Gap. That's where you're going to find the transnational terrorist networks. That's where their interior lines of communication are found'.[33] Something remarkable is assumed to happen here to the question of agency as all mediations on violence are effectively absolved of any human complicity. As Elaine Scarry writes, 'So completely have the formerly embodied skills of weapon use been appropriated into the interior of the weapon itself that no human *skill* is now required; and because the need for human skills is eliminated the human act of *consent* is eliminated. The *building in of skill* thus becomes the most triumphant form, the *building out* of consent'.[34]

The technical connect is, however, only one part of the complex interface. No sooner had military and security strategists started to appreciate the benefits of the informational revolution such that we witness a veritable revolution in military affairs, so the human and natural sciences offer a wider biospheric complimentary within the Anthropocentric frame. Nature itself begins to resemble a highly complex, adaptive, information-rich, emergent system that is open to the most micro-specific interventions. Indeed, it is the micro-specific which becomes integral to understanding major changes in macro-physical climatic conditions. While the connect to nature is often touted by activists as something that stands in marked contrast with the neoliberal pursuit of further techno-scientific progress, they have in fact proved to be wholly complementary to the broadening of concerns with underdevelopment, violence and environmental degradation. In sum, as human life begins to stand out alone only in terms of its connectivity and survivability within an already enclosed system that connects with it despite whatever attempts the subject may make to find lasting refuge, all that remains is an acceptance that one must partake in the world. It would be a mistake, however, to see the imperative to technically connect and the impossibility of the natural disconnect as being logically incompatible. They are fully revealing of the very notion that our systems are inherently insecure by design and, despite our best efforts, the catastrophe still awaits. Although we profoundly disagree with the claim, not least the abandonment of political agency, it is worth noting how evolutionary geneticists assess the intellectual implications of this equation of intelligence to catastrophic adaptation as if intellect itself runs a natural and turbulent evolutionary course which omits the deluded hallmarks of a 'descent of man':

> I would wager that if an average citizen from Athens of 1000 BC were to appear suddenly among us, he or she would be among the brightest and most intellectually alive of our colleagues and companions, with a good memory, a broad range of ideas and a clear-sighted view of important issues . . . The basis for my wager comes from new developments in genetics, anthropology, and neurobiology that make a clear prediction that our intellectual and emotional abilities are genetically surprisingly fragile.[35]

The Valorization of Adaptability

While security has functioned historically as the major rationality for the subjection of populations to liberal governance, the rationality which governs that subjection is fast becoming that of resilience. As such the policy problematic of liberal regimes of governance is undergoing a global shift from that of how to secure the human to how to render it resilient. When policy-makers engage in the discourse of resilience, they do so in terms which aim explicitly at preventing humans from conceiving of danger as a phenomenon from which they might seek freedom and even, in contrast, as that to which they must now expose themselves. This is because of the ways in which the modelling of neoliberal subjectivity reifies its biological status as the domain of agency and governance. Life, biologically understood, is an extremely difficult entity to secure. It has a habit of dying on you, undergoing change, eluding your grasp, defying your will to control it. Not only is it difficult to secure, the very attempt to secure it can, it is said, have deleterious effects on it. The more you try to secure life, the more you thwart its ambitions, even to the point of eventually killing it. Security, then, is dangerous, authors of risk acceptance say, paradoxically, because it defies the necessity of danger, preventing the necessary exposure to danger, without which the life of the neoliberal subject cannot grow and prosper.

Once the practice of freeing oneself from danger is rendered, as it has now become, a pathological disposition of humans who are not attuned to the dangerous realities of the times, the problem becomes not how to secure the human but how to enable it to outlive its proclivity for security. How to alter its disposition in relation with danger so that it construes danger not as something it might seek freedom from, but which it must live in exposure to in order to become more reasonably human. Resilient subjects embody these reasonable lives. They are subjects who have learnt the lesson of the dangers of the myth of lasting security, in order to live out a life of permanent exposure to dangers that are not only beyond their abilities to overcome, but necessary for the prosperity of their life. As Al Siebert proclaims in another of those self-help guides for the non-lamenting resilient subject:

> Sadly, some people get stuck in the victim/blaming mode when their lives are disrupted. They reject all suggestions on how to cope with what happened. They won't take steps to overcome their difficulties even after the crisis is over . . . Victim thinking keeps people feeling helpless, and by blaming others for their bad situations, they place responsibility on others for making their lives better . . . Highly resilient people [in contrast] are flexible, adapt to new circumstances quickly, and thrive in constant change.

Most importantly, they expect to bounce back and feel
confident they will. They have a knack for creating
good luck out of circumstances that many others see as
bad luck.[36]

Here, we now turn our attentions to the modelling of
neoliberal subjectivity, further, onto the terrain of another
concept and capacity, dear to the liberal tradition; that of
autonomy. Traditionally, we are used to thinking about
the liberal subject as the autonomous subject. By autonomous, we mean a subject defined by its disconnection from
other human beings, and a certain non-adaptivity or resistance to the will of others. Disconnection and non-adap-
tation were once understood as conditions of possibility
within the liberal tradition. As Isaiah Berlin describes in
his classic essay, 'Two Concepts of Liberty', the liberal
wishes 'to be a subject, not an object; to be moved by
reasons, by conscious purposes, which are his own, not
by causes which affect him, as it were, from outside. He
wishes to be somebody, not nobody; a doer – deciding,
not being decided for, self-directed and not acted upon by
external nature or by other men as if he were a thing, or
an animal, or a slave incapable of playing a human role,
that is, of conceiving goals and policies of his own and
realising them'.[37] In contrast with Berlin's classical vision,
when liberals engage today in promoting the life of human
beings, they do so in terms that aim at preventing us from
conceiving our capacities to determine our own ways of
life in freedom from others as a state to strive for and, in
contrast, as a potential risk unto ourselves. Autonomy, it
is said, equals a diminished capacity to connect with and
adapt to others, and so to be autonomous has become
conceived less as a condition to strive for, and more as a
source of danger to oneself and the life of others. Exposed
to the dangers on which its life is said to thrive, the neoliberal subject is nevertheless called upon to fend off the
formation of anything like an autonomously determined
way of life, on account of the risks said to be posed by

autonomy to the sanctity of life. These have become the paradoxical stakes of the contemporary and ongoing shift in discourses of governance and subjection characteristic of neoliberalism.

As with the pathologization of security under conditions of neoliberalism, so the pathologization of autonomy and subsequent valorization of adaptation has been fed by ideas and discourses deriving not just from outside of political science, but from beyond the social sciences strictly conceived. It is the life sciences that account for much of the thinking concerning the problematic nature of autonomy and importance of adaptation and connectivity as requisite capacities for the development of neoliberal subjectivity. The ongoing pathologization of autonomy began less in the political discourses of liberal practitioners or thinkers, but in the context of scientific studies of non-human living systems. To a certain extent, this pathologization of autonomy follows on from the pathologization of security and shift to resilience. As we saw in the previous chapter, ecology has played a powerful discursive role in enabling the rise of the latter concept. But the life science of biology has been equally important in shaping the critique of security within neoliberal discourse, as well as enabling the proliferation of ideas concerning the importance of adaptivity and correlating arguments for the diminishment of autonomy as something altogether abnormal. Understanding how neoliberalism has problematized and pathologized autonomy thus requires contextualizing that move within the deeper scientific problematization and pathologization of security such that we can begin to appreciate resilience as a key marker of neoliberal subjectivity.

Connecting with Danger

If it is ecology that has been most vocal in pronouncing the finitude of human life, the fragility of its dependence

on the biosphere, and its consequent exposure to the
dangers of ecological catastrophe, it is molecular biology
which has been most powerful in expressing faith in the
potential of the human to be able to go on living and thriving in a context of such finitude, vulnerability and potential catastrophe. Indeed the very idea of life as a phenomenon
of finitude, vulnerability and exposure to danger has been
valorized by molecular biology throughout its history as a
condition of possibility, rather than an obstacle, for human
development. This has happened to the extent that theories
of economic growth have, over the last ten years, tended
to merge and benefit from their intersection with theories
of how life grows and develops, at the molecular level,
through exposure to danger.[38] There are already some
excellent histories of this molecular history available.[39]
Significantly, it was in the 1990s that influential molecular
biologists such as Stuart Kauffman, for example, began to
argue that living systems cannot, by definition, be secured
from dangers, because their very capacity to go on living
depends, fundamentally, not on their *freedom from* danger
but on their *exposure to* danger. So the evolutionary development of living systems is dictated by the fundamental
law of 'emergence', which requires that they engage in a
continual process of exposure to danger even to the point
of potential catastrophe (Kauffman 2000: 157).[40] We may
even pre-emptively create the conditions for the catastrophic so that we can control its emergence on our terms,
rendering the event somewhat amenable. Without that
exposure to danger, living systems then cannot evolve, and
those which do attempt to disconnect themselves from
their dangers will lose touch with their own powers of
propagation, to the extent that they will finally wither
away and die. Standing still thus becomes the surest sign
of the subject sounding a fateful retreat.

The concept of resilience refers to the 'buffer capacities'
of living systems; their ability to 'absorb perturbations' or
the 'magnitude of disturbance that can be absorbed before
a living system changes its structure by changing the

variables and processes that control behaviour'.[41] Living systems develop not on account of their ability to secure themselves from dangers, but through their abilities to absorb the perturbations that occur on account of their necessary exposure to them. Exposure to danger is a constitutive process in the development of living systems, and thus their problem is never how to secure themselves from it but how to develop the resilience which enables them to absorb the perturbations, disturbances and changes in their structure which occur in the process of their exposure to that which may endanger. It is all about thriving in complex systems which promote radical connectivity and accept radical uncertainty. And so, it is said, once the human is conceived in accordance with the laws that determine the life of other living systems, so that life must develop the selfsame capacities for resilience, enabling it to avoid the temptation to secure itself from danger, exposing itself in contrast to danger, while learning how to absorb the perturbations that occur to it in that process of wilfully encountering what poses a threat to its very existence. This is not the armoury of sovereign protection. It is the armoury of exposure.

Such accounts of how life 'connects with danger' in the biological domain may well hold some validity. A political scientist is not necessarily well positioned to question knowledge and laws deriving from the life sciences as they are applied to the study of the interface between biological species and the ecological systems with which they are said to co-evolve. What concerns us, however, is what happens when such frameworks are transferred to the human world of peoples. The results we find are politically debasing, for it is on account of such an errant transfer of assumptions that the subject is denied the capacity to demand of the regime which governs it that it provide freedoms from the dangers which it perceives as threatening it. This element of the terms of legitimation of modern regimes of political power has, of course, been fundamental historically, and yet is now in the process of rapid erosion, on account of the influence of these scientific ways of thinking about life and danger within liberal discourse. The neoliberal subject is not a subject which can conceive the possibility of securing itself from its dangers. It believes in the necessity of life as a permanent struggle of adaptation to dangers. Indeed, since the resilient subject accepts the dangerousness of the world it lives in as a condition for partaking of that world, and accepts the necessity of the injunction to change itself in correspondence with the dangers now presupposed as endemic, building neoliberal subjects involves the deliberate disabling of the aspirations to security which peoples might otherwise nurture, and replacing them with adaptive ones. Resilient subjects have accepted the imperative not to secure themselves from the dangers they are faced with but instead adapt repeatedly to their conditions, in the same manner that living systems, right down to weed species, adapt continually to the changing topographies of the dangers they encounter.

This is one of the catastrophic outcomes of Anthropocentric thought. Once the catastrophic becomes the condition of possibility for partaking in the world, life is inevitably reduced to the level of a natural force. It actually omits no differential qualities whatsoever, despite scientifically verifiable claims to superiority in terms of its complex design and capacities for adaptation. Gone, then, are mediations on the human subjects' lone capacity for reason, along with the ability to connect language with thought. And so too are any claims that human life is uniquely endowed with the capacity to think and act metaphysically, i.e. that there may be something more than human to life. Obliterated by a new intellectualism or what we prefer to term post-metaphysical dogmatism, it is quite literally 'down to earth'. So while we may have become the principal architects of worldly affairs on account of the sheer volume of our systemic activity that is profoundly shaping the biosphere, our self-reductionism to a purely biological state of being denies us the prospect to think poetically as it renders us vulnerable and fleeting.

Once exposure to danger becomes a condition of possibility for the subject, so the question posed of the subject is no longer whether you can exercise freedom in securing yourself from the dangers that you are faced with in living. The question becomes whether you are able to construe your freedom to live in the form of exposure to danger. Can you, in other words, as Foucault detailed in his *Birth of Biopolitics* lectures, accept and rise to the neoliberal injunction to 'live dangerously'? At its classical origins, however, and as Foucault detailed in those lectures, the early liberal subject, while living on the basis of an understanding as to the necessity of and even stimulus of danger, nevertheless aspired to achieve a condition of 'least exposure to danger'.[42] Its exercise of freedom was problematized as a dangerous activity; one that could have dangerous effects, for itself and those affected by it, but which could nevertheless be governed in a way that enabled it to minimize the extent of its exposure. This led to the development of liberalism as an art of governance conditioned by what Foucault described as 'strategies of security'.[43] Today, in marked contrast, the displacement of the very aspiration to security and shift to a discourse of resilience signals the changing nature of liberalism as it comes to terms with the failures of its universal political aspirations, along with highlighting the extent to which the conflation between liberalism and neoliberalism promotes insecurity as the principal design for governmental reasoning. It is no longer a question of how to secure freedoms for the subject in the condition of their potential to become dangerous, either to the individual or the collective, but how the subject might practise freedom so that it achieves exposure to danger on behalf of itself and that population to which it contributes. Endangerment, it is now said, is productive of life, individually and collectively.

The submission of the subject to this injunction to expose itself to danger requires, however, its prior subjection to the biological lore that, in spite of its humanism and discourses on freedom, actually underwrites liberalism. In other words, conceptions of relations between its own life and the dangers it encounters must conform to the demands of liberalism's biological account of life. Because biological life cannot free itself from danger without endangering its very capacities to go on living, so, it is said, must the liberal subject accept the same terms and conditions for the exercise of its political freedom in determining its way of life. Its freedom to determine the way in which it lives must be circumscribed by the biological imperative to expose itself to danger. It cannot live a life premised upon achieving freedom from dangers since such an undertaking would be tantamount to opposing the fundamental laws of life as determined by biological necessity. Such an act would be treasonous to the positive empiricism which liberalism holds true. Recognizing, then, that a constitutive function of the biological lore of liberalism means we can only obtain a superficial grasp of how neoliberal regimes of governance achieve this dual debasement of the subject's capacities for security and autonomy, what is required is a more critical focus on the so-called economic dimensions of the injunction to 'live dangerously'. Only then can we begin to understand how resilience is an extension of neoliberal governance which displaces any sense of social responsibility and pastoral care with a care for the self that naturalizes the conditions of vulnerability.

Since the publication of *The Birth of Biopolitics* lecture series, it has been common to suggest that Foucault abandoned his prior ideas of how to approach liberalism and gave himself up to a quasi-Marxist understanding of liberalism as a regime of economy. Foucault's discussions of neoliberalism thus appear to suggest 'that the security sought by biopolitics is mediated by a fundamentally economistic horizon of thought'.[44] Whilst economy does appear like some divine force that changes the contours of liberal rule, the incitement of the subject to 'engage in risk taking and entrepreneurialism' must also account for the biologization of the subject that liberalism is founded on, and

subsequently, the shift in thinking concerning how biological life profits in the world through a continual process of
exposure to danger. Even if there is not much reference to
the 'biopolitics' of the liberal subject, Foucault's wider
engagement with liberal economy nevertheless remains
committed to revealing its biopoliticization. It is nonsense,
then, to suggest that 'the inculcation of an entrepreneurial
spirit'[45] should be considered the end of biopolitical governance. To think so is to fail to grasp the depth of the
concept of biopolitics. The incitement of the liberal subject
to take risks is the means by which the life of that subject,
it is assumed, can be saved from itself and all that threatens
its prosperity. It is life, not economy abstractly understood,
that mediates the horizons of liberal thought and practice,
for Foucault. The concept of economy is merely one powerful and important discourse within which liberal understandings of the nature of life, as such, operates.

   Discourses and practices of resilience are intimately tied
to neoliberal economic policies, dedicated to developing
and protecting neoliberal institutions, including markets
and market-based forms of governance. But the legitimacy
of these institutions, practices of governance, along with
the subjectivities they require all depend on the virtues they
are said to possess vis-à-vis the welfare of the life of the
liberal subject. It does in fact inaugurate a new discourse
around welfare which, rendering the social state naive in
its quest to guarantee lasting protections, promotes a
certain care for the self that valorizes adaptability while
remaining allegiant to the logic of risk. This is precisely
why, for example, the development of neoliberal economic
policies has become so vigorously correlated with strategies for disaster management. There is profit (monetarily
and epistemologically) to be made out of the encounter
with the catastrophic. And this is also precisely why the
development of resilient strategies has been matched by a
veritable explosion of self-help guides to better prepare
individuals for all eventualities. With the social state
stripped back for more than two decades, even though the

military-policing state has assumed an unquestionable status, to be prepared is a matter of personal responsibility that does not question whether it is radically possible to address political questions of inequality, but instead is content with compensation for just enough survivability. As one particular resiliently minded expert puts it:

What I suggest is that a 'functional' approach be taken where vulnerability and resilience are assessed on the basis of the ability of a person or group or community to work towards and to attain certain basic goals, such as the capacity to manage their own affairs, to have access to appropriate and appropriate levels of resources, including food, water, shelter, health care, education, and cultural activity, social inclusion, and information and other necessary and desirable services. This approach can also be applied to groups and communities. Can they meet their goals in the face of specified systemic shocks and disasters?[46]

– 3 –

The Poverty of Vulnerability

Sustainable Recoveries

The contemporary concern of global governmental policies and practices with the promotion of resilience is very much an expression of liberalism's changing fortunes. Rather than enabling the development of peoples and individuals so that they can aspire to secure themselves from whatever they find threatening and dangerous in worldly living, the liberal discourse of resilience functions to convince peoples and individuals that the dream of lasting security is impossible. To be resilient, the subject must disavow any belief in the possibility to secure itself from the insecure sediment of existence, accepting instead an understanding of life as a permanent process of continual adaptation to threats and dangers which appear outside its control. Resilient subjects have to accept this imperative not to resist or secure themselves from the difficulties they face. Instead they adapt to their enabling conditions via the embrace of neoliberalism and its attendant demands to thrive in times of radical uncertainty. Nowhere is this trend more prevalent than in the domain of development discourse and practice. As we will see, the paradigm shift from development to sustainable development in particular has been of fundamental importance to the growth of resilience discourse and neoliberal strategies for the depoliticization of the human. For it is within this field of development that we encounter the complementary processes that lead to the promotion of life as a political problem, and its potent cartography of human separation which puts the social burden directly onto the shoulders of impoverished subjects.

To explain these dual moves, it is important to chart how the discourse of resilience has been articulated, firstly through the emergence of the doctrine of sustainable development, and the allied rise in influence of ecology, which can itself be attributed partly to the success of the environmental movement in reshaping the agenda of liberal governance, by shifting the locus of concern from the issue of the security of merely human life to that of the biosphere, but which must also be understood as an aspect of the ways in which neoliberalism, as distinct from classical liberalism, is grounded in a posthuman understanding of the nature of life itself. Whereas resilience was originally conceived by proponents of sustainable development as a property that distinguishes the extra-economic 'life-support systems' which humans require to live well, gradually it has become reconceived as a property which humanity intrinsically possesses just like all other living systems. But as a property of human populations, its growth is said to be dependent on their interpellation within markets, their diversity as economic subjects, and their subjection to systems of governance able to ensure that they continue to use natural resources in sustainable ways. Thus, as we will see, did a doctrine which started out as a critique of neoliberal policy prescriptions for development transform into a doctrine which legitimates a neoliberal model of development based upon the constitution of markets and the interpellation of subjects within markets.

Sustainable development is proclaimed by its proponents to offer a more progressive way of framing the development problematic to that propagated historically by Western governments and international organizations. In contestation of the crudely economic rationalities that shaped the development policies of the West during much of the Cold War, and especially in protest at the implications of the reification of the economic development of societies for their environments, sustainable development seeks to secure the 'life-support systems' which peoples otherwise require in order to live well and prosper.[1] By privileging the security of the biosphere over and above the imperative to secure economies, 'life' is thus offered as an obstacle to 'economy' by the doctrine of sustainable development. But, as we will see, sustainable development was always likely to be re-appropriated by the economic rationalities of Western governments, because of the interface between its 'alternative' rationality of security and that of specifically neoliberal doctrines of economy. While sustainable development deploys ecological reason to argue for the need to secure the life of the biosphere, neoliberalism prescribes economy as the very means of that security. Economic reason is conceived within neoliberalism as a servant of ecological reason; claiming paradoxically to secure life from economy through a promotion of capacities of life for economy. This is the paradoxical foundation on which neoliberalism has constructed its appropriation of sustainable development. Sustainable development and neoliberalism are not the same, nor is the former simply a proxy of the latter, but they do come into contact powerfully on the terrains of their rationalities of security. This surface of contact ought to make for a tense and political field of contestation, but has instead made largely for a strategically manipulable relation between the two doctrines.

In recent years we can see, at the very least, how vulnerable the ecological reasoning that underpins sustainable development has been to the economic reasoning of neoliberalism. Indeed, we argue that the ongoing disarticulation of the concept of security in development doctrine and correlate emergence of the concept of resilience is an expression of this. Neoliberalism is able to appropriate the doctrine of sustainable development on account of its claims not to the 'security' but 'resilience' of specifically neoliberal institutions (significantly markets), systems of governance and, most importantly for this chapter, conditions of subjectivity. Resilience is defined by the United Nations as 'the capacity of a system, community or society potentially exposed to hazard, to adapt by resisting or changing in order to reach and maintain an acceptable level of functioning and structure'.[2] Academics concerned with correlating the promotion of 'sustainable development' with that of resilience define it as 'the capacity to buffer change, learn and develop – as a framework for understanding how to sustain and enhance adaptive capacity in a complex world of rapid transformations'.[3] The concept of resilience arose not as a direct product of neoliberal doctrines but as an element of the critique of neoliberalism which sustainable development itself pertained to be at its origin. This shouldn't surprise us. Neoliberalism is not a homogeneous doctrine, nor are its particular forms of dogmatism homeostatic. Its powers of persuasion and discursive prosperity depend on its own resilient capacities to adapt to the hazards of critique.

The current prosperity of the doctrine of sustainable development is also a vexed expression of the resilience of neoliberalism. In that sense, we may argue that resilience is becoming to the twenty-first-century development–security–environment nexus [DESNEX] of contemporary liberal governance what sustainable development was to the development–security nexus during its earlier post-Cold War phase. If 'security' functioned during the first two decades of post-Cold War international relations as a rationality for the subjection of development to Western states, enabling governance practices that proved essential to creating the conditions for neoliberal subjectivity, the rationality which governs that subjection today is increasingly one of 'resilience'. Voices from within International Relations calling for the dismantling of the sign of security because it is 'the supreme concept of bourgeois society and the fundamental thematic of liberalism'[4] therefore miss the point. Calling for a new politics to take us 'beyond security' does little to solve the problem; indeed it obfuscates the very nature of the problem, which is that liberalism itself is outgrowing its long-standing correlation with security, and locating new discursive foundations through the concept of resilience that openly promotes insecurity.

Beyond showing how the discourse of resilience legitimates neoliberal systems of governance and institutions, it is necessary to attend to the forms of subjectivity it attempts to bring into being. The account of the world envisaged and constituted by development agencies concerned with building resilient subjects is one that presupposes the disastrousness of the world, and likewise one which interpellates a subject that is permanently called upon to bear the disaster – a subject for whom bearing the disaster is a required practice without which he or she cannot grow and prosper in the world. This is what we believe to be most at stake in the discourse of resilience. The resilient subject is a subject that must permanently struggle to accommodate itself to the world. Resilient subjects have accepted the imperative not to resist or secure themselves from the difficulties they are faced with but instead adapt to their enabling conditions via the embrace of neoliberalism. Resisting neoliberalism in the present thus requires rejecting the seductive claims to 'alternative futures' offered by seemingly contrary doctrines of sustainable development and their political promises of resilience. A reinvestment in an account of political subjectivity is needed, and a rearticulation of a vernacular concept of security is essential for such a purpose.

Uncommon Futures

The ideas that shaped the doctrine of 'sustainable development' became influential in the 1970s, but they only took

concrete form with the 1987 publication of the Brundt-
land Commission report *Our Common Future*.[5] On the
surface of things, sustainable development appeared to
operate as the foundation for a powerful indictment of
hitherto dominant theories and practices of development.
Development policies were classically aimed at increasing
the production, consumption and wealth of societies.
What 'sustainable development' did was to pose the
problem of the implications of such economy-centred policies for the 'life support systems' on which societies
otherwise depend for their welfare.[6] The doctrine of sustainable development that emerged from *Our Common
Future* and which culminated in the 2002 World Summit
on Sustainable Development in Johannesburg was based
upon the seemingly contrary axiom that economic development had to be suborned to the need to ensure the
sustainable use of natural resources, healthy environments, ecosystems and biodiversity. Here, the utility and
value of 'life' in all of its complexities was offered by the
doctrine of sustainable development as an obstacle to
economy. Committed to securing life from the dangers
posed to it by unfettered economic reason, the doctrine
of sustainable development appeared to emerge in direct
conflict with the governmental doctrine of neoliberalism
which, during the 1980s, had become increasingly hegemonic, and which would have the opportunity to go
global with the end of the Cold War in 1989. The kinds
of 'pure liberalism' championed by Thatcherites and Rea-
ganites, said to reify the economy at all costs as both
means and ends of development, was subject to an appar-
ently new line of questioning, not on account of its equally
questionable implications for the economic welfare of
peoples, but on account of the threats it posed to something outside of the order of economy: life. Proponents of
sustainable development did not claim to question the
value of economic development in and of itself, but they
did aspire to offer a framework for the re-regulation of
the economy in alignment with the needs and interests

of the biosphere. And, indeed, its effects were palpable
during the 1990s, a decade in which a Senior Vice-
President of the World Bank, Joseph Stiglitz, was to be
heard making savage indictments of the implications of
liberal policy prescriptions, and in which the advice of
environmentalists was increasingly taken into account by
governments and international economic institutions.[7]

The relationship between sustainable development and
the crisis in liberal reason that began to trouble governments in the 1980s and 1990s was, however, highly
complex. Mark Duffield has shown how the shift from
strategies of development preaching modernization to sustainable development owed much to a specifically neoliberal framing of the problematic of development.[8] As
Duffield argues, sustainable development emerged as part
of a neoliberal counter-critique of modernization strategies
of development which, rather than undermining the
authority of liberal reason, gave it a new and even more
powerful footing. While recognizing the function of ecological reason in shaping the doctrine of sustainable development and its critique of modernization strategies,
Duffield draws attention to the neoliberal rationalities
which have nevertheless defined it. For one, the strength
of its challenge to traditional models of development owed
much to its alignment with the neoliberal critique of the
state.[9] Preaching that sustainable development would only
follow once peoples gave up on state-led modernization
strategies and learnt to practise the virtue of 'community-
based self-reliance', so sustainable development reflected
a neoliberal political agenda that shifts the burden of security from states to people.[10] Sustainable development functions in extension of neoliberal principles of economy,
Duffield argues, by disciplining poor and underdeveloped
peoples to give up on states as sources for the protection
and improvement of their well-being, and instead practise
the virtue of securing themselves. Thus does sustainable
development engage in the active promotion of a neoliberal model of society and subjectivity in which everyone

is demanded to 'prove themselves by bettering their individual and collective self reliance'.[11] In African states such as Mozambique, for example, it has provided 'a virtually free social security system offering the possibilities of adaptation and strengthening in order to manage the risks of market integration'.[12]

Revealing the convergences between sustainable development and the neoliberal critique of the state, the model of society and subjectivity it proposes as solutions to the problem of the state, and the economic pay-offs that follow, Duffield offers a powerful riposte to those narrative accounts of sustainable development as arising simply from the empowerment of ecological over economic reason. But how, then, should we understand the nature of the relation between sustainable development and neoliberalism? Is ecological reason just a proxy of the neoliberal rationalities which Duffield argues has shaped the agenda of sustainable development? If we understand sustainable development as a servant of neoliberalism, then what should we make of those voices arising from environmental movements, and the many other ways in which ecological reason has been mobilized, to critique economy-based strategies of development in the interests of sustaining life? Answering these questions requires grappling further with the complex correlations of economy, politics and security with life in neoliberal doctrine; what Duffield rightly names its biopolitics.[13] Neoliberalism is widely understood as a 'theory of political economic practices proposing that human well-being can best be advanced by the maximization of entrepreneurial freedoms within an institutional framework characterized by private property rights, individual liberty, unencumbered markets, and free trade'.[14] Less understood, however, is how its claims to be able to increase wealth and freedom are correlated with ways to increase the prosperity and security of life itself. Its capacities to correlate practices for the increase of economic profit and prosperity with those dedicated to increasing the profitability and prosperity of the biosphere are precisely why the doctrine of sustainable development is so compatible with it.

In the first instance, this is a problem of the neglect of the complexities of economic doctrines *per se*. If we examine the origins of economics we find that it was from its earliest usage conceptualized as a domain of knowledge concerned with the prosperity not just of human communities, families and subjects, but a knowledge which aimed to increase that prosperity in alignment with the needs of nature in its entirety. For Aristotle, economics, it was said, 'must conform to nature . . . in as much as nature has already distributed roles and duties within the species themselves'.[15] 'Implicit', therefore, 'within the economy is the notion of an organic objective and functional harmony . . . a providential and natural order to be respected while acting in the service of the greatest cohesion of utility and well-being'.[16] Moreover, and as Giorgio Agamben has demonstrated in his account of the theological origins of the concept, economy evokes the idea of an administrative praxis not only of the natural course of things, but which is itself, as praxis, 'adapting at each turn, in its salvific intent, to the nature of the concrete situation against which it has to measure itself'.[17] In other words, economy pertains not merely to a mode of governance of nature but was itself conceived from its very beginnings as a praxis of governance that functions naturally by adapting to the nature of the object of governance.

Neoliberalism breaks, however, from earlier liberalisms and traditions of political economy in so far as its legitimacy rests on its capacities to correlate practices for the increase of economic profitability and prosperity, not just with practices for the securing of the human species, but with the life of the biosphere as a wholly commodifiable element for appropriation, ownership and political rule. These correlations of economy, well-being, freedom, security and biospheric life in and among neoliberal regimes of practice and representation comprise some of the foundations of what have been named its biopolitics.[18] And if there is anything 'fundamental' to liberalism then it is this: one cannot understand how liberalism functions, most especially how it has gained the global hegemony that it has, without addressing how systematically the category of life has organized the correlation of its various practices of governance, as well as how important the shift in the very understanding of life, from the human to the biospheric, has been for changes in those practices.

Examining neoliberalism biopolitically means we can understand better how it is that ecological reasoning has enabled the growth of strategies for the promotion of market-based entrepreneurial capitalism in and among developing societies. Of particular importance here are the ways in which the very account of security deployed by neoliberal states and their development agencies has begun to alter through its correlation with ecological reason. Crucial to this story is the relatively recent emergence of the discourse of resilience. When neoliberals preach the necessity of peoples becoming 'resilient', they are arguing in effect for the entrepreneurial practices of self and subjectivity which Duffield calls 'self reliance'. 'Resilient' peoples do not look to states or other entities to secure and improve their well-being because they have been disciplined into believing in the necessity to secure and improve it for themselves. Indeed, so convinced are they of the worth of such capabilities that they proclaim it to be a fundamental 'freedom'.[19] But the emergence of this discourse of resilience within the doctrine of neoliberalism owes massively, we argue, to the power of ecological reason in shaping the very rationality of security which otherwise defines it. In other words, comprehending how a neoliberal rationality of security functions in shaping the agenda of sustainable development requires us to examine the constitutive function of ecological reason in shaping both. Far from being a proxy of the neoliberal rationalities shaping sustainable development, ecological reason has been formative of them.

Debasing the Subject

Having established how sustainable development, via its propagation of the concept of resilience, naturalizes neoliberal systems of governance and institutions, we need to consider how it functions to constitute subjects amenable to neoliberal governance. Every regime of governance invokes its own particular subject of governance. Producing subjects the liberal way has long since been a game of producing self-securing subjects. Subjects that are capable of securing themselves are less of a threat to themselves and in being so are not a threat to the governance capacities of their states nor to the governance of the global order either. And in this sense the correlation of development with security feeds upon the political imaginary of liberalism predicated, as it became, upon the belief that a global order of self-securing subjects would in turn deliver a more secure form of world order.[20] What, then, does the shift in the correlation of development with security to resilience tell us about the nature of the subject which development is now aimed at producing? What differences are entailed in being a resilient subject as opposed to a merely secure subject? Is the emergence of this new object of development just an extension of the liberal rationalities of governance that feed upon what is otherwise described as the development–security nexus?

There is, in fact, a considerable shift here. The major condition of possibility for the subject of sustainable development is that it sacrifices its capacity and desire for security. Security, here, is less that which liberalism demands of its subjects than what it forbids them. The resilient subject of sustainable development is, by definition, not a secure but an adaptive subject; adaptive in so far as it is capable of making those adjustments to itself that enable it to survive the hazards encountered in its exposure to the world. In this sense the resilient subject is a subject that must permanently struggle to accommodate itself to the world. Not a political subject that can conceive of changing the world, its structure and conditions of possibility, with a view to securing itself from the world; but a subject which accepts the disastrousness of the world it lives in as a condition for partaking of that world and which accepts the necessity of the injunction to change itself in correspondence with the threats and dangers now presupposed as endemic. One can see readily how this plays out in relation to debates, for example, over climate change. One enthusiast for resilience as an answer to the problem writes:

> What is vital to understand is not the degree of climate change that we should expect, nor necessarily the impact that we might anticipate on water resource management, coastal defence, food security, species survival, etc. What is important to grasp is that we do have the abilities to adapt and adjust to the changes that climate change will bring.[21]

Sustainable development is no longer conceived henceforth as a state of being on account of which a human is capable of securing itself from the world, and via which he or she becomes a subject in the world. Once development is said to follow ecological laws of change and transformation, and thus once exposure to hazard becomes a condition of possibility for development, so the question which sustainable development poses for the communities and individuals subject to it becomes: how to survive in the world without securing yourself from the world?

This is precisely why resilience has become so intimately tied in the policy, practice and theory of sustainable development not just to neoliberalism but to disaster management. Indeed the latter is also crucial in legitimating the former. The ability to manage exposure to hazard in and among developing societies is dependent, the UN says, on their maintenance of a healthy and diverse ecological system that is productive and life-sustaining, but it also demands a healthy and diverse economy that adapts to change and recognizes social and ecological limits.[22] It requires 'capturing opportunities for social change during the "window of opportunity" following disasters, for example by utilizing the skills of women and men equally during reconstruction'.[23] As fundamentally it requires making societies 'aware of the importance of disaster reduction for their own well-being',[24] because 'it is crucial for people to understand that they have a responsibility towards their own survival and not simply wait for governments to find and provide solutions'.[25] Disasters, thus construed, are not threats to the development of human beings from which they might aspire to secure themselves. They are events of profound 'opportunity' for societies to transform themselves economically and politically. They are events which do not merely expose communities to dangers from which they must be saved in order that they might be set back onto the path of development, but, rather, where communities, in their exposure, are able to undergo novel processes of developmental change in reconstitution of themselves as neoliberal societies. Exposure to disaster, in this context, is conceptualized in positive terms as constitutive of the possibility for the development of neoliberal systems of governance. But the working of this rationality depends on a subject that will submit to it. Sustainable development requires subjects, the UN report insists in a remarkable passage, to understand the 'nature' of hazards. The passage of societies to such knowledge must in turn involve, it states

> a consideration of almost every physical phenomenon on the planet. The slow movements in the earth's mantle – the convection cells that drive the movement of continents and the manufacture of ocean floors – are the starting and also the sticking point. They lift mountains and shape landscapes. They also build volcanoes and trigger potentially catastrophic earthquakes. Like those other invisible movements that take place on a vast scale through the atmospheric medium – the carbon cycle and the water cycle and the nitrogen cycle – volcanoes and earthquakes, along with

technological advancements, provide the bedrock of strong nations, rich industries and great cities. They do, of course, also have the potential to destroy them.[26]

The human here is conceived as resilient in so far as it adapts to rather than resists the conditions of its suffering in the world. To be resilient is to forego the very power of resistance. 'The imperative of adaptation rather than resistance to change will increase inexorably', two ideologues of sustainable development claim.[27] In their enthusiasm for the 'inexorable increase' of this 'imperative', theorists of sustainable development engage in some vivid discursive representations of the human. 'As a species, humanity is immensely adaptable – a weed species. We are also capable of considerable adaptability as individuals, and also as households (variously defined) – the latter being the perennial and universal human social unit'.[28] The combination of the imperative of humanity to adapt with the representation of humanity as a 'weed species' recalls the discursive currency of similar combinations within the concentration camps of Nazi Germany during the Second World War. Those camps were, as Barrington Moore has demonstrated in a still brilliant and wide-ranging historical study, sites for the constitution of precisely such resilient subjects and the honing of precisely such adaptive capacities. The inhabitants of such extreme spaces of suffering often failed to exhibit any sign of resistance, seeking to survive through the development of complex and ultimately failed strategies of 'adaptation' to the conditions of their suffering.[29] The 'conquest' of the perception of inevitability and necessity of circumstances is 'essential', Moore argues on the other hand, 'to the development of politically effective moral outrage'.[30] The making of resilient subjects and societies fit for neoliberalism by agencies of sustainable development is based upon a degradation of the political capacities of human beings far more subtle than that achieved in Auschwitz and Buchenwald. But the enthusiasm with which ideologues of sustainable development are turning resilience into an 'imperative' is nevertheless comparable with that of the SS guards who also aimed 'to speed up the processes of adaptive learning' among those Jews and other populations in their charge by convincing them of the futility of resistance.[31]

The Margins of Existence

We are not arguing against the idea that we ought to take seriously the fact of human impact upon the conditions of its biospheric environment. Our aim is to bring to the surface those points of contact between ecological modes of reasoning and a mode of economic reason that is complicit with the degradation of the biosphere, as well as which degrades the political capacities of human beings. While sustainable development, in particular, deploys ecological reason to argue for the need to secure the life of the biosphere, neoliberalism prescribes economy as the very means of that security, while pathologizing political subjectivity and any form of philosophical mediation on questions that might interfere with the sources of its legitimacy. Economic reason is conceived within neoliberalism as a servant of ecological reason; claiming paradoxically to secure life from economy through a promotion of capacities of life for economy. All the while it diagnoses politics as that tendency of the human most inimical to the needs of life to live out that life as such. If, then, sustainable development is to escape its appropriation, it would seem imperative that it contest the nexus of relations on which claims as to the necessity of neoliberal frameworks for the sustainability of life are based. This has to mean rethinking the ways in which we engage with the concept of resilience, for it is upon this discursive terrain that the contemporary battle is being waged. The problem here is less about the demands to improve the resilience of ecosystems which distinguished the agenda of sustainable development in its early years than it is the post-Johannesburg shift to propagating resilience as a fundamental property and capacity of the human. The ecological imaginary is colonizing the social and political imaginaries of theorists and practitioners of development in ways that are providing fertile ground for the application of neoliberalism as a solution to the problem of sustainability as catastrophically conceived. Understanding how that is possible requires understanding the biopolitics of neoliberalism; how its claims to be able to increase wealth and freedom are correlated with ways to increase the prosperity and security of life itself. Life for the resilient subject is always on the margins of existence. As teleological reasoning gives way to a complex topography of radically interconnected endangerment, we phase shift from threshold to threshold, catastrophic rupture to catastrophic rupture, fated to look into the unknowable void as the contingent event gives qualitative meaning and expression to the event of life as such. Living on the margins of existence is no longer, however, simply conceived as a state to be avoided at all costs. Marginal life is actively promoted. For it is only by venturing into the unknown, succumbing to the terror-event, internalizing its very uncertainty as a natural part of the onto-political reasoning that affirms our very sense of being as eventual, that we become more adept at facing down events to come. Ellen Langer and Jane Roth's[32] often cited psychoanalytical insight into the 'illusion of control' as such becomes altogether redundant. Not only do we accept that nobody is in control of worldly affairs, we also give up on the idea that chance events can be tamed. Pathologization as such is radically altered, for it is precisely those who hold true to Langer and Roth's illusionary state that are openly condemned for their lack of realism and mature reasoning. To live at the margins is simply the way things are naturally designed. Arguing otherwise is to offer a fabricated deceit which is more dangerous since it denies us of the right state of mind necessary for preparedness.

Nowhere has this idea been felt more than in the field of economics as the foundational assumption that stable points of equilibrium can be established has been all but abandoned. Building on Ilya Prigogine's pioneering work on thermodynamics, which radically altered our understanding of the dynamical nature of complex systems more generally, economics, now understood to be a complex and interconnected system capable of exhibiting its own self-organizing tendencies,[33] appears to function in a dynamic state that is *far from equilibrium*. What is commonly termed 'complexity economics' looks at the ways in which micro-specific 'shocks' – what we may term economic events – define the aggregate performances of economic systems.[34] Ideas of macro-stability are thus displaced by a more complex terrain of radically connected productive elements and circulatory flows which are inherently unstable and whose overall significance and consequences cannot be predicted with absolute certainty. The linearity as such so often associated with the now outdated Keynesian pursuit of stable states, along with its social aggregations and top-down interventions, is veritably destroyed by non-linear sequencing which gives priority to constant adaptation and short-termism. Such a system, as Nicolis and Prigogine would write, does not tend towards 'some kind of global optimum'; instead it functions through complex stochastic processes 'whose rules can in no way be designed in advance'.[35]

Actually Existing Resourcefulness

Development has always been politically qualified. Not all development is 'good' and worthy of promotion. Indeed, as Duffield shows, developmental concerns are not simply with the poverty experienced by local populations, but those forms of 'actual existing development' whose autonomy is to be rendered dangerous because it takes populations beyond the regulatory gaze of liberal power. Resilient lives are subjected to a similar assay. In times of crises, it is not sufficient to say that survival must take precedence above all else. Rather, what survives is subject to a powerful discursive frame that shapes the conduct of conduct despite the catastrophic shock to the system. The pathologization of 'looting', or what could otherwise be called 'spontaneous distribution', so obviously an expression of a survivability instinct, exemplifies the ways in which resilience is politically qualified and governed. However catastrophic the crises, private property always takes precedence over the rights of people to gain access to necessary resources such as food and water. Indeed, as experiences from New Orleans to Haiti testify, while private property is to be afforded political and military protection without qualification, such that it even comes to signify our civilizational credentials, what it means to survive in the face of adversity provides little relief for those for whom the stakes are the highest and have nothing to lose except their very existence. As Naomi Klein has written in respect to what she aptly terms the 'green zoning' and human partitioning of disaster capitalism:

> At first I thought the Green Zone phenomenon was unique to the war in Iraq. Now, after years spent in other disaster zones, I realize that the Green Zone emerges everywhere that the disaster capitalism complex descends, with the same stark partitions between the included and the excluded, the protected and the damned. It happened in New Orleans. After the flood, an already divided city turned into a battleground between gated green zones and raging red zones – the result not of water damage but of the 'free-market solutions'.[36]

The idea of austerity far predates the current economic crises facing Western economies. Much of its reasoning can be traced back to the period of structural adjustment, as organizations such as the IMF and World Bank imposed financial restraints upon impoverished countries in exchange for incorporation into the regulated sphere of global neoliberalized flows. The Latin American debt crises of the early 1980s, in particular, produced a pivotal moment as the global financial system was brought to the brink of collapse. This prompted a major rethink in terms of fiscal responsibility which, following an all too familiar pattern, problematized less the operation of the banking sector than it did the spending habits of national 'socialist' dictators. Ironically, then, with ideas of social justice altogether absent from policy deliberations, the debt crises provided the global banking sector with the unparalleled opportunity to introduce austerity measures and neoliberal reforms in response to crises that were the product of unregulated currency flows in the first instance. What is more, rather than offering to protect impoverished populations from the ravages of crises, such policies actively promoted the need for insecurity in order for society to learn from its past indulgences:

> Austerity programs typically include stern measures or 'shock treatments' aimed at market mechanisms to stimulate export production and increase the foreign exchange reserves of government . . . These programs embody clear distributional implications. The urban poor and the working class are affected by a combination of subsidy cuts, real wage reductions, and price increases stemming from devaluations and the elimination of public services. A reduced share of national income for labour and greater income inequality are frequently documented to ill effect.[37]

Sustainable development emanated out of this thinking about austerity as it sought to respond to minimal state interference. In many senses it sought to fill the governance void by working within this neoliberal architecture. Equally we find the logic of 'conditionality' emerging here, which, although often applied to the promise of development as a way to overcome the issue of 'bad creditors' (whether economically or politically conceived), has now extended into discourses on resilience as the very forms that endurance takes is conditioned. Resilience is subject to a biopolitical conditioning as the question of survivability is qualified in accordance with neoliberal markers that decide whether a survival response meets privately accepted criteria for human behaviour. As Bauman has provocatively questioned in the context of Hurricane Katrina, 'did not Katrina help, inadvertently, the efforts of the ailing disposable-industry of wasted humans, clearly not up to the task of coping with social consequences? Was not this help one of the reasons why the need to dispatch troops was not strongly felt until social order was broken and the prospect of social unrest came close?'.[38] Here it is argued that the private has fully conquered the public to such an extent that our only way of thinking politically is to assume the naturalness of insecurity, inequality and the sheer inexplicability of all things that would ordinarily appear inexcusable to even the most fleeting of compassionate reflections. Giroux presses home the biopolitical stakes:

> In Katrina's aftermath, the entire world was exposed to a barrage of images in which the poor black and brown populations appeared as the 'waste turned out in the ever rising volumes of our times'. Instead of living in a world of consumer fantasies and super-mall choices, these groups are caught in an existence filled with the nightmares of being left behind, criminalised, and consequently charged with the guilt of their exclusion, and left to fend for themselves (or die) in the abandoned space of the urban ghetto.[39]

While many have pointed out the marked differences in both urgency and finance committed when compared to the 9/11 response, Katrina is not in any way exceptional when compared to other natural disasters such as Hurricane Sandy which devastated New York with equal ferocity, for instance. One of the evident differences here is the non-discriminatory nature of natural events which, affecting a wider population, revealed more fully both the already existing poverty cleavages of a society, along with the intellectual poverty of calls to be resilient. Sandy proves most instructive in this regard. This event in particular showed how the idea of a natural catastrophe is itself open to many interpretations depending upon racial, class and gendered differences. Vulnerability was not a uniform, let alone universal, condition. Like Katrina before it, those already insured with the financial means and capabilities to 'escape' impending change in climatic conditions experienced the event as a mere inconvenience in the ongoing accommodation to rapid environmental change. For those, however, on the margins of existence, those populations violently contained within deeply segregated ghettos which offer no credible means for escape, the raw reality of the devastation was all too apparent. In the absence of social protections, such populations were precisely the ones asked to evidence their resilience capacities. There is no resilience asked of those who can afford to take flight. That was an exercise in security. It was also an effective exercise in disaster preparedness for those with the means to benefit from the investment that goes into such programmes. The resilient was the black old age pensioner living in a violent ghetto of Red Hook and the poor areas of New Jersey and the Rockaway Peninsula for over three weeks with little food, no electricity and no heating in the blisteringly cold winter conditions.[40] As Alex Koppelman wrote in *The New Yorker* on the plight of a poor community in Manhattan's lower East side, 'The people who live at the Baruch Houses were supposed to have evacuated before Sandy hit. Some did. Many did not, though, often because they had no good place to go'.[41] The resilient, in other words, were not security prepared; they had to learn to adapt and live through the catastrophe on account of the fact that their insecure predicament became altogether more amplified and, for a moment at least, brought into the public gaze before being left to their poverty as usual without questioning wider social implications.

More than highlighting how the experience of the catastrophic is wholly dependent upon the local and the particular, Sandy also illustrated how our societies are exhausted by images of suffering. To suffer no longer immediately invites compassion or an unconditional response on account of it being simply the ethical thing to do. The catastrophes which now plague the liberal landscape are bereft of any radically deontological response on account of their very normalization. All that remains is for the subject to learn to take care of their own endangered destinies. Again, Giroux has his finger on the pulse, being fully aware of the political stakes:

> These days Americans are quickly fatigued by natural catastrophe. Major natural disasters and their consequences are now relegated to the airborne vocabulary of either fate or the unyielding circumstance of personal tragedy, conveniently allowing an ethically cleansed American public to ignore the sordid violence and suffering they produce for those populations caught in the grip of poverty, deprivation and hardship. It gets worse. Catastrophes have not only been normalized, they have been reduced to the spectacle of titillating TV. Rather than analyzed within broader social categories such as power, politics, poverty, race and class, the violence produced by natural disasters is now highly individualized, limited to human interest stories about loss and individual suffering.[42]

We are more than aware here that our critique will be accused of condemning people to suffer a fate that is irresponsible at best and wilfully abandoning them at worst. However, just as we have faith in people's abilities to resist what they find intolerable, we also have faith in local populations' *actually existing resourcefulness*. If oppressed peoples have never required the universal theorist to equip them with the intellectual tools before they feel confident enough to resist, endangered populations do not need some outside intervention before they learn how to deal with the trials and tribulations of daily existence. They have far more knowledge and experience and certainly don't require reminding of the presence of some vaguely looming threat they have already learned to deal with. So let's be clear, discourses of resilience are not about local empowerment; they are a technology of governance. There is, then, a marked difference between the autonomy of the resourceful as opposed to the interventionist strategies of resilience. Whereas the former is premised upon the self-governing capacities of local populations for whom political agency is central, the latter pathologize such claims on account of knowing what is better for lives whose lack of protection fully validates an interventionist response.

– 4 –

Living Dangerously

The Anxious Mass

Following the horrors of twentieth-century fascism, it became common to warn of the dangers of linking political rationality to human emotions. If the masses learned to desire that which they should have reasonably found intolerable as a result of some frenzied visceral assault, so there was a need to purge the affective dimensions of politics out of the discursive arena. That desire functions politically is not a problem for us. Neither is the claim that emotions can be manipulated for terrifying ends. We do, however, take issue with the positivist notion that the political can be studied without any sense of the affective dimension to human experience. Such a claim is not only nonsensical. It is fully implicit in the debasement of the political subject as politics is reduced to a purely technical practice. What is more, this removal of the affective dimensions to power conceals the play of emotions that simultaneously orchestrates and shapes the conduct of lives in very particular yet no less effective ways. Technical solutions would in fact have no resonance whatsoever were they not to connect to a wider field of emotional drivers.

Power, after all, only appeals if it can meaningfully tap into our raw emotions. If a policy cannot be affected, it stands little chance of being effective. This becomes altogether more apparent when dealing with the question of resilience. While claims to security have always relied upon the emotional field to condition the possibility for political rule, the shift towards the promotion of insecurity as the principal design for human formation takes direct hold of the affective dimension to shape the conduct of lives whose existence is always brought into terrifying question.

Affect is an ontological category. It shapes us by virtue of its capacity to instigate certain performances. And it mobilizes us through an ability to call upon our various desires that invariably become amplified in times of crises. Affect, however, is far from perfect when viewed from the perspective of reasonable outcomes. We remain the most illogical and unreasonable of beings when viewed from the categorical imperative of pure reason. Indeed, despite Newton's forceful insistence, life cannot simply be prodded into action as if it conformed to linear laws of motion. How else can we account for the ways in which life constantly puts its destiny into question for the purpose of its own trans-valuations and trans-mutations?

Catastrophically speaking, the prevailing mode of contemporary affect is a state of normalized anxiety. Fear of course remains a constitutive element. But it is anxiety which is more apt in explaining the well-being of the resilient subject. Anxious conditioning is a default setting for a system which is insecure by design. Our anxieties, however, have taken on a radically new meaning in the post 9/11 world. It was once suggested that liberal societies are caught up in what was aptly termed 'statistical panic'. As Kathleen Woodward once noted,

> if we live in a visual culture where society is distinguished by the spectacle, we also live in a society of the statistic. Rather than anchoring us to a stable life-world, statistics that forecast the future engender insecurity in the form of

low-grade intensities that, like low-grade fevers, permit us
to go about our everyday lives but in a state of statistical
stress. Statistics are the very atmosphere we breathe, the
strange weather in which we live, the continuous emission
of postmodern media life.[1]

Such probabilistic reasoning fully implicated us in a world
of predictable measures albeit of a dark and troublesome
nature. This numbers game no longer provides us with
such worrying comfort. We only have to look at contemporary attempts at future scenario enactment to evidence
the sheer poverty of statistical measure as the disaster is
doubly reified as we try to read the signs from catastrophes which will never happen again and a future landscape of endangerment yet to be formed. The catastrophe
instead is precisely what we now imagine it to become.
This is a far cry from the claims of objective science. It
is a form of *catastrophic prophecy*. As Frank Kermode
once wrote:

> All plots have something in common with prophecy, for
> they must appear to educe from the prime matter of the
> situation the forms of a future. The best of them, thought
> Aristotle, derive from a *peripeteia* no less dependent than
> the other parts upon 'our rule of probability or necessity'
> but arising from that in the original situation to which we
> have given less attention.[2]

Our anxieties are what we make of them in all their
catastrophic permutations. Anxieties deriving from events
yet to materialize are pure fabrications or fantasies, ema-
nating from a certain image of thought. It is everything we
dream it to be and worse. And so we are compelled to live
out, with real narcissistic intent, a self-authoring violence
whose exact pathology is catastrophic unto oneself. These
imaginaries, however, are not abstracted from the conditions of the real. They are experienced in the minds of
the vulnerable. Anxieties of the potentially catastrophic
are fully internalized and produced as a visceral and

psychological reality in ways that profoundly influence our
ways of thinking about and relating to the world. Changing behaviours, while making subjects deeply suspicious of
their familiar *not-so-secure* environments, force us into
logics of catastrophic negation wherein the affirmative
possibilities which exist in any present state of affairs are
vanquished by an imagined encounter with violence cloud-
ing all judgement. This continues into a self-fulfilling narcissism. Should the devastation eventually arrive, the fact
that it *punctures* all preconceived fantasies about the foreboding event, revealing then how even the most horrifying
things never really go to plan, only serves to heighten the
sense of anxiety further. Just as the vulnerable subject is
therefore forced to accept that nobody is in control of their
lives, it also learns how nobody or nothing can truly tame
the catastrophic occurrence. It is an unknowable force of
nature whose impact and lasting effects can only be
assessed, after the event, to become the ownership of the
historical record.

Previously this would have been a source for lament.
However, anxiety and trauma are now both seen to be
learning processes which can positively enrich the resilient
subject. It is commonplace to assess anxiety as a clinical
problem. It is also common nowadays to suggest that
everybody suffers from anxieties in one form or another.
Nobody, it seems, is 'anxiety-free'. For Sally Winston, co-
director of the Anxiety and Stress Disorders Institute of
Maryland (ASDI), 'The presence of unpredictability, uncertainty and uncontrollability all provoke anxiety pretty
automatically'. And yet as Alice Park writes in the headline
article of *Time* magazine's dedicated coverage of the 'Two
Faces of Anxiety', 'that's not to say all anxiety should be
battled. Sometimes it should be embraced – even celebrated'.[3] Citing Winston once again, 'Anxiety itself is
neither helpful nor hurtful. It's your response to your
anxiety that is helpful or hurtful'. It is all then about learning from fear. This is a psychological and emotional journey
which cannot be ventured into without entering into a pact

with the source of one's anxieties in the first instance. As Parks explains,

> People with a phobia of, say, spiders will often react with fear and anxiety to a picture of one or simply the thought of one – never mind an encounter with the genuine crawly article. Learning to control the anxiety involves gradual exposure to spiders, from least scary circumstances to most, with the brain – and thus the body – growing sequentially desensitized with each encounter.[4]

So rather than being a source for lament or viewed as a clinical problem to be fully exorcized from human experience, anxiety may be constitutive of new experiences that allow us to connect more fully with the world. The 'coping strategies' it encourages as we become more adept at embracing anxiety may, as Parks concludes, be the source of our 'salvation'.

Trauma is also said by contemporary theorists to work in similar ways. As a mode of scientific enquiry that initially tried to come to terms with the horrors of the Holocaust, the advent of trauma theory in the Humanities sought to diagnose those subjects who were rendered catatonic by terrifying experiences, which seemed beyond reasonable explanation and yet remained all too real in the memory of the victims. Such concerns became more nuanced with the advent of Post-Traumatic Stress Disorder (PTSD) which rose to prominence in the public sphere throughout the 1990s as a mental condition notably afflicting casualties of conflict and military personnel returning from the theatres of war.[5] This would pose a direct challenge to Freud's antithetical claims about anxiety and trauma, as his fantasy-based explanations were displaced by theories which focused instead upon the complex and adaptive functioning of the brain.[6] Ideas of memory retrieval would also be challenged, or at least reworked, as explanations moved towards the reliving of the traumatic moment in different and contingent ways. This was already appreciated by the most celebrated of witnesses, Primo Levi, whose personal testimony warned against the purity of memory:

> Certainly practice (in this case frequent re-evocation) keeps memories fresh and alive in the same manner in which a muscle often used remains efficient, but it is also true that a memory evoked too often, and expressed in the form of a story, tends to become fixed in a stereotype, in a form tested by experience, crystallized, perfected, adorned, installing itself in the place of the raw memory and growing at its expense.[7]

Following Levi's intervention, the pioneering specialist on trauma, Cathy Caruth, developed her argument that '[w]hat returns in the flashback is not simply an over-whelming experience that has been obstructed by a later repression or amnesia, but an event that is itself consti-tuted, in part, by its lack of integration into conscious-ness'.[8] This effective undermining of the privileged position assigned to the role of the witness, whose words and expressions were understood to always fail to capture the true horror, led to the various debates about the 'unrepre-sentability' of events. This was epitomized in Theodore Adorno's claims about the questionable use of the poetic post-Holocaust. Leaving aside crass misreading of Adorno, which tend to offer a superficial reading of the death of the poetic subject, there is something critical at play here. If focusing on the traumatic event itself is rendered mean-ingless due to the complexity of the experience, along with the open temporality of memorization, as better under-stood as *lived through*, what matters more is the subse-quent attribution of meaning which, of course, may become deeply politicized on account of its pathologization. As Jean Laplanche and Jean-Bertrand Pontalis argue, it is what takes on meaning 'afterwards' that makes a particu-lar memory traumatic as such.[9]

Of significance here is the claim that it is possible to locate a theory of subjectivity within the field of trauma studies. Ruth Leys' work has been instructive in this regard as she challenged representational approaches to traumatic experiences:

> Hypnosis (previously) played a major theoretical role in the conceptualization of trauma . . . because the tendency of hypnotized persons to imitate or repeat whatever they were told to say or do provided a basic model for the traumatic experience. Trauma was defined as a situation of dissociation or 'absence' from the self in which the victim unconsciously imitated or identified with the aggressor or traumatic scene in a situation that was likened to a state of heightened suggestibility or hypnotic trance.[10]

Not only does this approach deny the traumatized subject any political agency, it tends to 'regard trauma as if it were a purely external event coming to a sovereign if passive victim[11]'. This position is shared by Jenny Edkins. For Edkins, 'What we call trauma takes place when the very powers that we are convinced will protect us and give us security become our tormentors: when the community of which we consider ourselves members turns against us or when our family is no longer a source of refuge but a site of danger'.[12] Crucially, trauma, for Edkins, is not established at the moment of its occurrence. It is articulated through *memories* that are not only reworked as life takes on new meaning and is refashioned through new experiences, but continues to challenge the official memorialization or truth of events. With trauma exhibiting 'performative' and 'social' qualities, it has the potential to create new bonds amongst vulnerable people. A sentiment shared by Alphonso Lingis who suggests that it is 'when one exposes oneself to the naked one, the destitute one, the outcast one, the dying one', that community can be built.[13]

Nobody is suggesting here that people don't suffer as a result of some devastating upheaval to their lives. Nor are we resistant to the idea that trauma could be politically transformative. To use trauma, however, to further validate the idea of the vulnerable subject is problematic to say the least. There is a marked difference between the traumas experienced from a life-shattering event to the contemporary condition that focuses more on a terrifying prospect; that is between the past trauma and what we term 'future trauma'. What does it mean, for instance, to suffer or mourn what is yet to materialize? How does it feel to inhabit the ruins of the future? And what does it mean to be traumatized by an event which in the present has no witness to speak of except in the mind of the anxious subject? As Susannah Radstone writes, 'testimony (to trauma) demands a witness and it is only within the context of witnessing that testimony to trauma is possible . . . What needs emphasizing here is trauma theory's moving beyond modernity's coherent, autonomous, knowing subject to a model of subjectivity grounded in the space *between* witness and testifier within which that which cannot be known can begin to be witnessed'.[14] Turning away from the memory of trauma, then, to the incommensurability of the event does more than refashion the meaning of the witness. Appreciating the limitations of past representations, trauma is opened onto an emergent terrain of affective relations with imagined experiences that are no less viscerally and psychologically experienced. Or to put it another way, if trauma is seen to be the basis of a singular theory of subjectivity, we need to develop a much better understanding of the political stakes, as contemporary anxieties are now projected into a future that is seemingly full of inescapable yet unknowable catastrophes.

The Full Life Crisis

Resilience is big business. We only have to look at the proliferation of self-help books that use the term to gain a sense of its claims to social responsibility as a matter of individual care and due diligence on behalf of the responsible subject. From dealing with early key stage childhood development, adolescent children, the ability for the traumatized to bounce back from shocks to self-confidence, on to the ability to become more entrepreneurial in work and life choices, building successful relationships that can survive inevitable turbulence, even through the ability to cope with the inevitability of loss, so the logic recognizes no disciplinary boundaries as it takes aim at life in all its forms and evolving stages of maturity broadly defined. None of this is incidental. If the social state promised to take care of life from cradle to grave, resilience logically inverts this by foregrounding the catastrophic such that every stage of the subject's development appears to be fraught with potential hazards that always and already threaten what existence may become. So rather than sounding an interventionist retreat upon the nature and performances of the individual subject, strategies of resilience demand continual vigilance of the vulnerable; albeit with the governmental retainer that, should things go wrong, you only really have yourself to blame. Caring for the self thus becomes the surest indicator of the politics of neoliberal rule, for it is through the learned and authenticated internalization of an all embracing sense of precariousness that we learn to partake in a liberalized world that has all but evacuated the social contract.

We can see this playing out in novel and somewhat disturbing ways. One of the most common life experiences for members of modern industrial societies was said to be the 'mid-life crisis'. This theory of personal trauma concerning one's status in life rested upon a certain sense of mortality and the realization that existence was finite. It was presented as a sort of 'coming to terms with it all' moment that could prove to be profoundly transformative – albeit in irrational ways (i.e. excessive consumption, adulterous sexual liaisons, searching for new intensive experiences) that tended to be derided as some immature transgression in which the subject temporarily takes leave of its senses. Although there were evident problems with the theory (not least in terms of empirical verification), it certainly resonated in popular culture, as the ageing male became a focal point for ridicule, along with a somewhat healthy lack of surety about his confidence and position in life. This was taken to the extreme in Ebbe Roe Smith's cult classic *Falling Down*, which had more than a touch of subversiveness to its plot. Not simply content with the regressing and downward spiralling pathology of the out-of-work and divorced character William Foster, it offers a poignant critique of the deeply commodified nature of contemporary life and the state of social decay which necessarily accompanies it. In doing so, the question of pathology was put into question (not without evident irony) as the wider structural violence ordinarily concealed was brought to light through Foster's schizophrenic rage against a system whose very psychosis proves to be self-fulfilling, as it thrives on the fact that nobody appears in control.

By the late 1990s, research started to emerge that would bring this theory into question or at least its applicability.[15] While increasing life expectancy had a part to play, also central were issues of 'locatability', as life no longer seemed to have the neat stages of progression which once hallmarked modern societies. There was real expectation in former industrial times that things could happen 'for life'. Jobs, life partners, places of residence, each of these retained a certain fixity, such that the more fleeting lifestyles were the exception and not the rule. Late liberalism has brought each of these into question. Hence, with life becoming more enmeshed in a complex web of entanglements that are insecure in their design, the conditions that give rise to a meaningful life are optimally unlocatable. That does not, however, mean the crisis has altogether dissipated. The resilient subject is always in crisis. It has no chance for a reprieve. There is no possibility for respite. Neither is there any real prospect of being able to fully secure a retirement which awaits the other side of the introspection. Behavioural psychologists have responded by advocating various sub-sets of crises evaluation within an overall full life crisis spectrum: 'On the whole, young people are much more stressed than previous generations were . . . Young people feel under so much pressure to prove themselves, and the constant struggle to keep up a certain image means you can end up with a sense of failure and emptiness. It's the notion that what you own is who you are which causes problems for today's young people'.[16] Pathologization invariably begins here at the earliest possible stages of development. As the subject is always at the point of a potential crisis, so the production of subjects deemed to be in permanent crises comes into full life effect. Little wonder that so much of the thought and practice of resilience targets younger children and adolescents, whose experience of trauma is a concern on account of its potential lasting effects, that may lead, it is assumed, to repeated patterns of unacceptable behaviour. Significantly developing out of earlier psychological studies of children with learning behavioural problems during the 1960s and 1970s,[17] resilience has gone from being an anomaly in psychotherapeutic study to now appear as a dominant term of art for qualifying the very meaning of success amongst vulnerable children who develop in spite of their catastrophic life experiences. We may argue here that the focus on children is both urgent and necessary. Studies continually show that children tend to be the most open to violence, abuse and many of the problems associated with wider social inequalities. They also show how these patterns tend to repeat themselves as the victims of these injustices tend to repeat behaviours across generations. It is here that resilience enters to offer a more optimistic future that offers a definitive break from a more traumatic past. Hence, for its advocates, resilience is precisely defined as 'the interaction of a child with trauma or a toxic environment in which success, as judged by societal norms, is achieved by virtue of the child's abilities, motivations, and support systems'.[18] The author takes inspiration from Sula Wolff who classically insisted:

> Resilience is an enduring aspect of the person. Genetic and other constitutionally based qualities both determine and

are in turn modified by life experiences. Good intelligence plays a major part, as does an easy, adaptable, sociable temperament that, together with an appealing appearance, attract positive responses from others which in turn contribute to that inner sense of self-worth, competence and self-efficacy that has repeatedly been identified as a vital component of resilience. The sources of such positive responses are threefold: primary relationships within the family; the network of relationships with adults and children outside the family; and competence and achievement.[19]

The significance of linking self-worth and achievement to the 'social norm' cannot be underestimated as it allows us to illustrate the differences between the learning processes of resilience as compared to a properly critical pedagogy which would encourage children to question the fundamental tenets of power and inequality in the world. Strategies of resilience when applied to children take the form of training exercises which enable them to deal with the localized effects of their vulnerability and the forms of attachments and dependencies they have created which amplify the problems. The examples of youths falling into membership of inner-city gangs become a prime example of a vulnerable child that has fallen through the cracks. Countering this is the idea of 'educational resilience', defined as the 'heightened likelihood of success in school and other life accomplishments despite environmental adversities brought about by early traits, conditions, and experiences'.[20] But how exactly do we measure success? Is the educationally resilient the vulnerable subject who goes on to fulfil their neoliberal potential, or is it the subject who goes to war with the system that seeks to render them resilient as such? Resilience, as we have learned, is more a code for social compliance than a political ambition to transform the very sources of inequality and injustices experienced by marginalized populations. We find this in early educational theories where resilience is again conflated with strategies of resistance such that the resilient child, individualistically conceived, pathologically outlives its conditions of impoverishment to exhibit social achievement in ways that are altogether in tune with the normal functioning of society.[21] Indeed, more than simply learning to cope in conditions of impoverishment and vulnerability, as Steven Condly succinctly puts it in an approving review of the prevailing mainstream educational approaches, the doctrine of resilience offers new ways to assess qualities, competences and capabilities, as 'resilient children tend to possess an above average intelligence and have a temperament that endears them to others and that also does not allow them to succumb to self-pity'.[22] What of course qualifies as 'self-pity' in another setting could easily be read as a conscious attempt to challenge that which is beyond the control or individual responsibility of the particular subject.

Sheila Martineau is attuned to this and writes of the political dangers of resilience in education with considerable foresight: 'Though resilience conveyed anomalous childhood behaviour in the context of traumatic events in the 1970s, it has become detached from the traumatic context . . . dangerously, resilience has become constructed as a social norm [. . .] modelled on the behavioural norms and expectations of the dominant society'.[23] Resilience, in other words, becomes a normalized standard for mapping out (ab)normal behaviours such that the very terms of success are loaded with moral claims to a specific maturity, wherein the maturity itself is qualified through one's ability to connect to the liberal order of things and partake in the world such that to resist means, without contraction, that one successfully learns to conform. Or to put it in more critical terms, since the 'solution' is to teach children to overcome 'obstacles' to personal development without ultimately challenging wider relations of power, the resilient child (which, although said to include all children, overwhelmingly concentrates on those from poorer, culturally and racially distinct backgrounds) encounters policies which, instead of 'treating the individual', end up by virtue of its logic 'blaming the victim'.[24] Disadvantage as such becomes once again the means to author new forms of discrimination that plays the vulnerable card to remove any political claims that things could be otherwise.

Today we can situate these earlier demands for resilience within the strategic context of what Henry Giroux calls the 'war on youth'. Indicative of the neoliberal assault on the education system more generally, Giroux maintains that youth has become a privileged object for power in a way that seeks to strip away any sense of critical awareness and political agency at the earliest possible stages of intellectual development. As he writes, since 'neoliberalism is also a pedagogical project designed to create particular subjects, desires, and values defined largely by market considerations', questions of 'destiny' become 'linked to a market-driven logic in which freedom is stripped down to freedom from government regulation, freedom to consume, and freedom to say anything one wants, regardless of how racist or toxic the consequences might be'.[25] This has a profound bearing upon education policy as 'Critical thought and human agency are rendered impotent as neoliberal rationality substitutes emotional and personal vocabularies for political ones in formulating solutions to political problems'.[26] Hence, within this 'depoliticized discourse, youths are told that there is no dream of the collective, no viable social bonds, only the actions of autonomous individuals who can count only on their own resources and who bear sole responsibility for the effects of larger systemic political and economic problems'. Whilst education therefore should have a pedagogical commitment to the globally oppressed, what takes its place is a substitution for education that produces vulnerable consumers whose very training renders the political impossible.

The Tragedy of Vulnerability

We find ourselves in a rather troubling predicament. Not only may we trace the genealogy of vulnerability to the

birth of liberal reasoning and its biopolitical account of
life as forever endangering unto itself, it also appears
central to some of the more considered works of radical
scholarship on the left of recent times. It is there, for
instance, in John Holloway's *Change the World Without
Taking Power*, which begins with an epic scream at the
deeply internalizing suffering of the world.[27] Life, Holloway insists, is metaphorically akin to the situation faced
by a fly trapped on a spidery web. We are not simply
thrown into the world; most of us land into conditions of
exploitation and entrapment which render us vulnerable
from the outset. Vulnerability is also at the heart of Alain
Badiou's speculative philosophy which not only demands
a continual journey into the void whatever the consequences; but also develops a theory of love that is precarious and fraught with dangers: 'The absolute contingency
of the encounter takes on the appearance of destiny. The
declaration of love marks the transition from chance to
destiny and that's why it is so perilous and so burdened
with a kind of horrifying stage fright'.[28] Not only is this
account of love perfectly in keeping with his singular
understanding of the subject as one driven by its own
disconnected fidelity to the truth (albeit in a way that
allows room for the vanguard performer to shine light on
a more truthful staging), Badiou's adventures in love are
all about suffering the encounter of such fidelity. Love as
such is akin to a vulnerable endurance, for 'in love, fidelity
signifies this extended victory: the randomness of an
encounter defeated day after day through the invention of
what will endure'.

While Badiou, in particular, has become something of a
darling of the intellectual Left, Judith Butler remains the
intellectual embodiment of vulnerability. 'Each of us is
constituted politically', she writes, 'in part by virtue of the
social vulnerability of our bodies'.[29] Exemplifying the bio-
philosophical tradition of thought that seeks to tear 'the
subject from the terrain of the cogito and consciousness'
and 'root it in life', Butler's ambition is to underscore the

embodied nature of the subject and, more to the point, the living of the life that embodiment entails. The subject is a thing that lives, indeed, which must live, in order to be and, in living, is a thing that must die and therefore can never aspire to the kinds of security promised to it by the false prophets of Western metaphysics. Security, once considered in light of the subject's finitude, must be dismissed as hyperbolic fantasy. Basic to the life of the subject is not its capacity to achieve security but its radical vulnerability. As Butler states,

> There are no conditions that can fully 'solve' the problem of human precariousness. Bodies come into being and cease to be: as physically persistent organisms, they are subject to incursions and to illnesses that jeopardize the possibility of persisting at all. These are necessary features of bodies – they cannot 'be' thought without their finitude, and they depend on what is 'outside themselves' to be sustained – features that pertain to the phenomenological structure of bodily life.[30]

Recognizing the vulnerability of the subject must mean, Butler argues, not just establishing a different way of theorizing subjectivity, but establishing a different politics, one that emerges from the recognition of our vulnerability.

Butler argues for the necessity of a 'new bodily ontology', underscoring vulnerability, for the development of a new form of leftist political subjectivity. The Left needs to understand vulnerability as 'a shared condition' and to develop coalitions between different vulnerable subjects to struggle against the violence by which populations are differentially deprived of the basic resources needed to minimize their vulnerability. Whatever we may think about the veracity of Butler's theory of vulnerability as predicate of life and precondition for subjectivity, it is necessary to note the degree to which this way of thinking about subjectivity is contemporaneous not with an incipient new leftism, but with the dominant episteme and regime of power relations that the Left today has to combat. The ontology of the social underlying Butler's account of vulnerability is deeply *liberal*. Vulnerability 'implies living socially, that is, the fact that one's life is always in some sense in the hands of the other. It implies exposure both to those we know and to those we do not know; a dependency on people we know, or barely know, or know not at all'.[31] However, rather than following Butler and embracing another reiteration of liberalism's understanding of the dangers posed to the subject's vulnerable life by the unknowability of the social, we can better pose the questions of why, when, and how it was that the life of the subject came to be so conceived. Butler, in other words, should be associated within the very tradition that the Left today is forced to think against. As these less critically minded set of academics put it, 'resilience and vulnerability are dialectically linked: that a people can be constituted as resilient precisely because they can also be coded as vulnerable. Resilience, then, not only makes sense primarily within the context of a perceived sense of vulnerability but also offers an appealing and constructive alternative vision'.[32]

One primary lesson that Foucault teaches us is the danger in practising philosophy by way of what he called 'an imperative discourse'. Rather than engaging in a philosophy that glibly attempts to pronounce the facts or truth about life, it is necessary to analyse the 'knowledge effects' produced by the imperative discourses that support the regimes of truth through which life is determined as life as well as to analyse how different forms of life are evaluated as worth living. Rather than pronouncing truths about life, Foucault examines the implications of what life is said to be and what conditions will enable it. Every imperative discourse on life, no matter its content, entails such implications. This is why we must, if we are to do justice to Foucault, practise circumspection when examining claims about the reality or facts said to concern life. Imperative discourses are never grounded in facts, no matter how much they may make recourse to 'the facts'. The 'fact' of 'vulnerability' is no different. It is an element within a discourse every bit as aesthetic as discourses that presuppose the possibility of security and on account of which Butler critiques their inauthenticity. This error owes to the debased ways in which Butler and others have engaged Foucault's concept of biopolitics. Life, as Foucault argues repeatedly, is not an ontological category. Rather than embracing Butler's argument for the ontological fundamentality of vulnerability, it befalls us to consider what are the implications for life when vulnerability is reified as the authentic basis for subjectivity? What forms of life will a vulnerable subject discount as unworthy and indeed declare permissible to kill in order to defend the sanctity of its own account of life as vulnerable? And, more affirmatively, why must we wait for the catastrophe and experience of suffering before staking an ethical or political claim?

Violently Exposed

That killing takes place in order to produce liberal subjects is now well established within critical theories of biopolitics. In order to promote and improve the species life of the human, so the body (as a micro-synonym for the wider 'body-politic') becomes the site upon which necessary forms of violence are openly declared. In this regard, we find some agreement with Butler that violence, biopolitically conceived, always amounts to a 'performance' that is integral to the formation of political subjectivities. Such violence may amount to the establishment of simple and reductionist identitarian claims, or it may author more sophisticated subjective stakes as the marked body evidences various signs of the subjugated, the complicit, the shamed, the inferior, the passive, the gendered and so forth, through the act of violation. But what becomes of this performance when we move beyond the biophysical in terms of its material and objective qualities? Indeed, how may we conceive of violence once our exposure to the fact moves us out of the realm of fixed elements such that we concern ourselves with the less locatable promise of violence to come? Violence, after all, remains poorly understood if it is accounted for simply in terms of how and what it kills, the scale of its destructiveness, or any other element of its annihilative power.

Roberto Esposito makes an important intervention here with his *Immunitas* thesis.[33] Extending his earlier thinking on the biopolitical as a political intervention upon the bodies of the living, he searches for a theory that is capable of addressing the violence which occurs as the subject moves from equilibrium to some consequent need for reconstitution. Key here is the understanding that violence occurs at the interventionary threshold, where life ceases to become what it was and yet has not quite revealed its new formative conditioning. While sovereignty has always revealed this form of violation as it marks out the domains so familiar to students of Schmitt, the realm of the biopolitical offers a more complex approach to the issue of contagion, such that the essentially passive defence of bodies by keeping threats at a distance is replaced by the active inducement of that which threatens to endanger. Life therefore 'combats what it negates through immunitary protection, not a strategy of frontal opposition but of outflanking and neutralising'.[34] This raises a number of significant issues. Firstly, since survivability is premised upon the belief that there are certain wounds the subject cannot fully secure itself against, the lethal principle is incorporated as part of one's defences. Violence, in other words, comes to 'characterise the immunitary processes themselves'.[35] Second, since this strategy places the body absolutely central to thinking about the political in terms of its inescapability from violence, 'life is reduced to pure material' that is 'abstracted from any form or right life or shared life'.[36] The violation of the subject cuts into and irreparably scars the very fabric of the body-politic. And third, since the body becomes both the instrument and terrain in a constant battle between life and death, the purpose of this violent intervention in the name of the living is to 'delay the passage from life to death as long as possible, to drive death from the farthest point from the presentness of life'.[37]

Not only does immunization expose the body to the catastrophic possibility of its dissolution before the impending risk has materialized, it inaugurates a pathogenic matrix that continually reworks the normative basis for the authentic self whose life politics ends up negating everything that is originally taken to be the source for protection – the *quality* of life:

> Here lies the terrible contradiction on which we should focus: what saves individual and collective life is also that which impedes its development, and indeed what, beyond a certain point, winds up destroying it. We could say, by using the language of Walter Benjamin, himself dead because of the closing of a border – that immunization at high doses is the sacrifice of the living, which is to say, every form of qualified life, to simple survival. The reduction of life to its bare biological layer, of *bios* to *zoe*. To remain as such, life is forced to give way to an outside power that penetrates it and crushes it; to incorporate that nothing that it wishes to avoid, remaining captured by its void of meaning.[38]

Anybody who has experienced immunization will appreciate the violence of the encounter. The whole process begins with the awareness of some vaguely looming threat which promises in the worst case an extremely violent ending. To pre-empt this happening, the subject is physically penetrated by the alien body with a controlled level of the lethal substance which, although producing violent sickness, is a fate less than death. Such violence unto oneself offers to counter violence with violence such that life may carry on living in spite of the dangers we are incapable of securing ourselves against. It is to give over to a form of self-harm albeit in a way that is actively desired and positively conceived. How else may we live otherwise? Resilience follows a similar logic. It encourages that we partake in the violence of the world to keep death at bay. For in the process of learning to live through the insecurity of the times, the subject is asked to incorporate the catastrophic intellectually, viscerally and affectively, thereby providing certain immunization against a more endangering fate. Indeed, since the ultimate litmus test is to bring to question the worst case scenario, the future cannot appear to us as anything other than completely monstrous. What, however, is actually slain as the future is wagered by the violence of the present may only become revealed with the passage of time. None of this operates outside of the realm of power politics. We only have to consider here (a) the moral judgements and political stakes associated with HIV as a pandemic that is more than simply biological, and (b) the development of viral analogies to explain more generally the problems 'infecting' societies from terror to criminality to evidence the point. Immunization is precisely about exposing oneself to something that is potentially lethal, thereby raising the threshold level for existence such that violence is normalized on account of our vulnerabilities to that which may be tempered but remains undefeatable.

We are drawn here to Stellan Rye's (1913) silent horror movie *The Student from Prague* (Der Student von Prag) which has inspired a number of compelling literary and cinematic classics. In this tragic tale of poverty and violence, the impoverished student, Balduin, makes a bargain with the Devil as he exchanges the reflection of image for more immediate compensations. Upon eventually seeing himself, however, the student is avenged by an angry double that begins to wreak havoc as it seeks out revenge in light of its betrayal. Following an eventual violent confrontation the student has with his double, Balduin shatters the mirror that is central to the plot, and invariably destroys the fantasy of endangerment which also became the source of his afflicted curse. Inevitably, however, since the double was an essential element of this Faustian agreement, in killing the violent double, so the student kills himself. Otto Rank famously related this to the narcissistic self whose very sense of loneliness and alienation is caused by an anguish of a fear of death; even though it is precisely the violence of the pact which pushes the subject further towards the precipice. Whilst it is tempting to read this in familiar dialectical terms, there is a more sophisticated double move at work here, as the violence is already encoded within the initial act of demonic violation *before* the tragic encounter. For the double merely highlights the self-propelling tendency, from the fantasy of endangerment to the reality of the catastrophic. There is also a semantic interchange at work in Rye's Doppelganger as it stakes out the choice between a violated/violent life and eventual death. Since reason or logic prove utterly incapable of explaining the condition of Balduin's existence, let alone offering any promise of salvation from the oppressive situation to which he is fatefully bound, the double serves as an important metaphor for the narcissism of the times, as the subject wilfully accepts a violation and all the violence this entails in exchange for an illusion or fantasy of security which proves in the end to have been imbued with the catastrophic from the outset. Our understanding of the fundamental tenets of violence is invariably transformed such that we are forced to think about forms of violation/intervention prior to any sense of dialectical enmity.

Premetic Violence

René Girard's thesis *Violence and the Sacred* offers a theory of violence that is exclusively bound to the desire to 'overcome' tragedy. To develop this theory, Girard specifically relates to the classic Greek play by Sophocles, *Oedipus Rex*, which he uses to illustrate the relationship between tragic dispossession and violence. It is through the tale of Oedipus and his return to reclaim the realm from which he was abandoned that we uncover a genesis of sacrificial violence that is linked to some 'past tragedy'.[39] Oedipus thus epitomizes the motif of the lost prince whose modes of contestation can be understood through competing claims to the 'same object of desire'. The story follows that when two uncompromising entities vie over the same object of desire, violence necessarily erupts. Through Girard's decoding of the Oedipus myth, what we therefore find is any attempt to re-possess the object of desire necessarily requires the guilt of those currently in possession – a sacrificial victim. Thus, to overcome tragedy one must come from the 'outside' – a violently destined return that can only be justified by making a claim to the original sin, or what Girard terms a return to the 'original scene'. However, as Sophocles tells it, such violence is more than simply a reclamation of that which has been taken. The violence of the already dispossessed desires to re-establish the authentic order which has been falsely appropriated – the paradise lost. Importantly, for Girard, such violence is not a relation of difference but is more defined by the logic of *mimesis*: 'At first, each of the protagonists believes that he can quell the violence; at the end each succumbs to it. All are drawn unwittingly into a violent reciprocity – which they always think they are outside of, because they all initially came from outside and mistake this positional and temporary advantage for a permanent and fundamental superiority'.[40] Plunging into an opposition which 'reduces the protagonists into a uniform condition of violence', all claims to 'difference' are effectively 'eclipsed' by 'a resurgence of reciprocity'.[41]

It has been common to read Rye's doubling as a clear example of mimetic behaviour. This has found clear applications from Hegelian-inspired revolutionary accounts of dialectical reasoning, to Frantz Fanon's theory of (post) colonial brutality, onto the exceptional violence of Schmitt's sovereign decisionism. While accepting how this logic has played a structural role in the demarcation of certain regimes of violence which came to hallmark distinct marks of separation, we need to depart from this logic if we are to make sense of the violence of the catastrophic imaginary. What, in other words, becomes of violence once we reconceptualize the idea of the original scene and its logics of exposure such that violence itself becomes virtually ordained? That is to say, what becomes of violence once it begins to precede any dialectical arrangement? Mimetic violence, we have noted, is objectifiable. Based upon establishing various forms of mystical foundations, it has a distinct materiality to it that permits clear lines of demarcation and embodiment. These work both spatially and temporally. The object for violence is locatable, while the time of its occurrence offers clear (if sometimes contested) conceptions as to its beginning and ending. It benefits, then, from the guarantees of identification and the ability to represent that which must be vanquished at a given moment 'in time'. The virtual nature of the violence endured by the resilient subject offers no such guarantees. Collapsing the space-time continuum of mimetic rivalry, it is merely projected into the future without the prospect of bounce-back. Internalized, however, into the very living conditions of the subject now permanently under siege, the violence is no less real. As any author of horror fiction will tell, the mind can be a terrifying place to inhabit. Once the source of endangerment becomes unknowable by definition, everything becomes the potential source of a violent encounter.

Resilience challenges the logic of mimetic violence, therefore, in two fundamental ways. Firstly, it shows us that our only way of dealing with endangerment is to absorb its lethal tendencies. That which has the potential to destroy must become part of society's make-up and its epistemic fabric. We too, in the process, become more lethally endowed as a result. Invariably, the more lethal we become, the more we end up embracing the biophysical conditions of our potential undoing as a principle form of human conditioning. The body accepts the lethality on account of preparedness. Secondly, there is an outward projection against that which could potentially threaten our existence. But this projection doesn't connect to any mimetic rival. We have no clear sense of what it is that so endangers in its particular guise, only a generalizable indication that something which is part of the integral whole will eventually bring about our final demise. Deprived, then, of the potential to 'at last stand' upon a terrain whose forms of endangerment were known in advance, we continue to walk through a veritable minefield of potential disasters of a multi-dimensional nature, not knowing when the explosion will happen, with little comfort provided by the intellectual comforts of the past, and with no fence on the horizon beyond which relative security may be achieved and freedom from endangerment realized. The only solution, we are told, remains to expose oneself to all its disastrous permutations so that we may be better prepared against those already charged and yet to detonate, along with those yet to even be inserted into this catastrophic topography.

But what does it mean to say that violence is now beyond representation? And what type of reality are we producing if we are calling into question the depths of field that once gave qualitative and quantitative meaning to our relations to violence? For Paul Virilio, whose work we may connect to the premetic, this inaugurates 'the futurism of the instant' whose *kairos* shatters all metaphysical meaning:

> This spells disorientation in knowledge acquired over the course of millennia regarding the spatial environment and the cycle of seasons; an *integral accident* in knowledge of history as well as of the usual concrete geography that goes with it, the unity of place and time of a secular history. No doubt this is the fatal novelty of the historic tragedy befalling humanity and a progress that will no longer be exclusively technologistical and extra-planetary, but merely human, 'all too human'. Masochism vis-à-vis an abhorred past that no longer passes muster is now symmetrically doubled with a masochism in relation to a future where, for want of fear, we will, this time, have space, all the space of a miniscule planet reduced to nothing, or as good as, by the progress of our discoveries.[42]

Nihilism Unbound

Writing in the nineteenth century, Nietzsche argued that nothing was more deeply characteristic of the modern world than the power of nihilism.[43] Nietzsche's intervention here allowed us to move beyond the well-rehearsed attack upon Platonic reason or Christian faith, to focus instead upon 'the radical repudiation of value, meaning and desirability'.[44] Nihilism, thus understood, referred to the triumph of *reactive thinking*. It was all about the negation of life as it appeared to be incapable of affirming that which is properly and creatively different to human existence. Hence, for Nietzsche, nihilism was not simply reducible to some historical event in time, i.e. an exceptional moment in history which could be shamefully written into annals of human suffering. Nihilism was the recurring *motor of history* as the operation of power leads to a will to nothingness that strips life of any purposeful meaning. Crucially, as Nietzsche understood, this repudiation of the affirmative realm of experience is something *we create for ourselves*.[45] Nihilism, in other words, is to be understood through a sophisticated manipulation of desires such that the individual subject depreciates itself to such an extent that it actively participates in a custom of political self-annihilation.

Central to Nietzsche's thinking on the perpetuation of nihilism is the notion of *ressentiment*. In his *On the Genealogy of Morality*, Nietzsche explains this in terms of the slave mentality. This produces a feeling of impotence which not only translates into vengefulness, but more problematic still, teaches the slave that the only way it can become free is to give over to the prevailing reason mastery has set in place. Sloterdijk equates this *ressentiment* with rage, the basis of all great theisms.[46] Such a condition, as Nietzsche understood, was 'paralysing' insomuch as it annuls the possibility of thinking and acting otherwise, and it was 'exhausting' insomuch as life was forced to compromise with the very lethality that put its condition originally into question. Through a 'spirit of revenge' what is lacking is therefore produced in a double movement, for lack is not some original gesture, it derives out of the *ressentiment* to deny us the opportunity to bring something different into the world. This raises a number of pressing questions: Could it be that not only have we become slaves to our biological existence, but in claiming false mastery of the earth we have given to ourselves an illusionary sovereignty? For how can we have mastery if that which we claim to be able to dominate as the principle force makes us increasingly vulnerable with each passing moment? Have we not, then, become slaves to ourselves and slaves to the earth, and resentful of them as a result?

Nihilism has never been alien to liberal biopolitics. It is arguably its most potent expression. Its early development can be traced to Kant's Copernican revolution of the mind. Placing life at the centre of its universe, Kant forced us to look for meaning beyond the realms of theological destiny. Whilst this moved us beyond the suffering and lament of the Christian subject which so irked Nietzsche, Kant's universal substitute proved to be no substitute at all. The universal was actually denied to us due to the limits of our reason and our imperfections as finite beings – imperfections that significantly proved incapable of moving us beyond the reductionism of metaphysical idealism and its crude representations, towards a more affirmative form of metaphysics that worked in practice. As Drucilla Cornell writes, 'Martin Heidegger famously wrote that Kant takes us to the limit of the very notion of critique and ultimately raises, but does not fully address, the question of 'who' is this finite being that must think through the transcendental imagination'.[47] In a remarkably potent yet tragic stroke, Kant wrote the death of the omnipotent God and the types of docile subjects it produced who were rendered immobile due to its vengeance and fury, while putting in its place a fallen subject that was fated to be forever incomplete because of the burdens of its own actions.

While Kant's thinking paved the way for new eschato-logical forms of power to emerge that took leave of tradi-tional sovereign moorings, the fallen subject was compelled to become resentful of its biological existence. *Bios* were to remain forever imperfect by design and fated to be judged accordingly. With life fated to live a biologically endowed existence, it is stripped of its capacity to have a meaningful existence beyond the limits of its bodily forma-tions, while political strategies operate by governing through the problem of finitude, even though the finite inevitably became a philosophical problem too difficult to comprehend. As a result, forced to endure a growing resentment of its unfolding drama, liberalism slowly became morally equipped to continually intervene upon the souls of the living simply by offering to prolong the subject's existence better than any other political rational-ity. Such was the realization of our finite entrapment in the bodily form that the ability to philosophically transgress the injunction between life and death became increasingly impossible. Indeed, as we shall point out later, while liberal societies have a particular relationship to the question of dying as our existence is continually put into question, such that with each passing second we learn to survive until we become truly meaningless in the end, the idea of death remains incommensurable to the liberal subject.

No longer does the resilient subject solely project its resentfulness onto the souls of 'Others'. It resents the living world, for it too is radically endangering. It is here that catastrophic imaginaries begin to truly thrive. The resilient subject is shaped and anxiously mobilized by the prospect of the coming catastrophe. It fears the transformation of the subject, just as it fears the transformation of the eco-system that gives sustenance to life. Our rage as such, to borrow from Sloterdijk, has become truly limitless. As everything becomes the source of our endangerment, we internalize the *ressentiment* and proliferate our impotence with unrivalled intensity and absolute necessity. Hence this produces a form of nihilism which is 'unbounded'. For no longer do we simply resent the teleological unfolding of history as we phase shift from masters to slaves to masters; there is no mastery to speak of and as a result all our lament filters into a politics of *ressentiment* as we are left to simply govern through our continually unfolding state of unending emergency.

This brings us to an important conceptual point that must be addressed in our critique. Adaptation in the face of the catastrophic is not the same as political transformation. The former accepts its conditions of insecurity and vulnerability. Adaptation conflates resistance with resilience such that politics becomes a sheer matter of survivability. Without challenging the fundamental tenets of a catastrophic existence, to adapt is to concede defeat to the avatars of liberal reason which continue to proclaim no political alternative except the pathological. Transformation, in contrast, finds enough reasons to believe in the irreducible spirit of the world such that we may affirm a different sensual and aesthetic relationship to its natural forces. This has nothing to do with a fatalism that accepts the inevitability of human extinction (even though it is inevitable). Nor does it seek to make light of the real experiences of oppression, destitution and daily struggle faced by the majority of the world's inhabitants. On the contrary, it has everything to do with reintroducing political meaning back into the world, such that our relations do not dismiss the sense of wonder of experience one enjoys in those poetic moments with fellow humans and the earth which cannot be reduced to the techno-scientific conceit of biopolitical rule. And it has everything to do with a willingness to challenge indifferences to the political with more affirmative expressions that demand replacing the vulnerability of catastrophic rule with a poetic confidence in the creation of worlds to come.

– 5 –
Atmos

Beyond *Bios*

Never before have we been so saturated by meditations on the life of things. Animated qualities appear everywhere. Nothing it seems is devoid of a certain vitality. This is the age of posthumanism – a profound shift in our sensibilities that requires us to think about the questions of agency in radically different ways. We are not in any way resistant to this shift in our understanding that enables us to appreciate the recombinant nature of existence. Neither are we resistant to the ethical possibilities posthumanism presents for us as an important digression from the sheer terror of the humanist traditions. We are, however, deeply suspicious of the novel forms of biopolitics that emerge from this connected terrain, especially the equation of 'the virtual' with technologically driven processes of connectivity such that 'the open' as a field of possibility is colonized by the catastrophes which define the radical interconnectivity of the times. Not only does this emergent form of biopolitics put the very meaning of the human as a metaphysically endowed subject capable of transforming its world into question. While the human is still central to

this survivalist dispositif, the contingency of life connec-
tivities are no longer capable of escaping the wider milieus
for uncontrollable change which surrender us to the
mercies of the world. There is an important point to stress here. Contemporary biopolitics is not the same as that originally conceived
by Michel Foucault. Whereas Foucault's earlier provoca-
tions talked about the manipulation of localized populations, liberal biopolitics has gradually moved on to the
problem of biospherical life complete. Whereas Foucault
was concerned with the immediacy of biopolitical interventions as they impacted upon the conduct of human
actions, it is now the virtual realm (understood as a future/
present terrain of infinite possibility) that dominates thinking on questions of security governance. And whereas
Foucault talked about the question of race as integral to
biopolitics, especially as it appeared against some perfect-
ible model of standardization, i.e. a pure race of species
that was logically superior on account of its biological
heritage, despite the continuation of liberal violence against
all illiberal elements, contemporary liberal biopolitics
starts from the less confident assumption that the species
is naturally endowed with vulnerabilities which it must
accept. These exclusively derive from the insecure design
of everything.

No life – even the most contemplative – can permanently exist outside of the many dispositifs into which it
is enmeshed. Nor should it wish to. Such a journey into
the void is neither affirmative, nor is it desirable, for the
positive enrichment of its existence is only made possible
through inter-subject interpellation. We are social and
political animals whose very sense of becoming in the
world can only be felt if our transformations connect in
a trans-valuative fashion. What matters more is whether
or not the inevitability of systemic transformation made
possible by the various creative flights of individual
elements are allowed to express their affirmative qualities, without suffering from the violence of some

pre-determined normalization that renders the affirmation some pathological abnormality. With this in mind, there is a need to bring together a number of further intellectual contributions which allow us to triangulate what we identify to be the *atmospheric-aesthetic-affective* dimensions to human existence and their concomitant biopoliticization. This reframing of the problem of biopolitics today represents an important departure. Not only does it allow us to better understand the operations of power in ways that cannot simply rely upon technical claims, it also allows us to rethink their terms of engagement such that their more irreducible qualities can be appreciated as integral to the creation of better ethical relations. If there is an alternative to the vulnerabilities of the resilient subject, it must be seen as something more than a reworking of the biopolitical.

That the atmosphere is part of, or at least impacts upon, our political thinking seems to be self-evident. Not only is our language full of references to such things as the 'climate of fear', often we comment that a particular event can be judged in terms of its atmospheric qualities. Success and failure is frequently accounted for in terms of some atmospheric contribution which, although difficult to quantify, is no less real in terms of allowing us to make sense of a particular situation. Atmosphere is more, however, than some element that exists independently of subjects and objects. It is precisely that which connects subjects and objects in ways that give qualitative and affective meaning to relations that are wholly contingent in space and time. Indeed atmosphere is not separate from the body; it penetrates the subject to profoundly influence both our visible and material realities, along with the ephemeral conditions that affect how we see and experience the world. Such atmospheres, of course, are never universal or static. We may write of many different types of atmosphere which are able to insert a presence upon us in affirmative or suffocating and toxic ways. Hence, what matters is how we conceive of the atmospheric in terms of its integral status to the human condition. As Gernot Böhme insists, the art of living is atmospheric by design.[1]

Like emotion, however, the atmospheric has equally been a casualty of the liberal revivalism following the horrors of the Second World War. If emotion was politically problematic, along with the aesthetics of fascistic power that still is said to symbolize decadence, madness, disease and perversion,[2] so the manipulation of atmospheric conditions, as imagined by the likes of Albert Speer, has continually been consigned to the realm of the dangerous or the unquantifiable. Atmosphere, however, matters – politically. Despite the fact that it remains elusive and irreducible to the narrow and self-serving enquiries of the positivist traditions, ignoring the politics of atmosphere is to gloss over the truly potent dimensions to anthropocentric thought and the contemporary nature of biopolitical rule. For it is with meditations on Atmos that the catastrophic imaginaries truly capture us. Indeed, we maintain that our critique of resilience makes no sense whatsoever unless we account for the manipulation of our active living spaces which are atmospherically charged, thereby aesthetically and affectively connecting to further authenticate the vulnerable subject's lament for its fated and catastrophic existence.

Peter Sloterdijk's work in promoting atmospheric thought is exemplary in this regard. Throughout his *Spheres* trilogy, he makes the compelling case for thinking about the atmospheric dimensions to life as no less important than other aspects which shape human thoughts and behaviours. To write of the atmosphere, indeed, is to also write of it as a social and political field of force that needs to be taken seriously as a critical area for study. The atmosphere as such is integral to any understanding of how we 'weather existence'. We may read this as an attempt to properly conceptualize the spatial ontology of existence in ways that move beyond the representable or visible aspects of epistemic certainty. It should be pointed out that atmospherics for Sloterdik are not only integral to thinking about questions of mood and temperament so often neglected in the operation of power. It holds the promise for a new politics that allows us to act 'still in the storm'. Hence counter to the Heideggerian claim of being thrown into the world, the most potent phenomenological articulation of survivability that shares an all too evident connect to the Kantian logic of fallen freedom, Sloderdijk's shift toward being-with-in-the-world works from the premise that there is something altogether more literary in the air that we breathe. This requires a new-found confidence to find quality, beauty and poetic transformation so that being-with-in-the-storm doesn't necessarily translate into a vulnerable retreat or lament for inevitable changes in atmospheric conditions. This is what he terms a 'critical theory of air and a positive notion of the atmospheric *res publica*',[3] which for Sloterdijk represents a kind of atmospheric third way to move us beyond the impasse of the pure terror of indeterminacy and the less than oppositional alternative of the environmental cage. This is delightfully captured by Nigel Thrift who explains:

> It all matters. These different aspects of space are brought together as landscaping organisms which both produce the world and hedge it in; forming within their orbit atmospheres that gradually take on a life of their own. They act as selective animations with their own dynamic momentum that resembles a climatic regime in that it both creates a new medium and makes it possible to breathe within it, whether the air be fresh or stale. Hence, the Sloterdijkian emphasis on atmospheres and what might be called the pursuit of air quality, and alongside this emphasis, the instigation of regimes of detoxification.[4]

Linking this to aesthetics, Jacques Rancière offers an important contribution by insisting that aesthetics should not be divorced from our understanding of power (the ability to affect and to be affected) – that is to say that, when we talk about the dispositif, it is also pertinent to write of the aesthetic dispositif that is no less meaningful and significant. Indeed, for Rancière, whilst it is possible to write of a specific partitioning of the sensible such that our aesthetic experiences are manipulated for the service of power and its regimes of truth (with knowledge itself depending upon and indeed creating its own aesthetic apparatus), the aesthetic dispositif allows us to understand the conflicts and tensions that exist within such regimes in a way that draws out distinctions between a partitioned sensibility and a more poetic orientation:

> What is called an image is an element in a system that creates a certain sense of reality, a certain common sense. A 'common sense' is, in the first instance, a community of sensible data: things whose visibility is supposed to be shareable by all, modes of perception of these things, and the equally shareable meanings that are conferred on them . . . [it is] a spatio-temporal system in which words and visible forms are assembled into shared data, shared ways of perceiving, being affected and imparting meaning.[5]

Being affected, as Rancière intimates, is integral to our understanding of power. Indeed, biopolitics makes little sense from the perspective of agency unless we factor in the notion of affect. For it is through the manipulation of desires made possible through claims to improve the human existence that the biopolitical gets tangible purchase. We give ourselves over to it on the promise of the more progressive existence it lays claim to. Such promises cannot simply be reduced to reason and its technical dreams of power. They must be felt. Biopolitics would, then, have no positive hold over us whatsoever, were it devoid of the ability to viscerally animate. It is, after all, a vital power; its strategies depend upon the ability to harness human potentials to condition affective relations within a social body. Affect, however, is always more *excessive* than the biopolitical will to rule. What biopolitics tries to achieve is precisely the regulation of desires such that life conducts itself in a way that is wilfully internalized. With this in mind, it would be a patent mistake

just to view the logic of affect through the prism of technical interventionism. We never were ghosts in the machine. Nor are we able to separate the capacity for reason
from sometimes inexplicable moods or aesthetic influences. All discussions of the human subject in the world
must begin from the position that it remains atmospherically-aesthetically-affectively irreducible to the operation
of regimes of power. This is its milieu. Why else would
power need to intervene if not to tame the irreducible
which appears to be beyond or in excess of its strategic
remit?

The Politics of Atmosphere

Catastrophic reasoning is all about rendering the invisible
visible. It demands a certain *exposure* to the fact before
the event of its occurrence appears for real. This virtual
inauguration of the catastrophe in the minds of vulnerable
subjects is not in any way divorced from the conditions of
reality as it pertains in the here and now. Whilst the visibil-
ity of its occurrence in relation to its catastrophic consequences may lack immediacy in terms of verification, what
is going to come to pass is already *happening*. Every potential terror in this age of extinction points to the inevitable
unfolding of a *slow catastrophe* – one whose very problematic actually denies us the comforts of epistemic proofing until it proves to be too late. This is pre-emption writ
large. It is also the terrain for power struggles today. For
if the atmospheric-aesthetic-affective dimensions to power
are essentially contested; their biopoliticization can be
understood as a form of 'climatic conditioning'. It is all
about manipulating the general crisis environments such
that indeterminacy nevertheless functions as a strategic
weapon for political rule.

It is no coincidence that we may trace the origins
of climatic conditioning to warfare. Certainly from the

twentieth century onwards, atmospheric war appears an
integral element of battles as ideas of spatiality become
much more sophisticated than simply the territory which
we occupied. The British were particularly adept. From
Winston Churchill's sanctioning of the use of gas in Meso-
potamia[6] to Bomber Harris's use of phosphorus in the
aerial bombardment of Dresden – a tragedy inflicted on a
target of no strategic or military importance which resulted
in more casualties than Hiroshima and Nagasaki combined, violence increasingly targeted the lived environment. As Duffield has observed, total war has always
demanded 'the destruction of an enemy's environmental
life-world'. Its targets have continually included 'the
climate regimes, vital urban infrastructures, ecological
systems, and social networks, together with the neurologi-
cal and cellular processes that collectively support life and
make it possible'[7]. Indeed, for Duffield, since environmental terror evidences most clearly the deeply embedded relations between war, nature and economy, it is here we can
detect the early seeds of resilience discourses as societies
learn to accept unpredictability and vulnerability. This
reveals a particular historically consistent feature of liberal
power. Rather than seeking to banish war and anxiety as
liberal peace advocates would maintain, liberalism actually thrives in conditions of pure uncertainty. This rein-
forces the need for greater militarism on account of the
fact of the very insecurities the system creates and promotes as 'natural'. As Duffield further explains, 'everything within the frame of environmental terror has a
potential dual use and latency; everything that touches or
supports life can be turned around. Everything can be
weaponized'.[8] Atmosphere included!

As the century developed, the United States and the
Soviet Union would be at the forefront of these monstrous
attempts to engineer the atmospheric for strategic gain.
Even before the Second World War, the Soviets established the Leningrad Institute of Rainmaking (1932) to
pioneer cloud manipulation for political, economic and

military reasons. The grandiose nature of these efforts was wonderfully captured in the concluding paragraph of *Man Versus Climate*:

> Our little book is now at an end. We have described those mysteries of nature already penetrated by science, the daring projects put forward for transforming our planet, and the fantastic dreams to be realized in the future. Today we are merely on the threshold of the conquest of nature. But if, on turning the last page, the reader is convinced that man can really be the master of this planet and that the future is in his hands, then the authors will consider that they have fulfilled their purpose.[9]

The United States was invariably horrified by such ambitions and potential capabilities. As Henry Houghton, chair of the MIT meteorology department, stated in 1957, 'I shudder to think of the consequences of a prior Russian discovery of a feasible method for weather control. Fortunately for us and the world we were first to develop nuclear weapons . . . International control of weather modification will be as essential to the safety of the world as control of nuclear energy is now'. While the designated 'fortune' in respect to Hiroshima is banal in the extreme, the response was altogether expected. The Vietnam War became a further experimenting laboratory as environmental terror became central to military strategy. In addition to the cloud-seeding sorties during Operation Popeye, as silver iodine was inserted into cloud formations in order to prolong the monsoon season, it is estimated that the United States dispersed more than 72 million litres of herbicide in central and southern Vietnam in order to defoliate the land and kill everything within range.[10] Agent Orange destroyed some 5.5 million acres of forest and croplands, resulting in widespread human and biospherical deformations, the scars of which are still most visible today. This resulted in the ratification of an International Convention on the Prohibition of Military or Any Other Hostile Use of Environmental Modification Techniques by the UN General

Assembly, which banned 'military or other hostile use of environmental modification techniques having widespread, long-lasting or severe effects'. Environmental modification techniques are being defined here as 'any technique for changing – through the deliberate manipulation of natural processes – the dynamics, composition or structure of the earth, including its biota, lithosphere, hydrosphere and atmosphere, or of outer space'[11]. The problem, of course, with this convention is that it is premised on the ability to mark out clear distinctions between civil and military applications. For as we have learned, liberal societies in their operations shatter such binary distinctions such that politics is normalized as the continuation of war by other means. What is more, as liberal power dictates, the term 'hostility' has no home or political resonance whatsoever in its defining lexicon.

The ending of the Cold War has fully removed the liberal pretence that its ambition is to banish war and anxiety. Not only is war openly declared on each and every social ill such that any micro-specific distinction between war and peace is rendered meaningless. So we have also learned how anxiety is integral to the creation of liberal subjects who are asked to embrace vulnerability as a necessary condition for partaking in this world. While the breaking up of the welfare state and the continued investment in the manipulation of climatic conditions for war and other strategic gains may therefore appear initially unrelated, they are in fact more revealing of a generalizable logic as the life-world system is open to limitless interventions on account of the vulnerabilities all living elements are said to display without distinction. In spite of these connections, however, it remains the case that the manipulation of the atmosphere for political purposes is absent from discussions of the environment. As Michel Chossudovsky notes, while 'the Intergovernmental Panel on Climate Change (IPCC) has a mandate "to assess scientific, technical and socioeconomic information relevant for the understanding of climate change"', including

'environmental warfare', '"Geo-engineering" is acknowledged, but the underlying military applications are neither
the object of policy analysis or scientific research in the
thousands of pages of IPCC reports and supporting docu-
ments, based on the expertise and input of some 2,500
scientists, policymakers and environmentalists'. Hence for
Chossudovsky, while 'Climatic warfare potentially threatens the future of humanity', it 'has casually been excluded
from the reports for which the IPCC received the 2007
Nobel Peace Prize'.[12] Of significance is the US government's HAARP (High-frequency Active Auroral Research
Program). HAARP is based in Alaska, and its website
states, 'HAARP is a scientific endeavor aimed at studying
the properties and behavior of the ionosphere, with particular emphasis on being able to understand and use it to
enhance communications and surveillance systems for
both civilian and defence purposes'.[13] This tacit appreciation of the dual latency of atmospheric manipulation is
revealing. It is also an inevitable cause for concern.

There is an important point to be made here concerning
the politics of atmosphere, which we may define as the
ability to ascribe a regime of truth to the atmospheric in
order to permit the authentication, intervention and
manipulation of its conditions upon the lives of human
subjects. As Bruno Latour explains, the strength of Sloterdijk's intervention is to make the atmosphere *explicit* in
political terms.[14] Now, while we should overlook the ways
'quantifiable value' is attributed to the atmospheric today,
not least in respect to its monetary costs/benefits as articulated in nearly every liberal government's attempts to bring
the environmental debate home to its subjects, the focus
we have given here to atmospheric war is deeply significant
to our contemporary predicament, as it highlights most
clearly the political stakes. Sloterdijk was fully aware of
this from the outset. As Latour writes:

At first we feel nothing, we are insensitive, we are naturalized. And then suddenly we feel not something, but the

absence of something we did not know before could possibly be lacking. Think of the poor soldiers on the front
line, deep in their trenches, the 22nd of April 1915 near
Ypres. They knew everything about bullets, shells, rats,
death, mud, and fear – but air, they did not feel air, they
just breathed it. And then, from this ugly, slow moving
greenish cloud lingering over them, air is being removed.
They begin to suffocate. Air has entered the list of what
could be withdrawn from us.[15]

Key to Latour's reading is the realization that through
conscious manipulation of the atmosphere, most notably
in times of war, we appreciate our climate on account of
its respective negation; while at the same time, through
these explicit manoeuvres, we begin to understand how its
political manipulation forces us into a condition wherein
our 'life supports' may be put into question. It *appears*
violently to us through its *disappearance*. Such logic has
been directly transposed into contemporary environmental
discourse to the point of its effective normalization. We
need to be climatically aware of all its negative and suffocating effects, for what used to belong to the battlefield
– gas masks included – will soon become a common feature
of twenty-first-century living. However, rather than simply
combating this with a familiar dialectical move such that
we negate the negation of the atmospheric conditioning in
order to move to a higher and more enlightened stage of
survival synthesis, why not reach for a more positive
account of the atmospheric? One, for example, that permits
a new phenomenological sense of who we are as living and
breathing subjects, and whose sense of perception learns
to account with ethical diligence that which remains irreducible to the presentness of existence. Atmospheres are
fully intertwined with bodily affects and our presence of
mind. They cannot be divorced from the affective or the
aesthetic. How, then, might we think, as Böhme once proposed,[16] the atmosphere as fundamental to conceiving of
a new aesthetics beyond the judgemental? How might we
relate this more affirmatively to the phenomenological fact

of being such that we may operate in a more poetic and imaginative way beyond the suffocation and lament of those catastrophic narratives into which we are atmospherically immersed? And how might we better produce atmospheric conditions that are matched by semiotic systems which don't fear but harness their transformative potentials?

A Pathological Earth

There is a well-rehearsed theory of power which argues that the more that power begins to wane, the more violence it necessarily requires. Following the work of Hannah Arendt, it is argued that power and violence are different strategies wherein the latter is revealing of the former's demise. Looking at this from the perspective of violent pathologies, it appears that the onset of violence and its continuation to the point of unlimited and unmediated delivery is synonymous with the failure to maintain *power over life*. In this sense, violence appears to be a sort of pathological revenge waged against unruly elements which question the supreme source of authority that gives life to the living as such. It is certainly there in Thomas Hobbes's *Leviathan*, for instance, where the sovereign itself is presented in terms of an 'artificial lung' that allows life to live in a way that gives meaningful quality and security to an otherwise wretched existence. And it is also there in theorizations of civilizational collapse, none more so than of the Third Reich, which for Paul Virilio became as pathological in its destructive intent as it reached a point of no return that only the term 'suicidal' would be appropriate. Whilst this is certainly not the only meditation on power and violence, for both can be written in many ways, this typology is useful for explaining how the earth now appears to have its own pathological disposition, as we seek to explain the violence it wages with increasing frequency and ferocity upon those elements it once provided security to.

Anthropocentric thought has displaced Gaia with the human species. We have become the planetary hegemonic force, albeit in a way that lacks any appreciation of the lasting implications of our actions, let alone respecting any natural laws to ensure the biosphere positively flourishes in ecological diversity. The Earth, we are told, is fighting back precisely because of the scars we have inflicted upon its surface. Here the very idea of a scorched earth policy assumes an altogether different meaning, for as we have consciously, or at least ignorantly, waged continuous war upon the biosphere, amassing a greater number of troops along the way, instead of negotiating a compromise, the Earth it seems is sounding a fateful retreat and slowly but surely taking us all with it. With the Earth as such enacting its revenge upon us as it slowly loses its capacity to have power over life (whether that power is of a tyrannical dependency or democratic reciprocity is a matter for debate), to suggest that the Earth has a violent pathology is not in any way removed or abstracted from contemporary meditations on environmental change as earthly violence becomes increasingly extreme in its non-discriminatory delivery. As Barack Obama reiterated during his second-term victory speech, we need to confront the 'destructive power of a warming planet'.[17]

It should be pointed out that there is a considered genealogy to be developed here between pathology and the atmospheric. Indeed, in terms of the history of madness, the more familiar French equivalent *lunatique*, which became of particular interest to Foucault's unparalleled studies of the emergence of pathology as a social and political phenomena, derives from the earlier Latin *lunaticus*, or moon-struck, as developed from the prefix *luna* (moon). While contemporary psychology has long since outlived any attempts at suggesting a direct correlation between lunar cycles and deviant behaviours, from psychoanalysis to politics, we are still yet to fully comprehend the recurring motif of the wolf (the beast with the most evident association) as a way of demonizing human characteristics

and indeed entire social forms of organization said to emit
pack mentalities. Building on Deleuze's earlier criticism's
of Freud, Jacques Derrida has shown how our entire understanding of modern politics, especially in terms of its
sovereign credentials, has been underwritten by the wolf-
like figure, to offer a distinction between politically qualified life and the life of nature; the collapse of these
distinctions, and indeed the shift in our focus to the
creation of new hot and frozen forms of desertification
as a result of climate change, once again promises to
connect the atmospheric with human and political devi-
ancy in perhaps more sophisticated but certainly no less
pathological ways to the reconstitution of (ab)normal
classifications.

For our purposes, it is clear that a pathologized earth
leads to the inevitable militarization of the life-world
system such that it becomes possible to rethink the biological notion of 'fitness landscapes'. While the fitness landscape offers ways to visualize the optimization of adaptive
biological systems that diagrammatically appear similar to
topographical environments,[18] we may extend the term to
refer to the politicization of the biospherical conditions
more generally, such that it brings together war and
weather, and everything in between. What becomes a
matter of fitness therefore blends the human and the
natural into one radically interconnected system demanding a more considered assay. Here, meditations on the links
between conflict, security and the environment appear less
important in terms of quantifiable support to evidence the
fact than they do for allowing interventions on the basis
that the potential alone for connecting the event of their
realization is sufficient to warrant action. Negative potentials can never be disproved. Whether it is a hurricane or
a terror event that creates a suffocating urban cloud of
despair, the longer it seemingly goes undetected or refuses
to happen, the more potency it actually promises. The fact
that it is yet to emerge only serves to heighten the stakes,
all the while rendering it altogether more dangerous on

account of the fact that its truly evasive qualities will continue to remain unknowable until it arrives.

Fitness landscaping requires certain subjectivities that are not simply physically trained but psychologically conditioned. No coincidence, then, to find the military at the forefront of contemporary thinking on building resilient subjects. A pioneering project for such purposes is the United States Comprehensive Soldier Fitness initiative. Developed as part of a comprehensive rethink in terms of the ability to perform war in a more humane way, as the soldiers involved evidence their preparedness to bounce back from the trauma of the experience, it is based on the PERMA matrix: positive emotion, engagement, relationships, meaning and accomplishment. These complementary elements for the development of soldiers that are aware of their own vulnerabilities and unavoidable anxieties *before* war takes place are seen by the military to be the building blocks of resilience and growth. As Martin E.P. Seligman, Director of the Positive Psychology Center at the University of Pennsylvania observes:

> When the legendary General George W. Casey, Jr., the army chief of staff and former commander of the multinational force in Iraq, asked me what positive psychology had to say about soldiers' problems, I offered a simple answer: How human beings react to extreme adversity is normally distributed. On one end are the people who fall apart into PTSD, depression, and even suicide. In the middle are most people, who at first react with symptoms of depression and anxiety but within a month or so are, by physical and psychological measures, back where they were before the trauma. That is resilience. On the other end are people who show post-traumatic growth. They, too, first experience depression and anxiety, often exhibiting full-blown PTSD, but within a year they are better off than they were before the trauma.[19]

What is particularly revealing about the US military approach to the building of resilient subjects is both the reworking of terms for hierarchy and the collapse of the distinction between military and family life (hence the time of war and time of peace). As Mark Neocleous observes, the programme 'offers a Performance and Resilience Enhancement Program (CFS2-PREP), run by Master Resilience Trainers and consisting of various aspects such as Universal Resilience Training and Institutional Resilience Training. More advanced Comprehensive Resilience Models include Building Resilience for the Male Spouse, Building Your Teen's Resilience, and Dynamics of Socially Resilient Teams'[20]. So not only, then, is the resilient subject presented to be of a universal disposition. From the battlefield to the household, it is possible to identify a generalizable logic for power and intervention that emanates from a perceived shared sense of vulnerability. In short, the ability to claim *power over* and act accordingly is not to be associated with the capacity for considered intellectual reflection or indeed to challenge the political basis/construction of the coming catastrophe. But since resilience is a learning process from which nobody is exempt – and since learning itself is less about pre-formed knowledge and more about intellectual and psychological capacities to adapt in times of crises which cannot be known in advance – judgements can be made about 'fitness of mind'. This makes it possible to evidence those who are more adept at leading *through* the crises-event to offer a deeply militarized vision that further authenticates the vulnerable ontology of the contemporary human condition.

Atmosis

So how may we think the atmospheric-aesthetic-affective register differently? Our engagement with this question leads us to what we elect to term *The Poetic Subject*. While our thinking on this will require more considered attention in a separate project, we must insist that a new ethics towards ourselves and the earth needs to look

beyond the sense of vulnerability that is continually promoted by contemporary regimes of power which, while
verifying our complex and adaptive states for being, take
this predicament to further validate an entire morphology
that is insecure by design. Rather than seeing transformation as a source for lament, we must begin our search
for alternatives so that we can look to the future with a
confidence that is atmospherically-aesthetically-affectively
enriching. Evidently, if such a poetic register openly positions itself in direct conflict with fascism in all human and
aesthetic forms, we may also ask what an atmospheric
politics that counters a fascistic earth looks like. We maintain that such a relationship has no respect for the wilful
desecration of the planet or the self-annihilating tendencies of neoliberal power that speaks 'conservation' precisely for the need to conserve existing relations of power.
Neither, however, can it begin without an appreciation
of atmospheric transformation whose metamorphosis
between recombinant elements is philosophically and scientifically accepted to be the source of new creations and
worlds to come. Just as we should not colonize a people-
to-come by seeking to thwart the open horizon of political
possibilities; we must be wary that, in our righteous indignation of environmental desecration, we don't become
earthly purists of a different kind.

Deleuze once asked 'who does the earth think it is?'. We
now prefer to ask 'what do we fear the earth may become?'.
In his masterly account of the Holocaust and its relationships to pathologies of modernity, Zygmunt Bauman
shows how state racism operated in a way that appeared
all too ecological. Critiquing the notion of the 'gardening
state', he related questions of purity with the tendency to
split the population into 'useful plants to be encouraged
and tenderly propagated' against the weeds 'to be removed
or rooted out'.[21] Weeds here appear to be that which
must be destroyed. Hence, for that reason, modern culture
is a garden culture – a veritable ecology of manipulation,
assigning to itself the mission to perfect human conditions

and destroy that which stands in the way of ideal cultiva-
tion. Social gardening thus exhibits for Bauman a way to
assess what happens when humans become the principal
architects of their social orders. They are 'worldly garden-
ers', who link political and ecological reasoning in ways
that appear frighteningly rational as they appeal to base-
level desires, altogether reasonable in their calculated
extractions, capable of producing the right social atmosphere for things to prosper, and not of the least importance, aesthetically pleasing. But what becomes of this
when it is accepted that humans are now the dominant
architects for planetary life and are yet incapable of dealing
with the enormity of the task? And what becomes of this
when its worldly vision for society is no longer one of
perfectibility but to simply conserve what is existent, all
the while knowing it is slowly but surely slipping away?

As we have argued elsewhere, the problem of fascism is
far too complicated to be simply reduced to historical or
ideological moorings.[22] Indeed, the fascism of our times is
all too liberal. But unlike twentieth-century fascism, which
justified its power over life for the purposes of social per-
fection and purification, liberal fascism operates in a temporal purgatory that renders all life 'bare' within a broader
Nomos of biopolitical circulations. Not, then, a suicidal
state as such, but a vision of humanity in which the human
appears fully as a wolf unto all fellows. Metaphysical
subjects who are dead and whom we have killed. Their
violence in return has been the repudiation of meaning.
And not some vision of a utopian ecology – of Motherland
or Fatherland – but a vision of a pathological earth that
is claiming victim to the precise life forms which once gave
the planet some meaning beyond the immediacy of existence. Gaia is dying and we are killing it. Its violence in
return is an environmental terror of epic proportions that
promises us the most catastrophic of Faustian pacts. What
remains is a hyper-paranoiac sense of foreboding that
insists upon a system of rule that governs through our
ongoing state of emergency, knowing full well that despite

our best efforts, another catastrophic event is on its way and could strike at any moment. The real danger here is the continuation of the liberal tendency to use a universal frame to conceal the contingency of its biospherical interventions. Like humanity before it, the perception of the biosphere as some conceptually unified whole, which naturally gravitates towards its own resolute foreclosure, purports a highly reductionist account of 'nature' as a regime for truth for the coming catastrophe. Such a framing not only politically glosses over, for the purposes of moral absolutism and prophetic vision disguised as scientific validation, the highly rich and deeply complex nature of our many biospherical systems, along with those already in the making, whose interconnections we are only beginning to scratch the surface of, let alone compute with any meaningful applicability; it further lends itself to a familiar subject-object orientated retreat, such that the only politics possible is that which exists within the liberal framing of the problem as properly conceived. Manuel De Landa already presented to us the wonders of our non-linear and highly complex history.[23] From geology to linguistics, we are the continued products of profound transformations, only to delude ourselves that somehow we have a principal hand in shaping them. It is clear that we now fear transformation. What we fear the world may become, however, we are incapable of answering with any degree of detail, for the future itself lacks all content. How might we imagine better worlds once robbed of any claim beyond extinction? However, what we do know, perhaps with the only certainty left as we read the catastrophic signs and listen to nature's vengeful call, is that we must fear any profound transformation and mourn each passing earthly event as a further indication of a fallen existence. All that remains is to further disbelieve in ourselves, while suffocating the naturalness of biospherical transformation out of some shallow ethical claim of necessity.

Felix Guattari's psycho-analytical work thus appears well ahead of its time. As he wrote back in 1989,

If today, human relationships with the socius, the psyche, and 'nature' are increasingly deteriorating, then this is attributable not only to objective damage and pollution but to the ignorance and fatalistic passivity with which those issues are confronted by individuals and responsible authorities. The implications of any given negative development may or may not be catastrophic; whatever the case, it tends today to be simply accepted without question.[24]

This demands the formation of new 'ecologies' (social, mental and environmental) that *move us* away from the pseudo-scientific entrapment of the subject. 'In this context', Guattari writes, 'there is an urgent need for us to free ourselves of scientistic references and metaphors: to forge new paradigms which are instead ethicoaesthetic in inspiration. The best cartographies of the psyche – or, if you will, the best psychoanalyses – are after all surely to be found in the work of Goethe, Proust, Joyce, Artaud, and Beckett, rather than Freud, Jung, or Lacan'. Guattari makes an important qualification here. As he explains,

I am not seeking here to revive the Pascalian distinction between *esprit de geometrie* and *esprit de finesse*; for I understand these as two modes of apprehension – the one via the concept, the other via the affect or percept – which are in fact absolutely complementary. What I am suggesting is that what I have called this pseudo-narrative detour *also* deploys mechanisms of repetition – infinitely varying rhythms and refrains – which are nothing more or less than the buttresses of existence, since they allow discourse, or any link in the discursive chain, to become the bearer of a nondiscursivity which, stroboscope-like, cancels out the play of distinctive oppositions at the level of both content and form of expression.[25]

Such a condition he believes to be the 'very condition of emergence and re-emergence of the unique events – incorporeal universes of reference – which punctuate the unfolding of individual and collective historicity'.

— 6 —
Endgames

The Coming Catastrophe

While political modernity always depended upon exposing the finite qualities said to constitute the human condition to sanction the will to rule the living as such, never before has the destiny of the species as a whole been brought into such contingent question. Of course, the end of days as a regime of truth, doctrine and system of belief far precedes the contemporary imaginaries of biopolitical rule. Yet in marked contrast to earlier apocalyptic narratives which prophesized about the end as a time for justice so that the faithful may thrive in more peaceful conditions beyond, the coming catastrophe is premised upon a notion of ending that is terrifyingly final. Everything is to be forgotten, for everything, in the end, proves to be nothing but a fleeting moment. This raises a number of questions: What does it mean to live dangerously unto the end? Is it not the case that the vulnerability subject is now the last refuge for liberal subjectivity as it faces the limits of its own problematic score? If we are to follow the claim of no outside to liberal rationality, what are the philosophical implications of denying the idea of a temporal beyond?

And how far should we go along with the logic of catastrophe as it plays out upon the lives of the vulnerable and onto futures that continue to appear littered with the corpses of catastrophes to come?

Let us be clear from the outset: all questions about the future are idiotic. We are incapable of seeing into the future, let alone shaping it in a vision that conforms to some universal blueprint. History continues to teach us about the horrors and violence of such attempts. That is not, however, to suggest that we cannot critique political rationalities and logically extend their implications beyond the here and now. Nor is it to refrain from having confidence to face the future in a way that attempts to create it on our own terms. We now find ourselves in a peculiar predicament. Either we are told to forget the science of climate change and absolve the Western world of any guilt, or we must accept the catastrophe and take a lead in changing worldly behaviours through our enlightened wisdom.

Samuel Beckett's (2011) dramatization of the seemingly miserable disposition of the figure of Clov in his masterpiece, *Endgame*,[1] might seem to capture the tragedy and terror of our present humanity perfectly. Life at the end times of human existence, when suddenly the impossible becomes possible, and we are left waiting merely for 'Him' to whistle us. If contemporary science is to be believed, we have already crossed at least three and are near to crossing as many as nine 'planetary boundaries': climate change, species extinction, the disruption of the nitrogen-phosphorus cycles, ocean acidification, ozone depletion, freshwater usage, land cover change, aerosol loading, and chemical use.[2] These rifts in planetary boundaries, which together determine the 'safe operating space for humanity',[3] are said to constitute a global ecological catastrophe of epic proportions.[4] 'Planet Earth, creation, the world in which civilization developed, the world with climate patterns that we know and stable shorelines is in imminent peril' such that 'the survival of humanity itself' is at stake.[5] Indeed some scientists declare that we are already in the period of what they call the 'sixth extinction'; the greatest mass extinction in 65 million years, since the time of the dinosaurs; only this time the mass extinction arises from the actions of just one species – us – the human species.[6] Should we burn just half of the world's proven, economically accessible reserves of oil, gas and coal, the resulting carbon emissions, it is prophesized, will raise global temperatures by 2°C, bringing us to an irreversible tipping point – after which it will be impossible to return to the preindustrial Holocene climate that nourished human civilization as we have known it. Irreversible changes such as the melting of the Arctic sea ice and the ice sheets of Greenland will become unstoppable. This will speed up climate change, while also accelerating the 'catastrophic effects' of rising sea levels and extreme weather. The effects of sea level rise especially, it is argued, are 'irreversible on any time scale that humanity can imagine' and 'adaptation to a large sea level rise is nearly impossible'.[7] As Al Gore declared in accepting the Nobel Prize in 2007, the human species is effectively now at war with the planet itself, a war which it itself has started and perpetuated, as well as a war that it cannot possibly win. A war on the very entity that, as it turns out, the human depends upon for its very survival, and which in being so, can only prove to be a war of suicidal self-destruction.[8] Catastrophe then, we are told, is upon us. The world as we have known it, and come to rely upon, it would seem, is ending. 'Finished, it is finished, nearly finished, it must be nearly finished?'[9]

The Truth of Catastrophe

Being political theorists rather than climate scientists means we are poorly positioned to question the veracity as such of the truth claims concerning the catastrophic nature of climate change and other environmental

processes. Obviously, in the contested terrain of complexity science, there is no end of ways by which one could
attempt to challenge the regimes of truth surrounding the
'global ecological catastrophe', targeting their exaggera-
tions, distortions and deceits, by revealing the political
economy and interests that fuel such catastrophe talk in
climate science especially, and by laying claim to a better
knowledge of the truth.[10] Such debates are now so well
rehearsed they appear tired and bereft of critical imagination. Instead, we want to address the question of what
follows should we accept the veracity of these claims, and
think in terms of the political and ethical implications of
this tragic condition. What does it mean to be a finite
thing, such as the human, in a world that is understood to
be ending, and for which the human understands itself as
responsible cause? And how may we make sense of this
suicidal self-destruction which is seemingly hopeless and
without possibility of redemption? In other words, with
the aim of thinking through, in order to move beyond,
extinction, we are less interested in telling the truth about
this human condition in its exposure to the catastrophic
effects of climate change, than the effects of its truth, and
questioning how we respond to that truth.

Foucault was the single most influential interrogator of
the politics of truth-telling of the twentieth century. It is
also apparent that he took a great interest in the historical
origins and development of modes of truth-telling concerned with foretelling the imminent end of the world, or
what is better known more simply as prophesy, which,
while ancient in its origins, remains absolutely fundamental still today for the framing of practically all political
phenomena, but which is perhaps most pronounced when
it comes to the phenomenon of climate change and the
wider 'global ecological catastrophe'. But Foucault's interest in prophesy was tangential to his yet greater concern
with the origins and historical development of another less
well-known modality of truth-telling, and the more precise
subject of his very last series of lectures, what the ancient

Greeks described as *parrhesia*, and which arose in a form of contestation of the prophetic mode of truth-telling in ancient Greece. That contestation emerged in the form of a different understanding of the temporality of truth, the position of the truth-teller within time, and the nature of the truth that it is being told by the parrhesiac in contrast with the prophet. The prophet, as Foucault detailed in these lectures, is always positioned between the present and the future, functioning to reveal what is hidden in the future, 'what time conceals from humans, what no human gaze could see and no human ear could hear without him'.[11] This intermediary position of the prophet, between present and future, is different, as Foucault showed, from the parrhesiast who absolutely is not concerned with fore-telling the future, but who

> reveals and discloses what people's blindness prevents them from seeing, but who does not unveil the future. He unveils what is. The parrhesiast [in contrast with the prophet] does not help people somehow to step beyond some threshold in the ontological structure of the human being and of time which separates them from their future. He helps them in their blindness, but their blindness about what they are, about themselves, and so not the blindness due to an ontological structure, but due to some moral fault, distraction, or lack of discipline, the consequence of inattention, laxity, or weakness'.[12]

Now if we examine the discourse around the global ecological catastrophe as it is currently articulated, it seems that we encounter not simply the prophetic mode of veridiction in which we are being told the truth concerning what is hidden from us in terms of our future, what time conceals from us, and what no merely human gaze upon the earth and itself could reveal, but this other, different form of truth-telling, *parrhesia*, mobilized as it has been since the Greeks, to help us in our blindness as to our errors, by showing us what we are, what we have done, and what we are thus responsible for, as well as duty bound to change in ourselves so that we might correct our faults. This combination of modes of truth-telling, the prophetic and the parrhesiastic, is, as Foucault's studies also detail, not novel but historical, and indeed pre-modern. It was a recurrent combination within medieval Christianity. These two modalities, that of telling the truth about the future, about what awaits humanity and the imminence of an otherwise hidden event-to-come, and that of then telling the truth to humans about what they are, were frequently combined in the discourses of Franciscan and Dominican preachers, who played such a powerful role throughout the Western world in the Middle Ages 'in the perpetuation, as well as renewal and transformation of the experience of threat for the medieval world'.[13] Such preachers played the role of both prophet and parrhesiast by warning 'of the threatening imminence of the future, of the Kingdom of the Last Day, of the Final Judgment, or of approaching death' at the same time as telling human beings what they are, what their faults and crimes are, and in what respects and how they must change their mode of being in order to be prepared for that last day and final judgment.[14]

Obviously fewer people believe today, literally, in Christian ideas such as the Kingdom of the Last Day or the Final Judgment, but the combination of these two modes of veridiction which underpinned medieval discourses upon them, warning people of what events were to happen to them, as well as what they must do in order to secure themselves from the devastating outcomes of those events, remain very much in play, in prevalent discourses on the perhaps less absurd but nevertheless politically charged prospect of the global ecological catastrophe. The modernity of the prophetic and parrhesiastic framing of the politics of ecological catastrophe owes to the different ways in which it poses the problematic of finitude. In the Middle Ages the legitimacy of Theocratic rule depended on the promise to human beings of salvation from the costs of their finitude, principally through the promise of eternal life, true peace and security in an other-worldly place called Heaven. Today, the discourses of hysteria and fear surrounding the coming catastrophe express the reaction of humanity, if not yet its coming terms with its own finitude, as well as that of the earth on which it lives. Facing this reality as a species, we possess no divine providence, no inherent right to the earth, nor preordained right to development or security here. But this coming to terms with the truth of finitude also takes the form of a kind of morality tale. The story goes that as a species we have failed historically to recognize 'the truth of finitude' because we have not recognized the finite nature of the resources which our civilization has depended on for its exploitation and growth. But through recognition of the realities and threats posed by climate change and the wider environmental catastrophe, there might, nevertheless, be a window of opportunity for us to change our ways by submitting ourselves, finally, to such a truth. If only we could learn, now, how to value biodiversity and that complex thing named 'nature', so we might be able to engage in some sort of successful adaptation to the devastating realities of climate change. This problem of how to get humans to understand the finitude of the biosphere is widely expressed today by ecologists, biologists, conservation groups, environmental lawyers, indigenous groups as well as, and not least in importance, economists.

There is a correspondence, then, and a fascinating one at that, between on the one hand, the ways in which the possibilities of human salvation under the Theocratic conditions of the Christian Church depended on human beings accepting the veracity of the prophetic truths of preachers as to the coming of the Final Judgment and the Kingdom of the Last Day, as well as accepting the *parrhesia* of the truth of those selfsame preachers, as to the need to recognize their faults and crimes, and obey their spiritual direction as to how they must change their mode of being in order to be saved, and, on the other hand, the ways in which the possibilities of human survival today under the modern conditions of liberal governance depend on human beings, both accepting the veracity of the prophetic truths of climate scientists as to the coming of the global ecological catastrophe, as well as accepting the parrhesiastic truth of those selfsame scientists as to the need to recognize our responsibilities as *the* species that has caused this catastrophe, and obey their directions as to how we must change our mode of being in order to have any chance at all of surviving this imminent and immanent event.

We are not in any way suggesting here that climate change is not happening around us. Nor are we committing ourselves to a biological and environmental will to nothingness in celebration of the end of times properly conceived. Our wager, in fact, is that the catastrophic imaginary of liberal rule is doing a good enough job of this on its own terms, as it stifles any serious debate about a radical transformation in who we are as political subjects. Having reasons to believe in our world, however, doesn't encourage us to mourn for the earth such that we enter into a biospherical politics of lament that is ultimately founded upon resentment for our destructive capacities as a species, and how the world in turn is killing us as a result. Instead, it demands a new ethical sensibility towards our continual connections into the world such that life-world transformations affirm the poetic and the beautiful beyond the suffocating clouds of catastrophic despair. With our political resentments now projected onto one another, the earth and the atmosphere that continues to precariously sustain us, so we are being forced to embrace a nihilistic programme that does more than claim to promote the human while making us learn to resent its very existence. Taking the biosphere as a whole in order to raise the stakes in a truly magnificent deception, so our resentments are projected onto an atmospherically charged plane that offers in return no ability whatsoever for meaningful philosophical *reflection*. Reflection is, after all, impossible without the ability to bounce back – a quality, as we have come to learn, now fully appropriated by the biophysical quest for human survivability.

Catastrophism

The structural underpinnings of the discourse surrounding the global ecological catastrophe are to be found articulated on both left and right sides of the political spectrum. The proposition that climate change is catastrophic and that it results fundamentally from our failures as a species to recognize the finitude of the world on which we depend is not only serving to reproduce, but extend, a neoliberal economic regime of exploitation and value; the very system of value on account of which the destruction of the earth has occurred in the first place. In the contemporary and growing neoliberal discourse on climate change, for example, we encounter the idea that the catastrophic effects of climate change can only be mitigated by human beings changing their ways of living so as to engage more fully in 'more authentic' liberal practices. Becoming resilient in these terms involves the deliberate giving up of any possibility that climate change can be understood as a threat from which we can secure ourselves, as well as expectation that the state or any other political authority might be able to protect us from its dangers. Instead, we are to learn the virtue of adapting to its enabling conditions via the embrace of neoliberalism; specifically through our further interpellation within markets, property-rights regimes and engagement in entrepreneurial practices of the liberal self. The acceptance of the idea of the 'catastrophe' of climate change and the incapacity of the state to protect its populations from ecological catastrophe, and indeed the danger which the idea that the state might be able to save us from climate change is said to pose, is a fundamental 'truth' on which the blackmail of neoliberalism currently depends for its extension.

Likewise the demands from anti-liberal thinkers and practitioners, on the Left, for more radical political and social change as a means to mitigate the effects of climate change, are no less tied to prophesies concerning the imminence of the global ecological catastrophe and the truth claim as to the need for human beings to see their faults and admit the stupidities of their mistakes with respect to what has been hidden from them or what they have failed to see. Fundamental to such articulations on the left is the claim that, as Dipesh Chakrabarty argues, 'whatever our socio-economic and technological choices, whatever the rights we wish to celebrate as our freedom, we cannot afford to destabilize conditions (such as the temperature zone in which the planet exists) that work like boundary parameters of human existence. These parameters are independent of capitalism or socialism'.[15] The finitude of the planet, understood in terms of the boundary parameters that climate science proclaims to determine the 'safe operating space for humanity',[16] is that which the Left have historically failed to see, and which it must now recognize as 'independent of capitalism' itself. As such, what becomes of the revolutionary subject of struggle when it must learn to accept the realities of the times and disavow any strategy for the transformation or defeat of liberalism and its capitalistic drivers? Underwriting both the regimes of truth of Right and Left today is an assumption as to the need to adapt to the realities of the global ecological catastrophe by recognizing the truth of finitude and the conditions of vulnerability that a finite existence is said to produce.

In this context of widespread acceptance of 'the truth of finitude', it is worth posing some fairly simple questions. One question to be posed at both the Left and Right is: how does one survive or adapt to catastrophe? If these processes, which are said to already be under way, are as truly catastrophic as indicated, what is the worth of our changing our ways in mitigation of them? What is the utility of this *parrhesia* in the context of this prophesy? The concept of catastrophe is non-equivocal. It derives, etymologically, from the Greek *katastrophe* meaning 'an overturning or a sudden end'. How, then, one might ask, naively, does one survive or adapt to the event of 'the end', sudden or not? In its earlier Christian context, the utility of *parrhesia* owed to the ways by which humans who heeded its truth could save themselves from prophesized doom and receive eternal life, true peace and security in Heaven. Obviously this is not the case in the context of the global ecological catastrophe. The human who accepts the truth of the globality of this coming violence, and changes its ways in order to mitigate its effects, tragically receives no security from those effects. At most the human who accepts responsibility and changes its ways, might derive a pleasure or satisfaction from the buying of time for the species that follows from such obedience to that truth. The promise, at most, is that the human, understood in terms of its species existence, may go on living, a little longer, and that other species and living systems, including the biosphere itself, may also be granted more and longer life, while all the while dying off. The threat of extinction may, in other words, be postponed, but ultimately not prevented. As Ray Brassier points out, while the natural sciences are pretty clear on this eventuality, the philosophical stakes are barely considered let alone brought to bear upon contemporary questions as to how we may live differently given the circumstances:

> Natural science produces ancestral statements, such as that the universe is roughly 13.7 billion years old, that the earth formed roughly 4.5 billion years ago, that life developed on earth approximately 3.5 billion years ago, and that the earliest ancestors of the genus Homo emerged about 2 million years ago. Yet it is also generating an ever increasing number of 'descendent' statements, such as the Milky Way will collide with the Andromeda galaxy in 3 billion years; [and] that the earth will be incinerated by the sun 4 billion years hence . . . Philosophers should be more astonished by such statements than they seem to be, for they present a serious problem for post-Kantian Philosophy.[17]

The concept of extinction as it is currently employed in claims concerning the already occurring process of the Sixth Extinction within the discourse of global ecological catastrophe is also non-equivocal. Of course, extinction can be a risk and possibility that one might successfully avoid. But this is not the truth we are told of our times, which in the end *will* result in extinction. We are told that we are already 'in' the Sixth Extinction; a moment in our life-world cycle that is already happening. Regardless of how much time we may buy ourselves now by recognizing the truth of finitude, recovery of biodiversity will not occur in any timeframe meaningful to people: evolution of new species typically takes at least hundreds of thousands of years and recovery from mass extinction episodes probably occurs on timescales encompassing millions of years.[18] So, despite our best efforts at adaption, we are merely enduring and living through the conditions of the event of the Sixth Extinction, not overcoming or preventing its occurrence. This to us seems to be a highly questionable deal once broached either politically or philosophically. We seem to be in good company. For this problem was already raised by Nietzsche, who once again proves his remarkable capacity to think in the most untimely ways to challenge that which initially seems insurmountable and the source for lament:

> Once upon a time, in some out of the way corner of that universe which is dispersed into numberless twinkling solar systems, there was a star upon which clever beasts invented knowing. That was the most arrogant and mendacious minute of 'world history,' but nevertheless, it was only a minute. After nature had drawn a few breaths, the star cooled and congealed, and the clever beasts had to die. One might invent such a fable, and yet he still would not have adequately illustrated how miserable, how shadowy and transient, how aimless and arbitrary the human intellect looks within nature. There were eternities during which it did not exist. And when it is all over with the human intellect, *nothing will have happened.*[19]

This infamous passage from *On Truth and Lies in a Nonmoral Sense* has often been read to further the charges of nihilism. Nothing will have happened, so what is the point to it all? Nothing, however, could be further from the truth. A central question Nietzsche put in this article was 'What does man actually know about himself?' Which also may be put in a more affirmative way to read 'How can man live differently once he accepts the "errors" of his ways?'. For Nietzsche, part of the genius of construction lies in our abilities to bring error into reason. We live, he maintained, by the error of our ways. And long may it continue. We also live in a magnificent fabricating universe where the power of fabulation produces different senses of perception that are no less true to the subject's existence. More than necessary for revealing the suffocating modes of being which are continually authenticated in modern times, it was essential to its *over-coming*. It is a mistake, therefore, to read Nietzsche's original provocation on the end of times as the triumph of resentment and negation. On the contrary, he provides an acute warning as to the dangers of living unto the end *as if nothing will have happened*. Or to put it another way, to continue to live beneath the suffocating clouds of despair is sure testimony to the fact that there is nothing to live of meaning: 'The most extreme form of nihilism would be the view that *every* belief, every holding-something-true is necessarily false because there is no *true world*'.[20] For Nietzsche, the counter to this will-to-nothingness could not be achieved by turning towards some conservative approximation of truth that reveals some immutable 'essence'. It demands a veritable courage to truth that weathers the storm in order to emerge transformed: 'When a real storm cloud thunders above him, he wraps himself in his cloak, and with slow steps he walks from beneath it'[21].

This raises a number of significant questions for us: If we accept the truth and reality of the global ecological catastrophe, then how else might we respond to it? If we accept, especially, our responsibility as a species for the creation of this catastrophe, how does such an acceptance affect our response? Ought we not to question the injunction to respond by merely seeking to adapt in order to survive longer? Given that it is the very ethics of species survival and development that accounts, at base, for the existence of human responsibility for the global ecological catastrophe, ought we not to be seeking alternative answers to the question of how we want to live out this self-fulfilling endgame of human existence? If there is such a thing indeed as a global ecological catastrophe, surely the question becomes one that seeks to stake out a more affirmative choice? How do we desire to live out these end times of human existence so that our end might no longer be conditioned by the fear of that end? If it is an end, and if it is true that there is no turning back from this tipping point of extinction time, why are we choosing to live out that end by adapting to the conditions of our own demise, rather than with experimenting with other ways of living less attached to preserving our life as such, and more attuned to the inevitability of death and extinction as realities that can contribute to the intensity of our experience of worldly living for the finite time that we are left with as a species already fated to extinction in the end?

These questions are profoundly philosophical. And rightly so! The assault we are witnessing on the political today is so intellectually catastrophic that the only solutions presented to us as viable propose changes so that everything ultimately remains the same. For what are we really conserving when we offer vulnerability to counter vulnerability and insecurity to counter insecurity? This is the real mastery of neoliberalism. For it has led us into a catastrophic quagmire that is fully in keeping with its need to reproduce conditions that are insecure by design; and yet it is managing to repackage itself as the most enlightened way to navigate the uncertain waters, albeit with a captainless crew, which ultimately accepts that the promised land will never be shored. So surely without the ability to step back from the catastrophic injunction with more consideration, and bring into question the framing of the debates which offer various technocratic solutions to the effects brought about by ecological change, however devastating, to begin questioning the philosophical and political stakes, how is it at all possible to even think about setting a new course of direction with a confidence in our abilities to live through these uncertain times, and view the troubled waters in a new, more exhilarating and aesthetically enriching light of day?

Dead Zones

A recurring motif within popularized representations of global catastrophes is the creation of uninhabitable spaces that prove to be inhospitable to human life. These 'dead zones' take on a particular form that offers a remarkable return to a Hobbesian state of nature, albeit with a more pronounced biospheric and atmospheric twist as the existence of all things deemed worthy of living (after all, not everything dies) teeters on the brink of possible extinction. Such representations tend to focus upon the extreme thresholds for survivability, evidencing, in particular, the breakdown of all natural laws for habitable existence, thereby instilling a capacity for terror and violence within the entire topography as a space of unrelenting if sometimes temporally suspended endangerment. Here we find the veritable collapse between human life and the spaces it has come to inhabit, as the violence of the landscape becomes the surest indication of savage indiscrimination which now defines contemporary notions of political inhospitability. Certainly amongst the most celebrated of these 'fictions' remains Andrei Tarkovsky's (1979) cinematic masterpiece *Stalker*. Often cited for its somewhat prophetic vision in relation to the subsequent Chernobyl disaster, Tarkovsky portrays the sense of alienation and abandonment which has come to hallmark de-populated 'zones' of devastation.

Such zoning is expected to become the norm as ecological changes in the earth's climatic conditioning move apace. The fate of climate change refugees is now becoming an acute political problem as ideas of displacement are increasingly linked to environmental catastrophe which, in some cases – from the current water levels engulfing the Carteret Islands onto the predicted problems faced by the Maldives, along with temperate warming of zones that may prove equally devastating in reverse effect – offer no possibility for a right to return. With extreme or exceptional weather patterns increasingly becoming the violent norm such that the 'catastrophic' now indicates a level of official assessment, the age-old idea that the environment has no political significance appears both illogical in terms of empirical verification, absurd in terms of quantifiable datasets, and pathological in terms of the lived realities of ecologically shaped and misinformed victims of the world. This is a sentiment shared by Professor Tim Flannery, the Chief Commissioner of the Australian Climate Change Commission:

> Australians have long rated fire risk on the MacArthur index. On it, a rating of 100 . . . represents 'extreme' risk. But after the 2009 fires a new level of risk was required. 'Catastrophic' represents a risk rating above 100. . . . Australia's average temperature has increased by just 0.9 of a degree Celsius over the past century. Within the next 90 years we're on track to warm by at least another three degrees. Having seen what 0.9 of a degree has done to heat waves and fire extremes, I dread to think about the kind of country my grandchildren will live in. . . . And large parts of the continent will be uninhabitable, not just by humans, but by Australia's spectacular bio-diversity as well.[22]

While this idea of the zoning of the uninhabitable and the inhospitable tends to be limited to localized effects, in the longer run it is understood that the catastrophic offers no real possibility for containment. This bleak and irreversible possibility is depicted in Cormac McCarthy's Pultizer Prize novel *The Road*, which narrates a post-catastrophic tale of human demise brought about by some unspecified event that has devastated plant and animal life. The aesthetic quality of this work is striking. Upon this monochromatic wasteland, as Charles McGrath wrote in a *New York Times* review aptly titled 'At World's End', 'The sky is gray, the rivers are black, and color is just a memory. The landscape is covered in ash, with soot falling perpetually from the air. The cities are blasted and abandoned'.[23] Not only is the notion that we are all fated to meet a brutish end presented in the starkest of terms, unlike the post-apocalyptic genre, McGrath's catastrophic vision does not appear to be logically incompatible with contemporary thinking about the end of times. This was appreciated by John Hillcoat who directed the cinematic adaptation: 'What's moving and shocking about McCarthy's book is that it's so believable . . . what we wanted is a kind of heightened realism, as opposed to the 'Mad Max' thing, which is all about high concept and spectacle. We're trying to avoid the clichés of apocalypse and make this more like a natural disaster'. Philosophically speaking, the story's meditation on the distinction between survival and imminent death provides a critical exposé of the inabilities of those who only find meaning in the finitude of a vulnerable existence to transgress the injunction. In one particular flashback, which disrupts the temporality of the otherwise fated attempt to survive, the wife asks the protagonist why they don't talk about death anymore. Compelled to answer her own question, she responds, 'It's because it's here. There's nothing left to talk about'.

The Last Empire

Catastrophe has to be understood as distinct from other conceptualizations of collapse, decay, decline or disaster. To speak of catastrophe, ecological and economic, is absolutely not the same as to speak of ecological and economic crisis, for example. A crisis is cyclical; a governable expression of vexed conditions that one can assume the potential ability to withstand. It is in the nature of crises that they pass and that we ourselves pass through them. A crisis may threaten our destruction, but such destruction is only a possibility, and should we meet with destruction then our condition will no longer be simply one of crisis, but will demand another name. Catastrophe, on the other hand, is a historical void, an end that one cannot escape, a road with no beyond.[24] It designates an event of destruction that is already taking place, already in action, and fully mobilized, such that there is no escaping the inevitable process of its unfolding effects. 'Catastrophe effects' as the ecologists speak of when they press the urgency of the 'Sixth Extinction'. The numerical classification of this occurrence is all too striking in terms of its relation to the prophetic, as we are all too familiar with; the often derided mediation on possible intuitions of a dangerous foreboding resonates with the idea of the 'Sixth Sense'. What of course matters is whether or not the prophecy has enough scientific weight, or at least that it plays into the strategies of dominant regimes of truth.

What sense does it make to speak of, and to ask people to participate in the practice of adapting to catastrophe? How does one adapt to catastrophe? Is there not an absurdity to such a discourse? An absurdity to such a discursive framing of how we, as humans, ought to respond to the event of our own catastrophe? And moreover, is there not a double absurdity in the idea that we should adapt to the ecological catastrophe that is unfolding by speeding up and enjoining further with the economic catastrophe that is responsible for causing the ecological catastrophe in the first place? What degree of not just absurdity but stupidity are we addressing when we consider such fatalistic and fanatical strategies for human subordination to catastrophic processes? The concept of the fanatic emerged in early modern Europe to describe what Luther and others named 'false prophets' – religiously inspired individuals whose prophesy, they said, was a prophetic vision that was both absurd and unwarranted. Today, it seems that such is the absurdity of discourses surrounding both the ecological and economic catastrophes, that we are in the midst of a new fanaticism. But a fanaticism of which the prophesy is not so much false in that it is wrong, but fallacious in that it conscripts human beings into ways of life that make no sense in the context of the futureless world which is being promised them.

But there are historical precedents to explain such absurdity. In a still brilliant book, the sociologist Barrington Moore describes how in the concentration camps of Nazi Germany, Jews and other doomed populations would be made to accept, by SS camp guards, the futility of their resistance. How they were convinced to accept the need to adapt to the realities of their fates and the impossibility of escape or rebellion. And indeed the inhabitants of such extreme spaces of suffering often failed to exhibit any sign of resistance, seeking to survive for the severely limited time that they were capable of, through the development of complex and ultimately failed strategies of 'adaptation'. Moore's account of the fatalistic adaptations of victims of the Holocaust was a stepping stone within his argument as to the necessity of the 'conquest' of the perception of inevitability and necessity of circumstances, as a precondition for the development of political subjectivity.[25] Politics is the art of the contingent. It cannot operate in a field of necessity. Accepting the claims as to the necessity of either economic or ecological catastrophe means that we are condemned to respond to it in a depoliticized manner, with politics itself becoming at best an inconvenient distraction or worse an ally to the catastrophe horizon.

The coming catastrophe is very different from theological ideas of the apocalyptic. Apocalypse, like so much of the discourse of disaster, has a conceptual history that is irrevocably tied up, also, with the historical development of Christianity. An apocalypse, traditionally understood, is an end, but one that occurs with the important addition of revelation; a 'lifting of the veil'.[26] In that sense, it is different from catastrophe, which is an end without escape, removal or road leading to a world beyond. The concept has a history within a specific literature called apocalyptic literature. In another brilliant book written in the mid-twentieth century, *Occidental Eschatology*, the political theologian, Jacob Taubes told that history. Through his analysis of the very first example of apocalyptic literature to come down to us in its complete form, the Apocalypse of Daniel, Taubes described in concise terms the elements that compose what he called 'the structure of apocalypse'.[27] The belief in providence, the outline of world history, the cosmic horizon against which world history is set, visions of a dreamlike nature, the concealment of the writer, a seething eschatology, the computation of the End Time, the apocalyptic science, a symbolism of numbers and secret language, the doctrine of angels and hope for an afterlife. All of these comprise the elements of the structure of the apocalypse within apocalyptic literature.

It is the dreamlike visions of the authors of apocalypses Taubes mentions that most fascinate. Every apocalypse, as Taubes describes, required its seer, its visionary. The seer of the apocalypse saw into the obscurity of the decrees of fate. The seer of the apocalypse saw the evil deeds of a monster that passed in front of its eyes, and then bore witness to the figure of a man, or manlike figure, who the seer thought would finally triumph over the monster and thus begin his neverending rule of the world. Apocalypticism entails, therefore, a fundamentally positive disposition towards disasters, underpinned by an understanding of their necessarily conflictual and divisive nature, and conviction as to the power of man to triumph in their face. It is itself a mode of prophetic truth-telling, but an avowedly political form, which assumes the necessity and positivity of division between times present and future. The apocalyptic prophet does not merely warn human beings of what is hidden from them concerning their future, but encourages them to engage with and ultimately welcome it, on account of the positive change it will bring, rather than thinking they have to change their ways in order to be prepared for it. The geographer Erik Swyngedouw is, for these reasons, quite wrong to describe the 'climate change imaginary' as 'apocalyptical', given that it has none of these hallmarks of proper apocalyptical thinking. In effect, the imaginary that Swyngedouw describes is catastrophic, which in turn also accounts for its depoliticizing effects, the latter which his own work captures very well.[28]

The concept of apocalypse has had a profound influence on the political development of humanity ever since its first articulation by Daniel. Taken up by the Zealot movement in the Jewish revolt against the Roman Empire, apocalyptic prophesy has nourished and stoked the flames of revolution and social transformation ever since. Christianity was not something new in this regard, and Jesus himself emerged out of the apocalyptic movement in Israel, fitting into the succession of itinerant preachers that came before him. Each of those preachers had essentially one thing to say. 'I am a divine spirit. I have come because the world is about to come to an end and an element of Humanity will be carried away because of their injustices. But I will save you and you will see me come again with the power of heaven'.[29]

Fundamental to the writing of apocalypse was this consciousness, this confidence, this absolute certitude of possession of the power to be able to confront the disaster. Today, in the context of the widespread and deep-seated belief in the inescapably catastrophic nature of the world, both economically and ecologically understood, such a consciousness and confidence in the abilities to confront it is liable to be diagnosed as a form of, what we moderns call, madness. But perhaps that is the point. The apparent extremity of not just belief, but confidence and even certainty in the possibility of apocalyptic division between worlds and between times, of present and future, is a sign of how detached we have become from this particular mode of truth-telling. We cannot agree with Benjamin Noys, for this reason, when he argues that the main problem facing the Left today is the excess of its 'apocalyptic tone'.[30] In effect the opposite is the case. For the question is not about some messianic totalitarianism; it is how to save and reconstitute the power of a more confident vision in the context of our widespread political submission to the ecologization of the political on which neoliberalism thrives and the discourse of catastrophe has grown.[31]

The world we live in is a world of radical contingency, in which the future is uncertain and impossible to calculate. Nevertheless, as human beings we are capable of investing our futures with profound beliefs and senses of certainty as to what may and can happen. Indeed what does climate science express other than a longing for a sense of certainty; claims to truth which can be said to be beyond doubt? The scientific imaginary out of which the belief in the incontestable nature of climate change emerged, the necessity and reality of its occurrence, the impossibility of arguing with or over its reality, is an expression of that longing. Such a longing is for a realm of certainty beyond the radical contingency of the world; a radical contingency that many branches of science itself now understand as the real. Climate science is constituted by a subject who is dependent for its reproduction on the belief in the existence of, as well as our abilities to see and speak of, such a world beyond the real. In other words, it is structured by the very same ontology of time that structures Christian Science and literature. And when we look at debates within climate science, and claims to knowledge as to the coming of the 'Sixth Extinction', we are looking at a world populated by prophets that operate within regimes of truth deeply similar to those occupied by the prophets of Christianity. Climate science is a religion.

Our intention here is not to contest the truth claims of climate science and the ideologues of climate change on the basis of their non-approximation to reality. It is to point at the conditions of possibility for such claims; conditions of possibility that are structurally similar to those that underpin prophesy in its Christian form. Further, our intent is to point out that a political discourse which posits the possibility of welcoming the coming of another world and another life beyond that which is diagnosed as at risk of extinction in climate science, the world and life of catastrophe as we experience it today, may have no less 'truth' to it. Climate scientists say that there is no way of escape from the dreadful and fearful realities of climate change; while economists say that there is no alternative to the further extension of the market in mitigation of the catastrophic effects of climate change. The Left meanwhile castigates humanity for not having recognized and respected the 'parametric conditions' on which our existence depends. All such claims reproduce a prophetic mode of truth-telling tied into a parrhesiastic mode of truth-telling which predicts a future which is awful and diagnoses the faults and crimes of human beings on account of which they must change their ways of living.

What is precisely missing here is a different vocabulary through which to articulate the necessity and reality of climate change, while being able to welcome this inevitable event as the process of passage to a new world and new life beyond that which we have known up until now. It is to welcome the departure of that which has conditioned our experience as a form of species life to date. Who ultimately knows what the future for life is beyond the Holocene? Not one of us. The Anthropocene is only just beginning. What we can know is that life will take different forms. There will be, as there is always assumed to be in irreducible thought, a division between present and future, and within that a division between life forms. Not between the saved and the damned, but between the life forms that will die off with the end of the Holocene and

those that will emerge with whatever comes into existence
after that time. Consider, for example, the phenomenon of
the 'Grolar' bear; the cross between a Polar and Grizzly
bear born of the sexual encounter consequent upon the
'catastrophe effects' of climate change, specifically the
breaking up of the Arctic sea ice. What is it about a civilization or a culture that manages to turn the wondrous
phenomenon of the emergence of new forms of life, consequent upon these dramatic changes in a milieu, into a
problematic of insecurity and threat? A team of ecologists
led by Brendan Kelly of the National Marine Mammal
Laboratory, in Alaska, argues that with this phenomenon
of the 'cross-breed', so 'endangered, native species' such
as the Polar Bear, from which the Grolar Bear is emerging,
will soon disappear. Furthermore 'the speeding up of evolutionary pressures, the forcing of animals into rapid
adaptive modes, may not produce biologically favorable
outcomes'. Quoting Kelly, from an interview with Live
Science: 'This change is happening so rapidly that it doesn't
bode well for adaptive responses'.[32] This cult of mourning
for the coming death of existing species life, consequent
upon the movement of the earth, and fear for the nature
of the new forms of life to come, expresses perfectly the
ways in which the ancient fear for the coming catastrophe
is now coupled with a modern biopoliticized fear of the
transformative effects of life's movement upon existing
species. 'Pure' and 'native' forms thus become threatened
by the emergence of impure, foreign, maladapted ones.

Rather than simply accept the injunction to fear processes of imminent global ecological catastrophe, as well
as accept claims as to the moral culpability of humanity
for this catastrophe, there is a need to recognize the ways
in which our understanding of this phenomenon are shaped
for us by prophetic and parrhesiastic modes of veridiction.
From this more or less ancient combination of modes of
veridiction follows the injunction that the human must
change itself in order to save itself and its world. In
these senses, the truths we tell ourselves concerning the

problematic of finitude remain embedded within modes of veridiction as old and moralizing as Christianity itself.

Submitting to the blackmail of global ecological catastrophe is to submit to a combination of the very same modes of veridiction that functioned in the Middle Ages to subject human beings to absurd ideas such as the Kingdom of the Last Day and the Final Judgment. The modernity of prophesy and *parrhesia* concerned with 'global ecological catastrophe' owes to the different ways in which they pose the problem of finitude. While in the Middle Ages the legitimacy of theocratic rule depended on an offer of security to humans from the costs of their finitude through the promise of eternal life, peace and security in Heaven, today the offer is one of 'successful adaptation' to the costs of our having failed to understand the full nature of the problem of finitude, in mitigation of the reality that as humans we have only just come to understand that we have no preordained right to the earth, no providential history, or guarantee of security and development. The promise held out to us should we be willing to submit to this new problematization of the truth of finitude, and accept the need to adapt, is not one of eternal life, nor even necessarily better life, but simply a little more life for our species and those that we exist interdependently with.

This is why, rather than submitting to the blackmail of the coming catastrophe, we argue for the need to develop an alternative and more poetic vocabulary by which to articulate a politics of the welcome in order for us to confront the reality of what Paul Virilio names rightly 'the finitude of (human) progress'.[33] Why is it we fear that which is fundamental to the course of the world as well as of ourselves? And what is to fear of an end? Fighting the debasements of human potentiality, and moving beyond the impasses which political Lefts and Rights have reached today, requires the development of a new regime of truth (discursively, sensually, aesthetically and atmospherically) through which to articulate the possibility of the coming catastrophe while being able to welcome this event as the process of passage to a new world and life beyond that which we have known up until now. A regime of truth that does not demand of us that we learn to fear more the course of the world and its transformative effects, with a view to being able to sustain ourselves for longer in the forms and ways that we have come to know and depend on, but which instils in us the confidence and courage to encounter and desire of it the very transformations it renders possible of ourselves.

How do we source the establishment of such a new regime of truth? Both prophesy and *parrhesia* are practices open to contestation and reformulation such that they can be put to different uses. In effect, this is what Foucault's analytics of truth-telling were set up to achieve, by demonstrating the complex intertwinements of different regimes of truth across historical time, amid the multiple struggles over how to use them, and their indispensability for politics and the conditions of the political subject. Rather than arguing for a wholesale rejection of prophesy and *parrhesia*, we argue for their renewed use, and aim to show how they are in effect already in use, in constitution and deployment of a more poetic aesthetic, the dictum of which is that in seeing the end we do not fear it, that we live out the end in full knowledge of it, while we renounce any call to organize with a view to trying to survive the end in a game whose rules are written against us from the start. In this sense, and in following that dictum, we establish the necessary conditions for conflict with liberal governance underpinned as it is by its biopolitical aesthetic, and rival dictum that we must change by adapting to the conditions of liberal governance in order to save ourselves from catastrophic processes outside our control and fundamental to our fears.

– 7 –

The Art of Politics

More Than Human

The history of the modern subject, we are continually reminded, is one of survival against all the odds. Thrown into the world, as Martin Heidegger once proclaimed, it has learned to adapt to whatever surroundings it found itself imperilled to inhabit, only to learn that the mastery of any given space was illusionary at best. The life of the subject upon this embattled terrain remained, as Nietzsche declared with more critical purchase than is often acknowledged, 'all too human'. To live has been a story of endurance unto the end. And if it has been possible to write of any sense of progress, this amounts to a prolonging of human existence so that we are able to cheat death for as long as possible. All the while, of course, the modern subject remained sure that its existence would eventually end albeit in some yet to be discerned event. But are these narratives of human evolution and its accompanying stories of survival against all the odds satisfactory? Could it not actually be the case that there is *more to life* than this ongoing survival? Indeed if the contemporary crisis of liberalism can be read as both a logical and altogether predictable expression of its narcissistic and self-destructive qualities, how may we think the political differently so that we may entertain the possibility of *out-living* its catastrophic imaginary?

In a wonderful book *The Psychoanalysis of Fire*, Gaston Bachelard offers a remarkably compelling and delightfully poetic alternative to the narrative of survivability.[1] Why, Bachelard muses, were the discoverers of fire rubbing sticks together in the first instance if it were not for a more affective performance that was all about intimacy and communion? Some may point out here that the focus on fire is a tad cliché. And yet in the contemporary condition, fixated as we have become with biospherical power, how we understand the elements is surely more pertinent than ever. As Bachelard notes, fire has always been more a social reality than a natural one. And while there are many social realities, the reality most often scribed is the tale of fire for survival. In Western culture in particular, from the introduction of the God Hephaestus in ancient Greece who was tasked with weaponizing Olympus; the burning of the beacon at the start of the *Oresteia*; the burning towers of Homer's *Iliad* during the fall of Troy; depictions of the Christian Hell as a place where the sinners are tormented by the flame; onto the eruption of Mount Vesuvius, which not only was seen as some vengeful act for decadent lives, but has continued to have significant impact for theorizations and representations of the catastrophic,[2] fire all too often appears in our historical present to reinforce the 'necessity for survival' narrative rather than one of communal gathering, performance and spontaneous expression akin to the elements of dance.

Even through a brief social detour on fire, however, we can see how the continual framing of life in terms of its biological vulnerability has a more contested history. Indeed, even though the compulsion to view life biologically developed to be one of the defining features of modernity, throughout this period there was nevertheless some belief that the subject was able to secure itself from the problems of the world. This was backed up by the proliferation of various myths about belonging that were central to the creation of political communities. Liberalism, in contrast, operates as if it is 'limitless'. Its reach, growth and development demand more, and more, and more. However, instead of relating this to a new-found metaphysical awakening that allows us to think that there is more to life than its biological endowment, contemporary liberal biopolitics turns infinite potentiality into a source of limitless endangerment such that all there is to think about is the sheer necessity and survivability of things. In this sense, it is more proper to describe liberal biopolitics as limitless. For rather than taking the open horizon as a space for the infinitely possible, everything is internalized such that it is haunted by whatever remains irreducible to its current sensibility. This inevitably brings us to the vexed question of a death well lived.

We don't need grand theorizing to make the point that mediations on death have a profound impact upon the way we live. Anybody who has known a person with a terminal illness and becomes anxiously consumed with the prospect of dying will appreciate how the thought and presence of death effectively stops them living. They cannot live because the very uncertainties (physical and intellectual) presented by the mere thought of death are a burden that proves too difficult to carry. Hence, working in an opposite direction to Heidegger's much debated claim that the 'absolute impossibility' of thinking about death constitutes the very possibility of being, the possibility of its occurrence is sufficient to instil what in fact is less a fear of death but more a *fear of living*. But we cannot simply stop there. As we have suggested, what makes the art of living so dangerously fascinating today is that it requires us to *live through* the source of our endangerment. Trauma and anxiety as such become our weapons, as vulnerability is amplified and played back to us with increasing frequency to their point of normalization. The political significance of this should not be underestimated.

Our argument is that the political debasement of the subject through strategies of resilience more than puts the very question of death into question by removing it from our critical gaze. In doing so, it represents nothing short of a profound assault on our ability to think metaphysically. This in turn represents a direct attack upon our abilities to transform the world beyond the catastrophic condition in which we are now immersed. After all, how can we even conceive of different worlds if we cannot come to terms with the death and extinction of this one? Resilience as such is what we may term a 'lethal ecology of reasoning', for in taking hold and seeking to intervene in all the elements upon which life is said to depend, it puts the living on a permanent life support system that is hard, soft and virtually wired into the most insecure of social fabrics to the evacuation of all possible alternative outcomes. To open, then, a much debated but still yet to be resolved conflict in the history of political and philosophical thought, we maintain that if the biopoliticization of life represents the triumph of *techne* over *poiesis*, and if this very biopoliticization today thrives on the technical production of vulnerable subjects which learn to accept that fate, there is a need to resurrect with confidence the idea that what remains irreducible to life can be the starting point for thinking about a more poetic alternative art for living. As Peter Sloterdijk writes on the all too gradual demise of metaphysics:

Ever since the end of the eighteenth century, this has become a twilight zone where it was also possible to see the growth of nihilism, and it was precisely because there that art began to assume an enormous importance, and precisely because art makes it clear that it has a non-nihilistic way of coming to terms with the fact that we ourselves are responsible for the creation of what we think of as the essential. Art defends the truth of life against flat empiricism and deadly positivism, which are no longer capable of an awareness of anything more than the facts and which are therefore incapable of culling the energy to create new inter-relationships of vital or living forces.[3]

Life as a Work of Art

So where does this leave us in our attempts to move beyond the resilient subject? How may we revitalize the very meaning of the political out of the torment of its catastrophic condition? What is further required so that post-biopolitical forms of living may be entertained? How, in other words, may we resurrect with affirmative vigour Nietzsche's delightful and no less poignant provocation that life itself may become a work of art? We are yet to truly grasp the magnificence of Nietzsche's work as it may play out in the field of politics. While the stylistic artistry of his particular interventions largely remained tied to the literary field, as witnessed most notably in the figure of *Zarathustra*, he nevertheless demanded with affirmative vigour rejoicing in the fullness of an experience that embraces the poetic and the aesthetic. Not only does this stake a claim to the creative power of transformation, it also gives over to life the political possibility that its aesthetical qualities may have both an affirmative and resistive potential to challenge dogmatic images of thought. Never has this calling seemed more pressing.

What is at stake here is not simply the 'aesthetics of existence' wherein life conforms to some glorious representational standard of beautification. Such constructed imaginaries always grey the magnificent colours of the earth. What is demanded is the formulation of alternative modes of existence that are not afraid to have reasons to believe in this world. As Deleuze succinctly put it, 'In every modernity and every novelty, you find conformity and creativity; an insipid conformity, but also "a little new music"; something in conformity with the time, but also something untimely – separating the one from the other is the task of those who know how to love, the real destroyers and creators of our day'. Deleuze invariably provides a purposeful nod here to the Nietzchean idea of a poetic subject:

> that he himself is really the poet who keeps creating this life . . . as a poet, he certainly has *vis contemplative* and the ability to look back upon his work, but at the same time also and above all *vis creative*, which the active human being lacks . . . We who think and feel at the same time are those who really continually *fashion* something that had not been there before: the whole eternally growing world of valuations, colours, accents, perspectives, scales, affirmations, and negations'.[4]

What Nietzsche acknowledges in this passage is that 'aestheticizing of life entails its artful, stylish disappropriation, a free fall into metaphor and un-self-ness. Autoaesthetics, the artful and chimerical fabrication of the (un)self, means development of strategies of self-mastery, power over one's art and production, a convergence with self at the *locus* of the creation (and interpretation) of art'.[5] This was not lost on Foucault, who was also of the opinion that 'from the idea that the self is not given to us, I think that there is only one practical consequence: we have to create ourselves as a work of art . . . We should not have to refer the creative activity of somebody to the kind of relation he has to himself, but should relate the kind of relation one has to oneself to a creative activity'.[6]

We may argue that conceiving of life as a work of art stands in direct contrast to the nihilism, indifference and alienation of the catastrophic subject. It resurrects Nietzsche's claim about the death of God in a way that seeks to find new forms of meaning to life that are necessarily revelatory in nature. And it challenges head on the positivist conceit that a meaningful life can only be progressively reasoned on account of its biopolitical existence. This demands an account of the subject that is more than a historical unfolding of survivability. As Simon Critchley puts it, by drawing upon one of his arch provocateurs, Oscar Wilde, 'When I think of religion at all, I feel as if I would like to found an order for those who cannot believe: the Confraternity of the Faithless, one might call it, where on an altar, on which no taper burned, a priest, in whose heart peace had no dwelling, might celebrate with unblessed bread and a chalice of empty wine. Everything to be true must become a religion. And agnosticism should have its ritual no less than faith'.[7] This acceptance that there is something to existence that is less explicable to the prevailing logics of secularity, as Todd May explains, requires a more nuanced understanding of philosophical enquiry that moves away from 'thinking metaphysics' and all its ways of stupefying and rendering incapable the subject, towards questioning how we might live differently:

> We don't want to reduce it simply to a morally good life, as though a meaningful life were simply an unalienated moral life. Meaningful lives are not so limited and are sometimes more vexed. So we must ask what lends objective worthiness to a life outside the moral realm. Here is where the narrative character of a life comes into play . . . There are narrative values expressed by human lives that are not reducible to moral values. Nor are they reducible to happiness; they are not simply matters of subjective feeling. Narrative values are not felt, they are lived. And they constitute their own arena of value, one that has not been generally recognized by philosophers who reflect on life's meaningfulness.[8]

There are a number of qualifications that need to be made here. We cannot be content to see artistic production as something which fosters a negative response to the realities of the world. Creativity must *precede* any account of the dialectic. Nor must we confuse the art of living with the conforming arts that merely perform a well-rehearsed dance. Life as a work of art is necessarily affirmative in a sense that it appeals to the yet to be revealed. It has no taste for the simulacrum. Neither is it content to accept the need to live dangerously such that we are forced to live with déjà vu all over again. The self is to be actively produced as a non-stable subject that does not seek to emulate some normative standard, but instead forcefully challenges the vulnerable ground which it is said to occupy. So believing in the irreducibility of existence? Certainly. Hostile to all reactive and enslaving forces? Undeniably. Unapologetic in willing the event of its ongoing emergent existence? Steadfast. Openly committed to the affirmative potential of the autonomous subject? Categorically. A believer in a more affective notion of history that is forever in the making? Unreservedly. A student of the eschatological? Earnestly. Appreciative of the transformative political power of fabulation? Truly. A lover of the poetic over the mathematical? Wholeheartedly. Welcoming our coming into the world? Without reservation.

It would be wrong, however, to argue here simply in favour of life as if its very nature exhibited something of the poetic. As we have insisted, never before have we witnessed so many mediations on the value of life. Life, it is now said, constitutes the very meaningfulness of existence as broadly conceived. Without any engagement with the problem of life, there is nothing but a retreat into the abstract deceit of sovereign entrapments. This is now the default setting for global liberal governance on a planetary scale. Whilst critical philosophers once argued that life holds the capacity and the will to resist that which it finds intolerable to its existence, no longer can we have such confidence in the subject as framed in terms of its living qualities alone. Life continually desires that which it should find oppressive. It wilfully gives over to processes of de-subjectivization on the promise of better futures to come. Life also shamefully compromises with power to the subjugation of both the self and others. It happily allows itself to be the principal referent object for political strategies which, promising freedom, render life with a difference thoroughly dangerous. Indeed, when power takes life to be its principal object, it often returns with claims to vulnerability that contemporary forms of power find easy to accommodate and turn to their own advantage. Neoliberalism, after all, thrives in situations that are insecure by design. What is at stake here is not simply some mediation on life such that the meaningfulness of life may be thought anew. However tempting this may appear to us, we need to focus more clearly on the affirmative and poetic qualities of existence that are by their very nature 'irreducible to life' against those strategies which take life in order to render it deducible – hence deductable as a living entity that demands continuous intervention on account of its endless imperfections.

Needless to say, this art of living that finds political value in those poetic expressions that remain irreducible to life as such stands in marked contrast to the conformist arts which seek to resemble the world. Much of contemporary art, it is fair to say, is what money makes of it. Indeed, if Andy Warhol epitomized what Walter Benjamin aptly termed the work of art in the age of mechanical reproduction, no artist resembles the resilient logic of the times better than Damien Hirst. Beyond his penchant for self-valuation and shameless taking of ideas for self-gratification and self-glorification, Hirst's work has a well-documented affinity with the medical and the taxidermical. His series of figures in formaldehyde, in particular, can be seen to represent the catastrophic topography of the times. Suspended in perfect animation, while suffocated beneath the weight of a liquid modern embrace, the various animalistic subjects of Hirst's choosing are devoid of any political agency. Spectacularly simplistic in their mundane and catatonic gaze, their manufactured commitment to a death without the chance of credible decay tells less a tale of philosophical enquiry than the story of a finitude that refuses to accept the notion that finality may be transformative. They are literally 'set' in a perpetually fixed catastrophic plot. Nothing original is produced here. Life is merely taken as something to be exhibited without agential content or capacity for transformation. All the while it is condemned to a suspended sentence that is imagined to last for infinity. Hirst's work thus resembles a Kantian dream and Nietzschean nightmare in the very same move. For here the object is completely immobile such that we become aware of our shared vulnerabilities without asking what we may do differently to challenge them, let alone move beyond the tragedy of their artificial supports.

Exhausted by Suffering

'If the era we have just left exhausted its remaining possibilities and attained the stage of culmination, the processes of thinking, of action, of will, have by no means reached their term . . . on the contrary, the drama of anthropology has only just begun'. So claims Sloterdijk in another of his phenomenal works, *Neither Sun Nor Death*.[9] Sloterdijk's underlining of the drama of anthropology is an important gesture. The human is not simply a constructed category or outcome of representation, but a 'drama'. Every account of humanity presupposes its theatre. We continue to remain heirs to the Greeks in this regard. The human is a staging, a performance, which comes into existence not just in the act of its representation, but arises in and through a performance. We may think of it indeed as a performative unfolding that not only assigns certain 'significations' or modes of 'subjectivization' to authenticate the meaning of lives, but a more profound awakening that opens onto the future in ways which cannot be anticipated in advance. But what genre of performance are we now to practise? What drama does the theatre of our humanity today presuppose? Who, indeed, does this body of humanity condemned to be a spectator on this fated earth think it is? What truths does it guide us to see? And what truths does it tell such that we may repeat them without questioning otherwise?

We do not accept the idea so widely propounded by others that the most urgent question of our time is how

The Art of Politics 177

better to relieve human suffering, or that of any other form of life defined by tales of survival. We are, it appears, or ought to be at least, exhausted by the discourse and aesthetic practice of suffering. Nothing seems to us more tiring than the representation of the human as that form of life which suffers, makes suffer, and consequently has to be concerned with relieving its suffering from a merciless world. Not only are publics immune to the spectacles of 'victims'. Suffering often translates into pity. Pity in turn all too often shifts into piousness. The pious then give unto them moral supremacy to the righteous indignation of others. Such moralizing often becomes the vehicle upon which interventions proceed to enter into the souls of the living. These interventions sanction a removal of political agency on account of the fact that the need for something to be done to alleviate the suffering is premised in part upon the victim's complicity in the regressive conditioning. This results in the politicization of suffering such that the victim becomes a problem to be solved without ever questioning whether they perceived their plight to be different from the standpoint of vulnerable subjects who require external assistance, instead of focusing on confronting the conditions which deny their abilities to express their own political desires and agencies.

Our theatre, which we inhabit now, is a compassionately narcissistic one. Its chorus is deafening. Our question – the question we would like a theatre of the human to respond to – is that of 'what is it to exhaust or be exhausted by suffering?'. What drama does the human perform when it has exhausted all of those tragic idioms of lament it has been forced to repeat in the theatres of liberal modernity? 'The exhausted is the exhaustive, the dried up, the extenuated, and the dissipated'.[10] To be exhausted is absolutely not to be tired. Tired people continue to perform that which they are already doing in a laborious way. They suffer that which they are and have to do. And tired people are tiresome in their suffering. We suffer their presence while all the while wishing to be exhausted of them as well as wishing that they might exhaust themselves, dry up and disappear. To be exhausted, in contrast, is to have done with what one has been. It is to be incapable of continuing to perform that which one has done so as to become capable of being otherwise. Thus to be exhausted is absolutely not to be passive. It is only in being exhausted that one can become active 'for nothing'.[11] And to be active 'for nothing' is not to be caught 'doing nothing'. It demands a lot of its subject. Samuel Beckett's plays are populated by characters who are fully exhausted by their suffering, while they remain positively active 'for nothing'. Characters that in seeing the end do not fear it, who live out their end in full knowledge of that end while renouncing any call to organization with a view to trying to survive the end. Their goals are not to do this or that in preparation for their end, but instead to refuse all plans as to how to survive the end. There is no dignity for them in the servitude of self-preservation. Such refusal requires an activity, vigilance, awareness and a learning to die. This is a theatre that, in actuality, is not miserable at all, but which celebrates the end of the possible as a condition for the beginning of the new. Beyond the possible, it posits the question of absolute freedom. One must exhaust the possible, and be prepared to be exhausted by it, in order to reach such freedom. And in effect the possible is accomplished by the exhausted characters who exhaust it.[12]

Obviously there exists no end of aesthetic representations of 'the world's end' from which we might draw for political purposes. Cinema, especially, has become preoccupied with the image of the world's end in recent years, projecting and aestheticizing a fear for the imminent and total destruction of human life.[13] This fear underpins what we call 'the biopolitical aesthetic'. The advance of this preoccupation is an expression of the increasing power of the biopolitical aesthetic in cinema and systems of aesthetic representation as a whole. If what Fredric Jameson calls the geopolitical aesthetic describes the embodiment of cinematic representations within the capitalist 'world system',[14] the biopolitical aesthetic describes the function of a cinema that fantasizes the potential destruction of that system and all that lives within it from the position of a life which cannot tolerate that destruction. But amid all the schlock movies that help constitute the biopolitical aesthetic, depicting the end of the world and all that depends on it, one in particular stands out as worthy of dwelling on for the ways in which it disrupts that aesthetic: Lars von Trier's *Melancholia*. *Melancholia* depicts the last days of the world in context of a 'dysfunctional' bourgeois family composed most significantly of two sisters, Justine and Claire. Justine has been widely represented in articles responding to the film as suffering from 'depression'; a claim that is no way attested to by the film itself other than in the discourse of her cretinous family relatives, who diagnose her in the context of her rejection of her banal and stupid newly wedded husband. Afraid of the life she is being committed to through the institution of marriage, and loathing the work milieu into which she is also being further interpellated (her husband is also the best friend of her boss at the advertising company where she works as Artistic Director), Justine takes solace in the presence and approach of the 'other world', Melancholia. She is in effect a seer in the classical sense that Gilles Deleuze attributes to the seers of 'modern cinema' that he claimed populate it, in that she sees the intolerability of the power relations into which she is interpellated.[15] Understanding the political qualifications of 'modern cinema', we have to grasp, as Deleuze instructed us, its aesthetic tendency towards the portrayal of characters whose lives are determined not just by their 'seeing the intolerable' but the polemical situatedness which such seeing entails. For these are characters whose lives are determined by a confrontation with the 'intolerable' nature of the power relations on which their lives are otherwise dependent; characters who each in their own way, find themselves at war with themselves and all that surrounds them. Their life is lived as art and their art is a conduct of an open battle declared against those who would seek to suffocate the subject by clouds of reason.

The Politics of Prophecy

Ecologic catastrophe, which is but one of the many visions of the future to hallmark the contemporary liberal imaginary, is more than some claim to truth. It is a politics of prophecy. Whilst we have no concern here to revisit the links we have explored elsewhere between contemporary liberal biopolitics, power and theology, we are interested in looking at the sites of resistance and artistic expression that may allow us to challenge those modes of verification that have become so central to the articulation of vulnerable subjects and resilient strategies which operate in their name. That is to say, if all politics from the apocalyptic to the catastrophic necessarily reveals certain claims about the future that by their very nature forever elude proofing or empirical verification, and if all questions about the future are in themselves necessarily absurd for we cannot answer what cannot possibly be known in advance, then how may we rethink the idea of a performative unfolding and to what intellectual tradition or creative style of thinking may it connect? What does it really mean, after all, to say that we are facing extinction? And how may we move beyond the temptation to simply fall back upon the contradictions of the claim, for if true, what is the point in trying to think imaginatively when there is no point to anything in the end?

Following on from the idea that life is an unfolding drama, it would be ridiculous to dismiss outright the Greek origins of theatre as we seek to find alternative intellectual resources. It remains, after all, an essential element of the history of our dramatic present. The figure of Oedipus is an obvious starting point. Oedipus has dominated our thinking on everything from politics of the household, the patriarchal nature of the State, to violent pathologies more generally, as famously articulated by Sigmund Freud. The Oedipal complex has also been shown to be more than some fixed structure. The ongoing naturalization of the forms of power violently embodied in Oedipus become more possible when seen as an ongoing and regenerative process.[16] Countering the tyranny of Oedipus, Antigone is presented as a means for rethinking the political.[17] Antigone's vulnerability, in particular, is presented as a more subversive politics. Whilst Creon (as Oedipus before him) embodied stately reason, until he came face to face with the realization that he was suffocated by his own sovereign enslavement, his daughter Antigone becomes a new site of suffering so central to thinking about a revolutionary praxis. This is what Bonnie Honig has termed a 'post-enlightenment humanism of lament and finitude' which proposes a universal framework of shared suffering and grief.[18] Lament, however, is more ambiguous than Butler and her followers want to concede. Could it not be the case that Antigone actually permits the resolution of the political (in her case the collapse of Creon's household) on account of the violence carried out in her name? Does her vulnerability and grief translate into a new form of terror that remains inescapable except in death? This is fully appreciated by Honig who describes how 'the play actually and repeatedly explores the question of how permissibly to grieve not just ungrievable life but grievable life as well . . . This suggests that the play does not get embroiled in the problem of burial because of the politics of enmity. Rather, it takes up the problem of enmity in order to broach (in a distancing way, starting with the burial of an enemy) broad political problems of which burial politics are a synecdoche'.[19] But if not Oedipus or Antigone, then to whom may we turn for intellectual resourcefulness?

Before answering this we want to turn to Foucault's insistence that modern art in its entirety ought to be considered 'the vehicle of Cynicism in the modern world'.[20] Cynicism, as he explored at length in his *Courage of Truth* lectures was the classical doctrine that took the practice of *parrhesia* to its most extreme; an extreme very different to its deployment as foundation for moralizing and norm-instilling discourses in the development of liberal modernity. For which reason modern art is to be understood as a major vehicle not just of *parrhesia*, but politics, in its modern form. *Parrhesia* is fundamentally a practice of *telling* truth rather than simply *seeing* truth. So, might we not expect, then, in examining modern art, to find the performers that populate it to be a people of parrhesiasts? A people who not only *see* the intolerable nature of the power relations in which their lives are invested but who in their speech tell the truth about that intolerability, and who, in doing so, forge new understandings of what is true? A people who not only live a life that in being so lived is forced into a situation of polemical confrontation with intolerable power relations, but who denounce as intolerable liberal ways of living?

Deleuze's analysis of the modernity of cinema in particular and its 'people' is more attendant to its seeing than its saying function, and influential interpretations of it have seized upon its account of the figure of 'the seer' to theorize the people to come.[21] But it is clear that, for Deleuze, comprehending 'the people to come' that populates modern cinema means addressing not just its capacities for sight. The 'speech act' of 'story-telling' is a fundamental means, as he describes, by which characters in postcolonial cinema produce collective utterances the political function of which is to emancipate the colonized from the myths that legitimized their colonization by the colonizers.[22] The films of the Brazilian filmmaker, Glauber Rocha, for example, 'isolate a lived present beneath the myth, which could be intolerable, the unbelievable, the impossibility of living now in "this" society, then seize from the unlivable a speech act which could not be forced into silence, an act of story-telling which would not be a return to myth but a production of collective utterances capable of raising misery to a strange positivity, the invention of a people . . . the story-telling of the people to come'.[23] For it is through these collective yet individually performed denunciations of power that they are delivered from positions of solitude and marginalization against intolerabilities that are otherwise hidden from the view of the audience whom they address. In this sense, the performer is equipped with a courage to truth, denouncing what is recognized as true life for its falseness, and arguing for a 'changing of the value of the currency' in the manner that Diogenes, the arch-cynic of Athens, was renowned.[24]

But as we have learned, the contemporary condition is not simply magnetized by the telling of truths. What brings together continental philosophy and liberal biopoliticians today is a shared yet politically conflictual interest in the idea of the event horizon, whose openness to that which is coming is either seen to be a source of irreducible wonder or a catastrophe in the making. So rather than simply looking to debates on the parrhesiastic moment of truths, there is also a need to engage with the idea that politics is now finally exposed for the prophecy it always has been. There is no concept of the political that doesn't stake some claim to the future, just as there is no politics which doesn't reveal remnants from the past. We are in that sense forever embodied as subjects whose immanent qualities are continually teetering on the threshold between what has happened and what is going to happen. This is the event of life. Embodied subjects, whose contemporary fabric is at the strategic inter-pass where pasts and futures collide. Hence, how we make sense of this critically requires questioning what is not questioned (the truth-telling exercise) about our historical present, along with looking to the future in absolute certainty that the future will arrive and will be shaped by our actions (albeit in ways that we cannot anticipate in advance). It is here that we are drawn to the much neglected figure of Tiresias who seldom features in contemporary political and philosophical mediations.

Tiresias, the blind prophet of Thebes, appears in several of the Greek tragedies. It is, however, perhaps his brief appearance in *Oedipus Rex* that strikes a particular chord. Called upon by Oedipus to reveal the identity of Laius's murderer, Tiresias's seemingly ironic approach wittingly forces Oedipus to confront his own violence such that Oedipus becomes aware of the crimes he was already committing. Without Tiresias's vision, the Oracle's message previously delivered by Creon of banishment would therefore have become a mere prophecy. For it is what Tiresias forces Oedpius to see that sets him on the road to self-discovery, which, as the story develops, ultimately ends up resulting in his death. Could it not be said that what Tiresias does see of Oedipus is his eventual fate? So rather than offering a certain vision of the future as possessed by the Oracle, could it not be that he simply sees in the present what others do not see? Not, in other words, a revelatory figure able to reveal the truth as pre-determined; rather, Tiresias is capable of questioning what is not questioned such that he is appreciative of Oedipus's nihilistic qualities which will ultimately lead him to blind ruination, for it is a blindness already being proclaimed by Oedipus's impossible and self-destructive ambitions.[25] This is a point questioned by Champlin who comments: 'Was Tiresias, as an exponent of truth, on the general level of an Old Testament prophet? Sophocles speaks of him as cognizant of ineffable heavenly matters. The strictures of the play demanded only that he possess a full awareness of past and future human affairs'.[26] Hence, even though he is blind, he has a confidence and courage to speak to the future in a way that is critically engaged with the violence of the past and the unfolding and self-destructive nihilism of the present. Tiresias thus appears to be a seer of truth in the most affirmative of senses, for in his explanations, it is possible to detect a challenge to incontrovertible destiny such that it becomes possible to confront the catastrophe head on and warn against its catastrophic outcomes.

Intriguingly, in his *The Memory of Tiresias*, Mikhail Iampolski describes how beholden classical cinema was to the prophetic mode of veridiction. The great directors of the classical era, such as D.W. Griffith and Sergei Eisenstein, both understood themselves as prophets; their mission, and that of their works, as leading humanity out of its blindness into the light of emancipation. Griffith thought of his work 'as a kind of mission aimed at creating an unprecedented universal language that would be capable of resolving the most acute social contradictions'[27] and ultimately of establishing the conditions for the emancipation of humanity. 'With the use of the universal language of moving pictures the true meaning of the brotherhood of man will have been established throughout the earth'.[28] Eisenstein too, was obsessed with the prophet Tiresias, and in the 1940s, at the cusp of the transition of classical to modern cinema, made a series of sketches on the theme of blindness, evoking the idea of blindness as a precondition for a subject capable of seeing 'beyond the visible'.[29]

Might we suppose, then, that while classical cinema was prophetic, confident in its mission of improving humanity, approximating ever closer to the truth of the world, so with the crisis in cinema that occurs with the Second World War, faith in the prophetic modality broke down, to be replaced by the parrhesiastic? Characters shift from a modality of truth-telling concerned with foretelling the future, and cinema shifts itself from a vocation of fulfilling the prophet's word, to a modality of telling the truth concerning human wretchedness, revealing the world in its chaos, indicating only the impossibility of fulfilling the prophet's word, and ultimately the falseness of all prophets. Isn't there indeed a fundamental conflict between the Parrhesiast and the Prophet in so far as their dispositions to the world are based on conflicting understandings of the nature of the world as such? The modernity of cinema is such that it must expel the Prophet, in order to welcome the Parrhesiac. This returns us to the question of what has happened to the prophetic modes of veridiction subsequently. It seems to us that when we look at cinema today, we are looking at a much altered regime – a regime in keeping with the tensions we have staked out, neither modern in the terms described, and which numerous others since have followed, utilized and embellished, nor classical, but which does bear witness to a return of the prophetic mode of veridiction so definitive of the classical, and expelled by the modern. Indeed, whilst a great deal of this cinema buys into the catastrophic prophesies of late liberal rule, we can also detect a renewed investment in the possibility of a subject confident in its ability to foretell the future, see into it, and fulfil actions accordingly.

The title of Jacques Audiard's most recent film, *A Prophet*, would suggest it is a case in point. This is a film made in 2009 and thus the critical reception remains scant. The title in itself is revealing. For this is not a tale about 'the prophet', i.e. the arrival of some righteous pre-ordained entity whose appearance is both expected and whose purpose is all too apparent, but simply 'a prophet' whose intersubjective singularity demands a different reading. The film is set in a prison and depicts the predicament of a young Arab male prisoner, Malik, to survive when caught up in a gang war between two rival factions of Corsicans and Arabs. Forced under threat of his own life to murder another Arab inmate called Reheb, Malik endures a rite of passage through which he becomes an abject member of the Corsican gang, learning their social mores, speaking their language, adapting to their norms, but never being accepted by the other Corsicans. At a critical juncture, he is exposed as the murderer of Reheb to the head of the rival Arab gang, but survives through an incredible act of prophesy; while sitting in the back of a car he literally foresees the appearance on the road of a herd of deer, which so impresses the leader of the Arab gang sitting next to him that he is accepted and treated with deference by them. Consequently, Malik embarks on a course that leads him to sever his relation with the Corsicans, gradually forming his own group, achieving predominance in the prison itself, and eventual release. But what is the significance of this?

The Guardian journalist Phil Hoad argues that '*A Prophet* shows us a multilingual future for cinema – Most of us now live in a globalised, polyglot world, and Jacques Audiard's prison drama is a rare film that reflects that'.[30] Malik's survival is facilitated by his ability to learn the languages and cultures of both Corsican and Arab worlds and move between them. And in this sense, as Jérôme Segal has argued, the whole script can be considered a 'Bildungsroman', a coming-of-age story describing the psychological, moral, and social development of Malik, portraying as it does Malik's success 'in building up his own network' and more fundamentally 'how cultural capital, in Bourdieu's sense, can be invested in social capital with the development of a complex social network'.[31] As Hoad also argues

> The globalised world needs more linguist cinema like A Prophet – limber, alert and opportunistic. . . . Malik is left to forge his own destiny – a lesson for us all in an increasingly complicated world. He is almost a proxy for the fast-growing mixed-race and multilingual masses who are the next step on from old monocultures. They are the ones placed to thrive as the patterns of world power grow more enmeshed and hard to fathom. It is the hour of the bagman, the intermediary, the ambassador, the middle manager . . . In other words: Malik is the future'.[32]

Hoad's analysis is too shallow and ideological to rely upon for much. Instead, we have to ask the question, what does Malik see? What is the nature of his prophesy? In contrast with prophets classically conceived, *A Prophet* doesn't depict a foretelling of a future by a disclosure of what's hidden from men. Malik sees only what's transparently possible, reading the signs of the present as literally as possible. He sees a road sign for deer, and then he foretells 'deer'. In other words, he sees purely what's in front of him. Malik is not 'the prophet' but just 'a prophet' in its quotidian form, and in effect *A Prophet* prophesizes the becoming of a people without prophets. A pure informed people disconnected from a prophesized world of peoples past, connected up to a people to come.

Here we return to *Melancholia* and consider, once more, Justine. For she is also a prophet; she 'knows things' from the banal (678 beans in the bottle) to the profound ('life is only on earth and not for long'). Ultimately, we see Melancholia, including the end of the world; its approach heralds the fulfilment of Justine's prophetic conception of the necessity of the present world's end. Certainly the shot in which the earth is actually destroyed is among the most beautiful in cinematic history, and in its setting to Wagner's *Tristan und Isolde*, and viewed from the abstract vantage point of outer space, eroticized not as collision but attraction and fatal encounter. In *Melancholia*, the viewer encounters the fantasy and wonder of the potential destruction of the world, but in seeing it with Justine, from the position of a subject exhausted by the life that depends on that world. Justine's disposition is in this sense portrayed in radical contrast with her sister, Claire, who lives in neurotic fear of the end of the world, as the planet Melancholia draws closer to the earth and the moment of total destruction nears. What Melancholia depicts in Justine is not the fear of a subject for the end of the world, nor the disastrous consequences for life of the end, or how life somehow does survive. In effect, Melancholia initiates a post-biopolitical aesthetic; an aesthetic of life's exhaustion. A cinema which does not limit itself to proclaiming that 'another world is possible' as the card-carrying Leftists of Occupy Wall Street still bleat like lambs, but that grants subjectivity to that world such that the other world is in effect represented as not just possible but 'coming to get you'. Here, political subjectivity emerges in affirmation of the finitude of this world and active welcoming of another world which is not just coming to you, in effect, as some kind of eschatological gift, but which is coming for you, in order to take you out.

The conflict between the biopolitical aesthetic of Claire and the exhausted aesthetic of Justine mark the film at crucial points. 'The earth is evil, we don't need to grieve for it . . . life on earth is evil' says Justine, while John, the husband of her sister Claire, remonstrates that they should 'raise a toast to life' when Melancholia appears to have passed the world by. The cool demeanour of Justine contrasts with the neurotic fear of Claire and the repressed fear of John throughout the latter part of the film, as Melancholia approaches. But the most significant scene of all occurs between Justine and Claire, following John's death, once the inevitability of Melancholia's arrival and the total destruction of the world become altogether clear. Claire concerns herself with the preparation for the moment of destruction. She desires and proposes 'a plan'.

Claire: 'I want us to be together when it happens . . . I want to do this the right way'.
Justine: 'Then you better do it quickly'.
Claire: 'A glass of wine on the terrace?'
Justine: 'You want me to have a glass of wine on your terrace?'
Claire: 'Yes, will you do that, sis?'
Justine: 'How about a song? Beethoven's Ninth, something like that? Maybe we could light some candles. You want us to gather on your terrace to sing a song and have a glass of wine?'
Claire: 'Yes. That would make me happy'.
Justine: 'Do you know what I think of your plan?'
Claire: 'No, but I was hoping that you might like it'.
Justine: 'I think it's a piece of shit'.
Claire: 'Justine, please, I just want it to be nice'.
Justine: 'Nice? Why don't we meet on the fucking toilet?'

Here the intertextuality between *Melancholia* and Beckett's *Endgame* is striking. Both offer depictions of subjects who are exhausted by their suffering, and yet in their becoming active 'for nothing', affirm something that is wondrously optimistic to deny the tendency for lamentation. There is nothing fatalistic about this. The end, we are told, is already foretold. They are subjects, then, that in seeing the end do not fear it, but who live out their end in full knowledge of that end while renouncing any call to organization with a view to trying to survive the end. Justine does not want to do this or that in preparation for the end of the world and refuses all Claire's plans as to how to survive the end. Such a course of action would of course be futile and catastrophically suffocating unto the end. Her refusal requires a certain activity, her vigilance, her awareness. Hers is not a depressed condition of passivity but an activity, and the execution of a plan to have done with Claire's preparations for the end of times that suffocates all optimism or belief that things may be thought and lived differently. As such, we can take from von Trier's cinema a celebration that the end of the possible reveals the conditions for the beginning of the new, and beyond the possible, the darkness of an absolute freedom; Justine's freedom, underwritten by an aesthetic of exhaustion that, exhausted by suffering of the world, finds in the briefest of moments a confidence to live – albeit in ways that liberal theorists would find altogether pathological on account of its irreducibility to the prevailing virtues of a survivability instinct which, proclaiming the future to be an endemic terrain of ongoing catastrophe, demands certain behavioural conformity such that catastrophic reasoning cannot be reasonably denied, let alone intellectually challenged.

Beyond the End of Times

Some may read this meditation on the art of living dangerously as fatalistic. They may even argue that its narrative is apologetic to those who refute climate change. That is certainly not the intention, although we do find many of those debates tedious and bereft of political imagination. Our hunch is that strategies of resilience thwart a genuine love for the biosphere as planetary endangerment becomes a source of lament for a human species that has lost all hope in its ability to transform the world for the better. How can we better conceive our futures without a politics that accepts the existence of irreducible qualities like aesthetics (especially beautification that defies description); emotions (especially of love which does not simply endure); non-categorical imperatives (especially the ability to welcome the unknowable); atmospheres (especially those which are positively charged); and affective experiences (especially events that continue to highlight the limits of our discourse)? Moving beyond the end of times, then, demands a confidence to look into the future not with a catastrophic image of thought that forces us into some already pre-conceived quagmire, but with a commitment to believing in the world that requires an entirely new ethical relationship with the human as an irreducible entity, and the world that is forever transforming to the creation of new ecologies.

The ability of learning to live with one's ability to become different unto oneself such that loss is not a cause for mourning or lament but a joyous and affirmative experience demands coming to terms with the death of the subject. Learning to live, finally, requires learning how to die. It is to see the finite as a political condition of possibility rather than a way of rendering the emergent subject as a problem to be solved. It is, then, to replace the catastrophic void and its deeply embedded suspicions, with the poetic subject whose allegiance to the open horizon of possible existences is not afraid to summon forth peoples yet to come. As Jacques Derrida would maintain, 'One must love the future. And there is no more just category for the future than that of the "perhaps". Such a thought conjoins friendship, the future, and the *perhaps* to open on to the coming of what comes – that is to say, necessarily in the regime of a possible whose possibilization must prevail over the impossible'.[33] Here a demand is to be placed on the impossible such that a truly exceptional politics beyond the normative condemnation of catastrophists can be imagined and performed on the world stage.

It is here we most clearly see the advantages of shifting our political focus from discourses of vulnerability towards the critical pedagogy for the globally oppressed. Discourses, ideas, values and social relations that push against the grain, redefine the boundaries of the sensible, and reclaim the connection between knowledge and power in the interest of social change, too often become not only inconvenient but rapidly accelerate to being viewed as dangerous or pathologically absurd. As Gilles Deleuze shrewdly reminded us, however, nobody is ever put into prison for powerlessness or pessimism. It is the confidence to truth that so perturbs. Power does not fear vulnerability. Nor does it feel threatened by those who lament. It does, however, find troubling those who are acutely aware that their subjectivities and creative energies are being oppressed, and are willing to actively resist in order to release a potential which was already there in the making. For it is there that power detects the possibility for the creation of peoples yet to come. That is why there is solace in the wisdom of the earnest founder of critical pedagogy, Paolo Friere:

> The more radical the person is, the more fully he or she enters into reality so that, knowing it better, he or she can transform it. This individual is not afraid to confront, to listen, to see the world unveiled. This person is not afraid to meet the people or to enter into a dialogue with them. This person does not consider himself or herself the proprietor of history or of all people, or the liberator of the oppressed; but he or she does commit himself or herself, within history, to fight at their side.[34]

So what does it mean to speak not only of a confidence for the oppressed of the earth, but a confidence to the future? Just as we are not content to view the entire history of human evolution as various stages of survivability such that in the end, it seems, that from the outset we were fated to be vulnerable after all; neither do we accept the altogether complementary reasoning that the political is born from a sense of endangerment or enmity. Despite their apparent differences, both political realists and liberals still take endangerment to be the starting point for all theorizations of the concept of the political. We maintain, however, that if it were not for some more original love for the Other – a poetic connection that allows one to have confidence in their communion, that all subsequent bonds based upon a sense of vulnerability and endangerment would be superfluous. How else may we entertain the welcoming of kinship if not for something that exists amongst peoples prior to suspicions? Some may, of course, reason against this with the reason of the survivability instinct that brings together life out of strategic necessity. If that is the case, what a terrifyingly hollow, reductionist and unimaginative account of the human subject! Our challenge, then, is not only to have the confidence to create better ethical relations amongst the world of peoples and towards the biosphere in all its transformative wonder. It is to challenge the regime of truth surrounding the ways in which subjects and communities interact. From the term confidence we can, of course, extract the verb 'to confide', which in both original Latin usages was more about trust than secrecy. How might we confide with one another such that we have the confidence to challenge all encounters with all fascistic relations, including those that lead to the creation of a fascistic earth? Our parting shot, then, from this particular Nietzschean inspired bow is realized by the confidence we have in the idea of the poetic subject, for it is here we detect the possibility to create an entirely different atmospheric-aesthetic-affective registry to take us beyond our catastrophic times.

End of a Start

Liberal regimes have moved way beyond the security imperative so foundational to their origins, centuries ago, as the promise of security which once appeared to legitimate them back then has been disintegrated by a catastrophic imaginary that promotes what we have called *insecurity by design*. What once appeared to be the promise of progress and worldly transformation has given way to a full life crisis that offers us no means for escape. This way of treating liberalism, as a regime founded on catastrophic promises and ruinous images, does not mean we are in denial of the reality of the disastrous nature of the world we now inhabit and which liberal regimes understand themselves as responding to. But it would be wrong to think we can distinguish between the real and the imaginary. There is no hard and fast distinction, even though the fact that we speak of the real *and* the imaginary indicates that they are different. We perceive and make sense of the real through images. We are continuously interpellated within 'regimes of signs' that profoundly influence our affective registries and hence our sense of any given situation as it unfolds before us. And so the maps we construct to navigate the real are composed only of images. Liberalism itself, including its contemporary idea of the resilient subject, is a product of the imaginary. And so now we inhabit its nightmarish effects.

Nor are the images through which we make sense of and give representation to the real simply dependent on the real. If anything, the images precede the real, making and shaping it into what we come to name and know as the real, producing it, fabricating it, into the worlds we come to inhabit. The catastrophic nature of the world we now do not so much possess as find ourselves exposed and vulnerable to is of our own creation. It is a world which appears every bit as much in our heads as much as our heads are in this world, drowning in its images of impending disaster, species extinction, tipping points and catastrophe effects. The image and reality of catastrophe are ceaselessly interchanging such that the two are forever interfused. What we have learnt to call 'the world' is the manifestation of that interfusion. Politics is an art of worldly transformation, and transformation demands, first of all and fundamentally, a subject capable of conceiving the possibility of worldly transformation. A subject that sees the intolerability of the world as it is presently imagined and demands the seemingly impossible; the creation of a new one. A subject which affirms and follows the paths opened up to it by the visions of other worlds which the play of images creates for it. And a subject which affirms the reality of the existence of different worlds, their antagonisms, as well as tangibility and reachability, so to say. What we call *the poetic subject* therefore seeks to have a faith beyond that which arises simply from endangerment, as well as rekindling long diminished understandings of political subjectivity. Its diminishment owes everything not to the realities of a world which demand an evacuation of the political, but to the overwrought influence of liberalism over our own self-understandings of the limits of this world, its planetary boundaries, the weight of finitude, and the dangers which liberalism believes, and has preached for some time, that the imagination poses to a species equipped more than any other to transcend each and every boundary, each and every limit, and lose all sense of its own finitude and that of the world itself; the human.

We are now governed by Ministries of Anxiety of multiple kinds, whose dominant strategic mantra of resilience stems from the catastrophic imaginary of late liberal rule. We only have to step back ever so slightly from this blackmail, however, to see the political narcissism at work here. If we take, for instance, the idea of the full life crises seriously, how might we conceive of the governance of the subject such that it may once again conceive of better worlds to come? Instead of demanding, for example, that impoverished children, who are increasingly subjected to surveillance and lockdown conditions far beyond the reaches of earlier penitentiary systems, accept the vulnerabilities of their fate; what if they were instructed on the virtues of critical pedagogy such that the confidence and the poetic freedom to radically transform their lived condition was merited? That is a situation which begins at the earliest stages of development, wherein the transformative and critical power of imagination is welcomed, and the quality of lives assessed in terms of its poetic contributions. Pablo Picasso stated that 'all children are artists. The problem is how to remain an artist once he grows up'. This was not only a reflection on the power of the imagination. It is also acknowledgement of the power of a critical subjectivity which, as anybody who has a young child will testify, overwhelmingly appears when the former is suffocated such that the latter is expressed as a form of discontent for otherwise affirmative performances. But it also needs to be more than this. That is why exhaustion is fundamental to thinking about the poetic, for it allows us to take it out of the realms of fleeting abstraction. The art for living poetically needs to be crafted as a lifetime work. It must not be reduced to some Warholian commodifiable chancery that lasts but 15 minutes.

In this sense, the diagnosis of the contemporary degradations of human experience, which we have sought to provide here, remains an argument with the legacies of Immanuel Kant. The Kantian enlightenment, if we want to give it that absurdly paradoxical name, gave licence to human beings to speculate on the possibility of other worlds but always with the insistence that this world, as it is supposedly known, is the only world that can be. The possibility of another world is thinkable only within this world we inhabit, Kant said, and thus the possible has to always be suborned to the actual. The corollary of the possibility of us conceiving another world is the impossibility of us moving beyond this world, the world, as it is known and said to be. Thus understood, it was and still is a powerful and demeaning discourse on limits, one which forces us to accept our sense of the limits of this world as an imperious necessity without which we cannot think or act or indeed, imagine. Its influence goes some way to explaining why the world we live in has becomes so depoliticized, so absent of any sense of tangible alternatives, and crucially, subjects capable of creating and establishing them. When one reads back through the history of liberal thought, what's striking is the extent to which this project of constituting a subject of limits required a wholesale pathologization of the human imagination. Kant was a very sober man, for a reason. What existence beyond the harmonious regulation of the faculty of reason was to be feared; its abilities to incite the imagination, the wildness of what we see and feel, the freedom it gives us, and sense of increased vital force which leads us to follow the trajectories it opens up for us. We all know, or should know, the experience that arises from freeing ourselves and welcoming new experiences, and the ways in which it enables us to see the world differently, as well as act and speak differently, on account of the images it induces in us. There has to be an art to these imaginaries, and we have to be able to discern the differences between the subjective states we encounter in ourselves and each other under their influence.

The war on the imagination Kant and his disciplines inaugurated was also an attempt to govern truth, practices of truth-telling, and human relations to truth. It is not that the Enlightenment forbids us to tell truth, but that it sought to govern its production, and to subject it to a new regime of biopolitical power relations. For truth to be truth, Kant said, it had to be allied not simply to the world, but to the life of the world, or better understood, a world which itself is finite and living, requiring care and protection, vulnerable to the destructive potential of the maps and trajectories human beings impose on it on account of the power of their visions of what it can become. Today it is apparent, and we have sought to reveal, that the name we give to that Kantian conception of the world as a living being is the biosphere. Biospheric life is the vulnerable guide of the Kantian subject of liberal modernity. As living beings, so the story goes, our time cannot be indifferently dispersed and scattered. We have not just a path to follow, but a movement by which we might learn to follow life along that path, by accepting the reality that we owe our life, its sustenance and survival, finitely, to the world on which our paths are inscribed. Sustainable development is the name we give, today, to the Kantian conception of truth. The discourse on worldliness, and the prescription of the limits of the human imagination, is underwritten by a claim as to the infinite debt of all finite beings to the biosphere. The truths we can tell of this world and those to come have to be said in recognition of our debt and responsibility to it in all its finitude, vulnerability and limits. Now it seems to us that this original investment of Kant and others in biospheric life is what accounts for the fundamental antinomy between political and liberal subjectivity. An antinomy which continues to shape the antagonism between the neoliberalism analysed here in this book, the subject it calls into being globally today, and the erstwhile political subject of modernity that we have attempted to recover the lost signs of in this text.

Because the telling of political truth demands an affirmation of the conflict between worlds, a breaking through, without due care for what the implications will be for the world we inhabit and believe we somehow possess. Violence unto life which dispossesses the world we inhabit of the life which preserves it. A severing of the life-support systems which make the world we know possible. Because political truth cannot be told simply out of care for life! That idea is the great conceit of liberal modernity, and has been manifestly proven wrong by the long history of war and violence done unto life supposedly out of care for life. We have both written on that paradox extensively. We need an entirely different way of apprehending the relations between truth, life and death if we are to recover the politics of subjectivity. Because political truths are told by subjects that risk life, their own, that of others, and the world itself, in telling the truths which they do. They respect not the truth of biological life which Kant insists on, it being a phenomenon of finitude and vulnerability, but the life of truth. For truth has life only in so far as it outlives us while being spoken by us. Its vitality has to outstrip us for it to be worth telling. Fundamentally, the Kantian enlightenment understands none of these categories and their relations; life, world, death, politics, truth. More, in fact, than failing to understand them, it is responsible for the installation of a world in which their miscomprehension continues to reverberate powerfully and politically. Neoliberalism is the manifestation of the power of that miscomprehension. So, more fundamentally still, our battle against neoliberalism remains, in essence, a struggle against the legacies of the Kantian enlightenment. Obviously that declaration is not an incitement to 'forget Kant'. Kant is not understood or read well enough. But we need other textual resources. There is a rich tradition of thought which explores and affirms the imagination, which we have only been able to cursorily unearth in this book, but which we will be making much more use of for political purposes sequentially. It is pointless sticking with the canon.

Revalorizing the imagination, and stressing its importance for the equipping of a subject capable of transcending the limits of the catastrophic imaginary, does not mean, either, that we are somehow in ignorance of the importance of the exercise of political reason for the manifestation of resistance to neoliberalism, now and in the future. It would be daft to want to wish away reason and the forms of knowledge it provides, or even to think that one could dispense with it, should one want to. It is reason that tells you when you are being abused, it is reason that tells you the life you are living is limited, the laws you are subject to are unjust, the disciplines you are made to conform to absurd, the power relations you are captured within suffocating, and so on. The conditions of suffering out of which political subjects emerge are not imaginary; they are real, material, known and felt. Kant did not invent reason. It does not belong to 'the Enlightenment'. It is an archaic instrument of human struggle and intelligence, honoured and celebrated in Western literature, poetry, thought and art, going back at least to Homer. It is also a discourse unto itself; a multiplicity and practice, constantly reinvented and redeployed to serve different purposes and signify different forms of intelligence at different times, as well as in different ways at the same time. Kant effectively degraded Reason, limiting it, trying to draw boundaries around it, deploying it discursively to signify the limited, finite nature of the human, and in the process limiting and degrading human understandings of the potentiality of progress and politics. We have to reappropriate it, once more. It would be an insult to those who most suffer the catastrophic nature of the world we now inhabit to suggest that they have to exercise their imagination to experience the cold blooded anger and hate out of which political subjectivity emerges. You know when you are being oppressed because reason speaks to you and tells you that 'this is how it is here'. But when it comes to the question of 'what is to be done?' about your suffering, the limitations of your form of life, reason will do little for you. Of course it will try to help you if you ask it, carefully calculating for you the particular ways and means by which you might proceed out of your conditions of injustice and subjection on the basis of what it knows and can tell you of this world. But on that basis, it will only ever lead you back, one way or another, to this world, and forms of life conditional to this world.

That is the story of reason which Homer's *Odyssey* told us more than 2,000 years ago. If you want to be Odysseus, go round in circles, reason then is the very best of friends. To paraphrase Oscar Wilde, the reasonable subject always knows where he is going and he always gets there because he ends up going nowhere in particular but here.[35] He clings to the life that he possesses, and the world he inhabits, being very successful in navigating the twists and turns of this world, forever adapting its form of life to the challenges and obstacles the world throws at it. But when it comes to the question of giving you access to another life, and another world, he cannot help you. That requires the taking of a subjective path and the transformative powers of the imagination. Reason imagines nothing. It cannot create and thus it cannot transform. And, of course, reason also knows that. It is reason which tells you that these are its limits. It is not made for opening up new worlds, but enabling us to survive present ones. That is all it is tasked with and intended for. So don't ask it to do or perform that which it is not crafted for, even if it will try to help, should you ask it. There are plenty of problems in the course of life for which reason is perfectly adequate. But collective political transformation is not one of them. For that we need to turn to the imagination. Reason itself tells us of this inadequacy. It says, 'I am Reason, ask me to help you, and I will do my best, because I am reasonable, but know that in being reasonable, I am also limited, and know that there is another power, different to myself, defined indeed by everything which I am not, and which you should ask, if the transformation of the limits of this world is your problem. Its name is the imagination'. That turn, from reason to imagination, is itself founded upon rational knowledge of the limits of reason, and thus it is a product of the evolution of reason, its maturity, capacity to disincline itself, and abdicate responsibility for political subjectivity and action. We owe it to reason and its own self-deprecation to follow the path of Imagination.

There is a further utility to reason which we want to highlight here, in concluding. What fascinates and disturbs us, when we look today at so-called radical political thought, and what has partly incited us into writing this book, is not just the poverty, but the inadequacy of its imaginaries, the emptiness of the visions of what new forms of political subjectivity and ways of being together it provides for us, and thus the weakness of new fronts being opened up, in conditions of struggle. These are, we think, strategic mistakes being made today by the Left, which can only lead people suffering at the brunt end of neoliberal governance down dead ends. The inadequacy of those visions is also something which we can only recognize through the deployment of reason. We can see, through the deployment of a higher more savvy form of political reason, the extent to which our imaginations remain governed, complicit with dominant liberal epistemologies of power. In a sense, that is precisely what this book has been aimed at doing; showing how discourses of vulnerability, resilience and adaptivity cannot provide for a form of political subjectivity capable of outliving, meaningfully, the neoliberal subject. And yet it is precisely these discourses, these ways of imagining what the human is fundamentally, and can become, that are fuelling the so-called imagination of counter-liberal thought. Mere talk of the imagination, imaginaries and visions is cheap. We have to deploy the coldness of reason to sort out the good from the bad prophets, and govern, ourselves, the circulation of cliché in the dream life of the subject, such that the imagination can be quality controlled. Every idiot dreams; the question is which image of thought works, the destruction of cliché, and the production of new worlds and new forms of life. And that is a strategic-poetic problematic for which reason is indispensible; we have to know back to front, and inside-out, the subject against which we are struggling, such that we do not merely recuperate it. Poetry does not emerge free forming, it is itself a craft. Thus there has to be a kind of constant frenetic audit, and analysis even, of the function of the imagination. We have to know ourselves back to front and inside out. The risk is that we place unrequited faith in what goes by the name of imagination, but which is all too reasonable in its conformity with dominant and disempowering images of the human.

But this is not to say that the problem of politics today is simply a question of constructing, philosophically, an alternative image of the human, replete with political potentiality, in the practical reality of its absence. The liberal image of the human, degraded and incapable of action and meaningful creation, is the real chimera. Liberal regimes are putting so much effort into imagining the necessity and possibility of the resilient subject, equipped only ever to adapt to a world outside its control, because in reality the real world is a human one, replete with politics, creativity, action, imagination and transformative potential. Liberalism imagines the possibility of a world where humans are stripped of their imaginations, and led to live merely resilient, adaptive lives. But the reality is that life is not led that way, anywhere, by anyone. Odysseus, as he himself said, is 'no-one' and 'nothing'. He does not exist and cannot be found, anywhere. We are living out the final scenes of the liberal nightmare in all its catastrophic permutations. It is obvious that its images are imploding and that the idea of the liberal subject is exhausted. One would have to believe political philosophers to think otherwise. Think practically, pay attention to the realities of the world we live in, the struggles which are building, the new forms of human life and politics that are erupting, and we can see the conceit on which the image of the human still sheltered in the liberal academy rests. It may be that, as Deleuze argued, and as is attested to in the epigraph to the book, 'believing in this world, this life' is the most difficult task facing philosophers and political thinkers today. But the reality is that this world and this life imagined for us by liberal philosophers and political thinkers is already, if not yet finished, then so nearly finished. Our task, the political task of our times, remains learning to live finally, to thrive beyond the catastrophe of our times, such that we may announce the death of liberalism and welcome with confidence a more poetic subjectivity.

Notes

1 Anthropocene

1 Friedrich Nietzsche, *On the Genealogy of Morals* (Indianapolis, IN: Hackett Publishing, 1998).
2 Brad Evans, *Liberal Terror* (Cambridge: Polity Press, 2013).
3 Paul Crutzen and Christian Schwagerl, 'A New Global Ethos'. Available at: http://e360.yale.edu/feature/living_in _the_anthropocene_toward_a_new_global_ethos/2363/
4 Johan Rockström, Will Steffen, Kevin Noone et al., 'Planetary Boundaries: Exploring the Safe Operating Space for Humanity', *Ecology and Society* 14(2) (2009), Article 32.
5 See Manuel De Landa, *1000 Years of Non-Linear History* (New York: Zone Books, 1997).
6 Slavoj Žižek, *Living in the End Times* (London: Verso, 2011), p. 331.
7 Intergovernmental Panel on Climate Change (IPCC), *Managing the Risks of Extreme Events and Disasters to Advance Climate Change Adaptation* (Cambridge: Cambridge University Press, 2012), p. 3.
8 IPCC, *Managing the Risks of Extreme Events and Disasters*, p. 32.
9 Žižek, *Living in the End Times*, pp. 332, 333.

10 IPCC, *Managing the Risks of Extreme Events and Disasters*, p. 33.

11 IPCC, *Managing the Risks of Extreme Events and Disasters*, p. 38.

12 See Giorgio Agamben, *Homo Sacer: Sovereign Power & Bare Life* (Stanford, CA: Stanford University Press, 1998).

13 Brad Evans and Mark Duffield, 'Bio-Spheric Security: How the Merger between Development, Security and the Environment [Desenex] is Retrenching Fortress Europe'. In P. Burgess and S. Gutwirth (eds) *A Threat Against Europe? Security, Migration and Integration* (Brussels: VUB Press, 2011).

14 http://www.un.org/esa/population/publications/longrange2/WorldPop2300final.pdf

15 Rockström et al., 'Planetary Boundaries', pp. 461, 472.

16 The British Government's *Stern Review* is an excellent example of this. Nicholas Stern, *The Stern Review: The Economics of Climate Change* (Cambridge: Cambridge University Press, 2007).

17 For excellent examples of Anthropocentric aesthetics (particularly the section on thresholds and boundaries), see http://www.anthropocene.info/en/home

18 http://www.stockholmresilience.org/publications/artiklar/howdefiningplanetaryboundariescantransformourapproachtogrowth.5.1e6281dd1341fd2212c80001738.html

19 Rockström et al., 'Planetary Boundaries'.

20 http://www.stockholmresilience.org/publications/artiklar/steeringawayfromcatastrophicthresholdsplanetaryboundariesforhumansurvival.5.fb3ee2f125e9da349a80002141.html

21 Alan Weisman, *The World Without Us* (New York: Picador, 2007), p. 4.

22 Sophocles, *Oedipus Rex* (Cambridge: Cambridge University Press, 2006).

23 Astra Taylor, *Examined Life* (New York: Zeitgeist Productions, 2008).

24 See Zygmunt Bauman, *Collateral Damage: Social Inequalities in a Global Age* (Cambridge: Polity, 2011).

25 Susan Neiman, *Evil in Modern Thought: An Alternative History* (Princeton, NJ: Princeton University Press, 2002).

26 Walter Benjamin, *Selected Writings: Volume 2 Part 2 – 1931–34* (Cambridge, MA: Harvard University Press, 2005), p. 538.

27 Fredric Jameson, 'The Politics of Utopia', *New Left Review* 25, January–February (2004).

28 Fredric Jameson, 'The Politics of Utopia'. Online at: http://newleftreview.org/II/25/fredric-jameson-the-politics -of-utopia

29 Martin Coward, 'Network-Centric Violence, Critical Infrastructure and the Urbanisation of Security', *Security Dialogue* 40(4–5) (2009), 399–418.

30 See Stephen Graham (ed.) *Disrupted Cities: When Infrastructure Fails* (Abingdon: Routledge, 2010).

31 Department of Homeland Security, The National Plan for Research and Development in Support of Critical Infrastructure Protection (2004), p. xi. Available at http://www.dhs .gov/xlibrary/assets/ST_2004_NCIP_RD_PlanFINALApr05 .pdf

32 Department of Homeland Security, The National Plan for Research and Development in Support of Critical Infrastructure Protection, p. 2.

33 Michael Dillon and Julian Reid, *The Liberal Way of War: Killing to Make Life Live* (London: Routledge, 2009), p. 130.

34 Mark Duffield, 'Total War as Environmental Terror: Linking Liberalism, Resilience, and the Bunker', *South Atlantic Quarterly* 110(3) (2011) 757–69.

35 Gilles Deleuze, *Desert Islands and Other Texts: 1953–1974* (New York: Semiotext(e), 2004), p. 17.

36 Friedrich Nietzsche, 'Ecce Homo'. In K. Ansell-Pearson and D. Large (eds) *The Nietzsche Reader* (Oxford: Blackwell Publishers, 2006), p. 514.

37 See Peter Sloterdijk, *Thinker on Stage: Nietzsche's Materialism* (Minneapolis, MN: University of Minnesota Press, 1989).

38 Juliette Kayyem, 'Never Say Never Again', *Foreign Policy* 10(9) (2012), Available at http://www.foreignpolicy.com/ articles/2012/09/10/never_say_never_again?page¼full# .UFIslAvZ-RY.twitter

39 http://blogs.wsj.com/washwire/2011/09/11/obamas-speech -on-the-anniversary-of-911/

40 Alain Badiou, *Infinite Thought* (London: Continuum, 2005), p. 48.

41 W.N. Adger, 'Social and Ecological Resilience: Are They Related?', *Progress in Human Geography* 24(3) (2000), p. 349.

42 Jeremy Walker and Melinda Cooper, 'Genealogies of Resilience: From Systems Ecology to the Political Economy of Crisis Adaptation', *Security Dialogue* 42(2) (2011) 143–60.

43 Cooper and Walker, "Genealogies of Resilience," 155

44 United Nations Development Programme, United Nations Environment Programme, World Bank and World Resources Institute, *World Resources 2008: Roots of Resilience – Growing the Wealth of the Poor* (Washington, DC: World Resources Institute, 2008), p. xi.

45 Mark Duffield, *Development, Security and Unending War: Governing the World of Peoples* (Cambridge: Polity Press, 2007), p. 103.

46 Duffield, *Development, Security and Unending War*, p. 69.

47 C. Folke, S. Carpenter, T. Elmqvist, L. Gunderson, C.S. Holling and B. Walker (2002), 'Resilience and Sustainable Development: Building Adaptive Capacity in a World of Transformations', *Ambio* 31(5), p. 438.

48 Folke et al., 'Resilience and Sustainable Development', p. 437.

49 United Nations Environment Programme (UNEP), *Exploring the Links: Human Well-Being, Poverty and Ecosystem Services* (Nairobi: UN Publications, 2004), p. 39.

50 Folke et al., 'Resilience and Sustainable Development', p. 439.

51 UNEP, *Exploring the Links*, p. 13.

52 UNEP, *Exploring the Links*, p. 15.

53 P. Pingali, L. Alinovi and J. Sutton, 'Food Security in Complex Emergencies: Enhancing Food System Resilience', *Disasters* 29(Suppl. 1) (2005), p. S18.

54 Pingali et al., 'Food Security in Complex Emergencies', p. S18.

55 UNEP, *Exploring the Links*, p. 39.

56 UNEP, *Exploring the Links*, p. 5.

57 UNEP, *Exploring the Links*, p. 20.

58 Nidhi Tandon, 'Biopolitics, Climate Change and Water Security: Impact, Vulnerability and Adaptation Issues for Women', *Agenda* 21(73) (2007), pp. 12–14.

2 Insecure by Design

1 Michel Foucault, *The Birth of Biopolitics: Lectures at the Collège de France 1978–1979* (Basingstoke and New York: Palgrave, 2008).
2 Foucault, *The Birth of Biopolitics*, pp. 271–2.
3 Tom Peters, *Thriving on Chaos: Handbook for a Management Revolution* (New York: Knopf, 1987).
4 Zygmunt Bauman, *Liquid Times: Living in an Age of Uncertainty* (Cambridge: Polity, 2007), p. 26.
5 Filippa Lenztos and Nikolas Rose, 'Governing Insecurity: Contingency Planning, Protection, Resistance', *Economy and Society* 38(2) (2009), p. 243.
6 Zygmunt Bauman, *Collateral Damage: Social Inequalities in a Global Age* (Cambridge: Polity, 2011), p. 48.
7 Henry Giroux, *Twilight of the Social* (Boulder, CO: Paradigm, 2012), p. 36.
8 Giroux, *Twilight of the Social*, p. 46.
9 Bauman, *Collateral Damage*, p. 17.
10 Mark Neocleous, ' "Don't be Scared, Be Prepared": Trauma, Anxiety, Resilience', *Alternatives* 37(3) (2012) 188–98.
11 Michel Foucault, *The Order of Things: An Archaeology of Human Sciences* (New York: Pantheon, 1971), p. 387.
12 J. Katz, 'The Digital Citizen', *Wired* (December 1997).
13 Manuel Castells, 'The Network Society: From Knowledge to Policy'. In Manuel Castells and Gustavo Cardoso (eds) *The Network Society: From Knowledge to Policy* (Washington, DC: Center for Transatlantic Relations, 2006), p. 11.
14 James N. Rosenau, 'Information Technologies and the Skills, Networks and Structures that Sustain World Affairs'. In James N. Rosenau and J.P. Singh (eds) *Information Technologies and Global Politics: The Changing Scope of Power and Governance* (Albany, NY: SUNY Press, 2002), p. 278.
15 See, in particular, James N. Rosenau, *People Count! Networked Individuals in Global Politics* (Boulder, CO: Paradigm Press, 2008).
16 Norbert Wiener, *The Human Use of Human Beings: Cybernetics and Society* (Boston, MA: Da Capo Press, 1954), p. 58.
17 Lily E. Kay, *Who Wrote the Book of Life?: A History of the Genetic Code* (Stanford, CA: Stanford University Press,

2000); N. Katherine Hayles, *How We Became Posthuman: Virtual Bodies in Cybernetics, Literature, and Informatics* (Chicago, IL: University of Chicago Press, 1999); Peter Galison, 'The Ontology of the Enemy: Norbert Wiener and the Cybernetic Vision', *Critical Inquiry* 21(1) (1994) 228–66.

18 Wiener, *The Human Use of Human Beings*, p. 64.

19 Galison, 'The Ontology of the Enemy'.

20 Lily E. Kay, *The Molecular Vision of Life: Caltech, The Rockefeller Foundation, and the Rise of New Biology* (Oxford: Oxford University Press, 1993).

21 Donna Haraway, *Simians, Cyborgs and Women: The Reinvention of Nature* (New York: Routledge, 1991).

22 Anthony Miccoli, *Posthuman Suffering and the Technological Embrace* (Lanham, MD: Lexington Books, 2010), p. x.

23 James Rosenau, 'Governance and Democracy in a Globalization World'. In Daniele Archibugi, David Held and Martin Kohler (eds) *Re-imagining Political Community: Studies in Cosmopolitan Democracy* (Stanford, CA: Stanford University Press, 1998), pp. 28–57.

24 Rosenau, 'Governance and Democracy in a Globalization World', p. 33.

25 Michel Foucault, *Security, Territory, Population: Lectures at the Collège de France 1977–78* (Basingstoke and New York: Palgrave, 2007), pp. 10–11.

26 Foucault, *Security, Territory, Population*, pp. 16–17.

27 Martin Heidegger, *The Question Concerning Technology and Other Essays* (New York: Harper & Row, 1977). See also Michael Dillon, *Politics of Security* (London and New York: Routledge, 1996).

28 Michael Dillon and Julian Reid, *The Liberal Way of War: Killing to Make Life Live* (London and New York: Routledge, 2009); Julian Reid, *The Biopolitics of the War on Terror: Life Struggles, Liberal Modernity and the Defence of Logistical Societies* (Manchester: Manchester University Press, 2006).

29 Miccoli, *Posthuman Suffering*, p. x.

30 Sugata Mitra, 'Self Organising Systems for Mass Computer Literacy: Findings from the "Hole in the Wall" Experiments', *International Journal of Development Issues* 4(1) (2005) 71–81; Sugata Mitra and Vivek Rana, (2001) 'Children and

the Internet: Experiments with Minimally Invasive Education in India', *British Journal of Educational Technology* 32(2) (2001) 221–32.

31 Thomas P.M. Barnett, *America and the World after Bush* (New York: Putnam, 2009), pp. 429–31.

32 Daniel Kennelly, 'Q&A with Thomas P.M. Barnett', *Doublethink* Summer (2003), p. 17.

33 Kennelly, 'Q&A with Thomas PM Barnett', p. 18.

34 Elaine Scarry, *The Body in Pain: The Making and Unmaking of the World* (Oxford: Oxford University Press, 1995), p. 152.

35 http://www.independent.co.uk/news/science/human-intelligence-peaked-thousands-of-years-ago-and-weve-been-on-an-intellectual-and-emotional-decline-ever-since-8307101.html

36 Al Siebert, *The Resiliency Advantage: Master Change, Thrive under Pressure, Bounce Back from Setbacks* (San Francisco, CA: Berrett-Koehler, 2005), pp. 1–2.

37 Isaiah Berlin, 'Two Concepts of Liberty'. In *Four Essays on Liberty* (Oxford: Oxford University Press, 1969), p. 131.

38 Melinda Cooper, *Life as Surplus: Biotechnology and Capitalism in the Neoliberal Era* (Seattle, WA: Washington University Press, 2008), pp. 45–50.

39 Kay, *Who Wrote the Book of Life?*; Hayles, *How We Became Posthuman*.

40 Stuart A. Kauffman, *Investigations* (Oxford: Oxford University Press, 2000), p. 157.

41 W.N. Adger, 'Social and Ecological Resilience: Are They Related?', *Progress in Human Geography* 24(3) (2000), p. 349.

42 Michel Foucault, *The Birth of Biopolitics: Lectures at the Collège de France 1978–1979* (Basingstoke and New York: Palgrave, 2008), p. 66.

43 Foucault, *The Birth of Biopolitics*, p. 65.

44 Nicholas J. Kiersey, 'Neoliberal Political Economy and the Subjectivity of Crisis: Why Governmentality is Not Hollow', *Global Society* 23(4) (2009), p. 365

45 Kiersey, 'Neoliberal Political Economy and the Subjectivity of Crisis', p. 381.

46 Philip Buckle, 'Assessing Social Resilience'. In Douglas Patton and David Johnson, *Disaster Resilience: An*

Integrated Approach (Springfield, IL: Charles C. Thomas, 2006), p. 101.

3 The Poverty of Vulnerability

1 Sanjeev Khagram, William C. Clark and Dana Firas Raad, 'From the Environment and Human Security to Sustainable Security and Development', *Journal of Human Development* 4(2) (2003) 289–313; Thomas N. Gladwin, James J. Kennelly and Tara-Shelomith Krause, 'Shifting Paradigms for Sustainable Development: Implications for Management Theory and Research', *The Academy of Management Review* 20(4) (1995) 874–907; Edward B. Barbier and Anil Markandya, 'The Conditions for Achieving Environmentally Sustainable Development', *European Economic Review* 34(2–3) (1990) 659–69; C. Folke and N. Kautsky, 'The Role of Ecosystems for a Sustainable Development of Aquaculture', *Ambio* 18(4) (1989) 234–43.

2 United Nations Office for Disaster Risk Reduction (UN/ ISDR), *Living with Risk: A Global Review of Disaster Reduction Initiatives* (Geneva: United Nations, 2004), Ch. 1, S. 1, p. 17.

3 C. Folke, S. Carpenter, T. Elmqvist, L. Gunderson, C.S. Holling and B. Walker (2002), 'Resilience and Sustainable Development: Building Adaptive Capacity in a World of Transformations', *Ambio* 31(5), p. 437.

4 Mark Neocleous, *Critique of Security* (Edinburgh, Edinburgh University Press, 2008), p. 186.

5 World Commission on Environment and Development (WCED), *Our Common Future* (Oxford: Oxford University Press, 1987).

6 Khagram et al., 'From the Environment and Human Security to Sustainable Security and Development', pp. 296–7.

7 Robert O'Brien, Anne Marie Goetz, Jan Aart Scholte and Marc Williams, *Contesting Global Governance: Multilateral Economic Institutions and Social Movements* (Cambridge: Cambridge University Press, 2000), pp. 109–58.

8 Mark Duffield, *Development, Security and Unending War: Governing the World of Peoples* (Cambridge: Polity Press, 2007), pp. 67–70.

9 Duffield, *Development, Security and Unending War*, p. 67.

10 Duffield, *Development, Security and Unending War*, p. 69.
11 Duffield, *Development, Security and Unending War*, p. 69.
12 Duffield, *Development, Security and Unending War*, p. 93.
13 Duffield, *Development, Security and Unending War*, pp. 4–8.
14 David Harvey, 'Neoliberalism as Creative Destruction', *The ANNALS of the American Academy of Political and Social Science* 610 (2007) 22–44.
15 Marie-José Mondzain, *Image, Icon, Economy: The Byzantine Origins of the Contemporary Imaginary* (Stanford, CA: Stanford University Press, 2005), p. 19.
16 Mondzain, *Image, Icon, Economy*, p. 19.
17 Giorgio Agamben, *The Kingdom and the Glory: For a Theological Genealogy of Economy and Government* (Stanford, CA: Stanford University Press, 2011), p. 50.
18 Michael Dillon and Julian Reid, *The Liberal Way of War: Killing to Make Life Live* (London and New York: Routledge, 2009); Duffield, *Development, Security and Unending War*; Melinda Cooper, *Life as Surplus: Biotechnology and Capitalism in the Neoliberal Era* (Seattle, WA: Washington University Press, 2008); Julian Reid, *The Biopolitics of the War on Terror: Life Struggles, Liberal Modernity and the Defence of Logistical Societies* (Manchester: Manchester University Press, 2006).
19 United Nations Environment Programme (UNEP), *Exploring the Links: Human Well-Being, Poverty and Ecosystem Services* (Nairobi: UN Publications, 2004).
20 James N. Rosenau, *People Count! Networked Individuals in Global Politics* (Boulder, CO: Paradigm Press, 2008); James N. Rosenau, 'Information Technologies and the Skills, Networks and Structures that Sustain World Affairs'. In James N. Rosenau and J.P. Singh (eds) *Information Technologies and Global Politics: The Changing Scope of Power and Governance* (Albany, NY: SUNY Press, 2002); James N. Rosenau, 'Citizenship in a Changing Global Order'. In James N. Rosenau and Ernst Otto Czempiel, *Governance Without Government: Order and Change in World Politics* (Cambridge: Cambridge University Press, 1992), 272–94.
21 Nidhi Tandon, 'Biopolitics, Climate Change and Water Security: Impact, Vulnerability and Adaptation Issues for Women', *Agenda* 21(73) (2007), p. 12.

22 UN/ISDR, *Living with Risk*, Ch. 1, S. 2, p. 18.
23 UN/ISDR, *Living with Risk*, Ch. 1, S. 2, p. 20.
24 UN/ISDR, *Living with Risk*, Ch. 3, S. 4, p. 1.
25 UN/ISDR, *Living with Risk*, Ch. 3, S. 4, p. 20.
26 UN/ISDR, *Living with Risk*, Ch. 2, S. 1, p. 4.
27 John W. Handmer and Stephen R. Dovers, 'A Typology of Resilience: Rethinking Institutions for Sustainable Development', *Organization & Environment* 9(4) (1996) 482–511.
28 Handmer and Dovers, 'A Typology of Resilience'.
29 Barrington Moore, *Injustice: The Social Bases of Obedience and Revolt* (White Plains, NY: M.E. Sharpe, 1978), p. 66.
30 Moore, *Injustice*, p. 459.
31 Moore, *Injustice*, p. 66.
32 Ellen J. Langer and Jane Roth, 'Heads I Win, Tails It's Chance: The Illusion of Control as a Function of the Sequence of Outcomes in a Purely Chance Task', *Journal of Personality and Social Psychology* 32(6) (1975) 951–5.
33 Paul Krugman, *The Self-Organizing Economy* (Oxford: Basil Blackwell, 1996).
34 W. Brian Arthur, Steven Durlauf and David Lane (eds) *The Economy as an Evolving Complex System II* (Menlo Park, CA: Addison-Wesley, 1997).
35 Gregoire Nicolis and Ilya Prigogine, *Exploring Complexity: An Introduction* (New York: W.H. Freeman, 1989), p. 238.
36 Naomi Klein, *The Shock Doctrine: The Rise of Disaster Capitalism* (London: Allen Lane, 2007), p. 414.
37 John Walton and Charles Ragin, 'Global and National Sources of Political Protest: Third World Responses to the Debt Crisis', *American Sociological Review* 55(6) (1990), p. 877.
38 Zygmunt Bauman, *Liquid Fear* (Cambridge: Polity Press, 2006).
39 Henry Giroux, *Stormy Weather: Katrina and the Politics of Disposability* (Boulder, CO: Paradigm, 2006), p. 30.
40 John Leslie, 'After Sandy: Political Storm Coming?' *Socialist Organizer*, 5 November 2012.
41 Alex Koppelman, 'Sandy's Forgotten', *The New Yorker*, 1 November 2012. Available at http://www.newyorker.com/online/blogs/newsdesk/2012/11/the-baruch-houses-after-sandy.html#ixzz2HZanQKui

42 Henry A. Giroux, 'Hurricane Sandy in the Age of Disposability and Neoliberal Terror', *Truthout*, 3 December 2012.
   Available at http://truth-out.org/opinion/item/13025-hurric
   ane-sandy-in-the-age-of-disposability#VII

4 Living Dangerously

1 Kathleen Woodward, 'Statistical Panic', *Differences: A
   Journal of Feminist Cultural Studies* 11(2) (1999), p. 180.
2 Frank Kermode, *The Sense of an Ending: Studies in the
   Theory of Fiction*, 2nd edn (Oxford: Oxford University
   Press, 2003), p. 83.
3 Alice Park, 'The Two Faces of Anxiety', *Time Magazine*, 5
   December 2011. Available at http://www.time.com/time/
   magazine/article/0,9171,2100106,00.html#ixzz2HeiRoQAS
4 Park, 'The Two Faces of Anxiety'.
5 Cathy Caruth (ed.), *Trauma: Explorations in Memory*
   (Baltimore, MD: Johns Hopkins University Press, 1995).
6 Jeffrey Prager, *Presenting The Past: Psychoanalysis and the
   Sociology of Remembering* (Cambridge, MA: Harvard University Press, 1998).
7 Primo Levi, *The Drowned and the Saved* (New York:
   Random House, 1989), p. 24.
8 Caruth, *Trauma*, p. 152.
9 Jean Laplanche and Jean-Bertrand Pontalis, *The Language
   of Psychoanalysis* (London: Karnac Books, 1988),
   pp. 467–8.
10 Ruth Leys, *Trauma: A Genealogy* (Chicago, IL: University
   of Chicago Press, 2000), pp. 8–9.
11 Leys, *Trauma*, p. 10
12 Jenny Edkins, *Trauma; Memory, Trauma and World Politics:
   Reflections on the Relationship between Past and Present*,
   2nd edn (Basingstoke: Palgrave Macmillan, 2010), p. 4.
13 Alphonso Lingis, *The Community of Those Who Have
   Nothing in Common* (Indianapolis, IN: Indianapolis University Press, 1994), p. 12.
14 Susannah Radstone, 'Trauma Theory: Contexts, Politics,
   Ethics'. *Paragraph* 30(1) (2007), p. 20.
15 Sally Squires, 'Midlife Without a Crisis', *Washington Post*,
   19 April 1999. Available at http://www.washingtonpost.
   com/wp-srv/health/seniors/stories/midlife042099.htm

16 Fiona Macrae, 'Quarter-life Crisis Hits Three in Four of Those Aged 26 to 30', *Mail Online*, 5 May 2011. Available at http://www.dailymail.co.uk/news/article-1289659/Quarter-life-crisis-hits-26-30-year-olds.html

17 Sheila Martineau, *Rewriting Resilience: A Critical Discourse Analysis of Childhood Resilience and the Politics of Teaching Resilience to 'Kids at Risk'* (Vancouver: University of British Columbia Press, 1999).

18 Steven J. Condly, 'Resilience in Children: A Review of Literature with Implications for Education', *Urban Education* 41(3) (2006), p. 214.

19 Sula Wolff, 'The Concept of Resilience', *Australian & New Zealand Journal of Psychiatry* 29(4) (1995), p. 568.

20 Margaret C. Wang, Geneva D. Haertel and Herbert J. Walberg, 'Educational Resilience in Inner Cities'. In Margaret C. Wang and Edmund W. Gordon (eds) *Educational Resilience in Inner-City America: Challenges and Prospects* (Mahwah, NJ: Lawrence Erlbaum, 1994), p. 46.

21 See, in particular, Norman Garmezy, 'Vulnerability Research and the Issue of Primary Prevention', *American Journal of Orthopsychiatry* 41(1) (1971) 101–16; and Norman Garmezy, 'Resilience in Children's Adaptation to Negative Life Events and Stressed Environments', *Pediatric Annals*, 20(9) (1991) 459–66.

22 Condly, 'Resilience in Children', p. 219.

23 Martineau, *Rewriting Resilience*, p. 2.

24 Martineau, *Rewriting Resilience*, p. 9.

25 Henry A. Giroux, *America's Education Deficit and the War on Youth* (Boulder, CO: Paradigm Publishers, 2013), p. xiii.

26 Giroux, *America's Education Deficit*, p. xiv.

27 John Holloway, *Change the World Without Taking Power: The Meaning of Revolution Today* (London: Pluto Press, 2005).

28 Alain Badiou, *In Praise of Love* (London: Serpents Tail, 2012).

29 Judith Butler, *Precarious Life: The Powers of Mourning and Violence* (London and New York: Verso, 2006).

30 Judith Butler, *Frames of War: When Is Life Grievable?* (London: Verso, 2009), pp. 28–9.

31 Butler, *Frames of War*, p. 14.

32 Hamilton Bean, Lisa Keränen and Margaret Durfy, ' "This Is London": Cosmopolitan Nationalism and the Discourse of Resilience in the Case of the 7/7 Terrorist Attacks', *Rhetoric & Public Affairs* 14(3) (2011), p. 424.
33 Roberto Esposito, *Immunitas: The Protection and Negation of Life* (Cambridge: Polity, 2011).
34 Esposito, *Immunitas*, p. 8.
35 Esposito, *Immunitas*, p. 10.
36 Esposito, *Immunitas*, p. 33.
37 Esposito, *Immunitas*, p. 113.
38 Roberto Esposito, 'Immunization and Violence', p. 7. Available at http://aphelis.net/immunization-violence-roberto-esposito-2008/
39 René Girard, *Violence and the Sacred* (London: Continuum, 2005), p. 73.
40 Girard, *Violence and the Sacred*, p. 73.
41 Girard, *Violence and the Sacred*, pp. 74, 76.
42 Paul Virilio, *The Futurism of the Instant* (Cambridge: Polity Press, 2010), pp. 74, 75.
43 Virilio, *The Futurism of the Instant*, p. 3.
44 Friedrich Nietzsche, *The Will To Power* (New York: Vintage, 1968), p. 7.
45 Gilles Deleuze, *Nietzsche and Philosophy* (London: Continuum, 2006), p. xii.
46 Peter Sloterdijk, *Rage and Time* (New York: Columbia University Press, 2012).
47 Drucilla Cornell, 'The Thinker of the Future – Introduction to *The Violence of the Masquerade: Law Dressed Up as Justice*', *German Law Journal* 6(1) (2005), p. 126.

5 Atmos

1 Gernot Böhme, 'Atmosphere as the Fundamental Concept to a New Aesthetics', *Thesis Eleven* 36(1) (1993) 113–26.
2 See Kriss Ravetto, *The Unmaking of Fascist Aesthetics* (Minneapolis, MN: University of Minnesota Press, 2001).
3 Peter Sloterdijk, *Spheres II: Globes* (New York: Semiotext(e), 2010), p. 353.
4 Nigel Thrift, 'Peter Sloterdijk and the Philosopher's Stone'. In Stuart Elden (ed.) *Sloterdijk Now* (Cambridge: Polity Press, 2012), p. 142.

5 Jacques Rancière, *The Emancipated Spectator* (London: Verso, 2009), p. 102.

6 Jonathan Glanecy, 'Our Last Occupation', *The Guardian*, 19 April 2003. Available at http://www.guardian.co.uk/world/2003/apr/19/iraq.arts

7 Mark Duffield, 'Total War as Environmental Terror: Linking Liberalism, Resilience, and the Bunker', *South Atlantic Quarterly* 110(3) (2011) 757–769.

8 Duffield, 'Environmental Terror'.

9 Nicolai Rusin and Liia Flit, *Man Versus Climate* (Moscow: Peace Publishers, 1966).

10 Le Thi Nham Tuyet and Annika Johansson, 'Impact of Chemical Warfare with Agent Orange on Women's Productive Lives in Vietnam: A Pilot Study', *Reproductive Health Matters* 9 (2001) 156–64.

11 Available Online at: http://www.un-documents.net/enmod.htm

12 Michel Chossudovsky, 'Weather Warfare: Beware the US Military's Experiments with Climatic Warfare', *The Ecologist* (December 2007).

13 http://www.haarp.alaska.edu/haarp/gen.html

14 Bruno Latour, *Air*. Available at http://www.bruno-latour.fr/sites/default/files/P-115-AIR-SENSORIUMpdf.pdf

15 Latour, *Air*.

16 Böhme, 'Atmosphere as the Fundamental Concept to a New Aesthetics'.

17 Barack Obama, 'Transcript: Obama's Victory Speech'. Available at http://politicalticker.blogs.cnn.com/2012/11/07/transcript-obamas-victory-speech/

18 See Sergey Gavrilets, *Fitness Landscapes and the Origin of Species* (Princeton, NJ: Princeton University Press, 2004).

19 Martin E.P. Seligman, 'Building Resilience', *Harvard Business Review* (April 2011). Available at http://hbr.org/2011/04/building-resilience/ar/1

20 Mark Neocleous, 'Resisting Resilience', *Radical Philosophy* (April 2013). Available at http://www.radicalphilosophy.com/commentary/resisting-resilience

21 Zygmunt Bauman, *Modernity and the Holocaust* (Cambridge: Polity Press, 1991), p. 21.

22 Brad Evans and Julian Reid, *Deleuze and Fascism: Security, War, Aesthetics* (London: Routledge, 2013).

23 Manuel De Landa, *1000 Years of Non-Linear History* (New York: Zone Books, 1997).
24 Felix Guattari, 'The Three Ecologies', *New Formations* 8 (1989), p. 134.
25 Guattari, 'The Three Ecologies', p. 131.

6 Endgames

1 James Hansen, *Storms of my Grandchildren: The Truth about the Coming Climate Catastrophe and Our Last Chance to Save Humanity* (London: Bloomsbury, 2009); Samuel Beckett, *Endgame* (London: Faber & Faber, 2009).
2 Johan Rockström, Will Steffen, Kevin Noone et al., 'Planetary Boundaries: Exploring the Safe Operating Space for Humanity', *Ecology and Society* 14(2) (2009), Article 32.
3 Rockström et al., 'Planetary Boundaries'.
4 John Bellamy Foster, 'Capitalism and Environmental Catastrophe', *Monthly Review*, 29 October 2011. Available at http://mrzine.monthlyreview.org/2011/foster291011.html
5 Hansen, *Storms of my Grandchildren*, p. 11.
6 Foster, 'Capitalism and Environmental Catastrophe'.
7 Hansen, *Storms of my Grandchildren*, p. 144.
8 Al Gore, 'Nobel Lecture', Oslo, 10 December 2007.
9 Beckett, *Endgame*, p. 1.
10 As attempted by, for example, Patrick J. Michaels, *Meltdown: The Predictable Distortion of Global Warming by Scientists, Politicians, and the Media* (Washington, DC: Cato Institute, 2004).
11 Michel Foucault, *The Courage of the Truth* (trans. Graham Burchell) (New York: Palgrave Macmillan, 2011), p. 15.
12 Foucault, *The Courage of the Truth*, p. 16.
13 Foucault, *The Courage of the Truth*, p. 29.
14 Foucault, *The Courage of the Truth*, p. 29.
15 Dipesh Chakrabarty, 'The Climate History: Four Theses', *Critical Inquiry* (Winter 2009), p. 218.
16 Rockström et al., 'Planetary Boundaries'.
17 Ray Brassier, *Nihil Unbound: Enlightenment and Extinction* (New York: Palgrave Macmillan, 2007), pp. 49–50.
18 Anthony D. Barnosky, Nicholas Matzke, Susumu Tomiya, Guinevere O.U. Wogan, Brian Swartz, Tiago B. Quental,

Charles Marshall, Jenny L. McGuire, Emily L. Lindsey, Kaitlin C. Maguire, Ben Mersey and Elizabeth A. Ferrer, 'Has the Earth's sixth mass extinction already arrived?', *Nature* 471(7336) 51–7.

19 Friedrich Nietzsche, *On Truth and Lies in a Nonmoral Sense* (Chicago, IL: Aristeus Books, 2012).

20 Friedrich Nietzsche, *The Will To Power* (New York: Vintage, 1968), p. 15.

21 Nietzsche, *On Truth and Lies in a Nonmoral Sense*

22 Tim Flannery, 'As Australia Burns, attitudes are changing. But is it too late?' *The Guardian*, 12 January 2013, p. 34.

23 Charles McGrath, 'At World's End, Honing a Father-Son Dynamic', *The New York Times*, 27 May 2008. http://www.nytimes.com/2008/05/27/movies/27road.html?_r=0

24 Evan Calder Williams, *Combined and Uneven Apocalypse* (Winchester and Washington: Zero Books, 2011), p. 4.

25 Barrington Moore, *Injustice: The Social Bases of Obedience and Revolt* (White Plains, NY: M.E. Sharpe, 1978), p. 459.

26 John R. Hall, *Apocalypse: From Antiquity to the Empire of Modernity* (Cambridge: Polity Press, 2009), pp. 1–3.

27 Jacob Taubes, *Occidental Eschatology* (Stanford, CA: Stanford University Press, 2009), p. 43.

28 Erik Swyngedouw, 'Apocalypse Forever? Post-Political Populism and the Spectre of Climate Change', *Theory, Culture & Society* 27(2–3) (2010) 213–32.

29 Taubes, *Occidental Eschatology*, p. 48.

30 Benjamin Noys, 'Apocalypse, Tendency, Crisis', *Mute* 15 (2010). Available at http://www.eurozine.com/articles/2010-05-26-noys-en.html

31 Julian Reid, 'The Degraded and Politically Debased Neoliberal Subject of Resilience', *Development Dialogue* 58 (Spring 2012) 67–79.

32 Quoted in '"Grolar" Bears & "Narluga" Whales? – Arctic Warming May Promote Hybrid Animals. Available at http://planetsave.com/2011/02/24/grolar-bears-amp-narluga-whales-arctic-warming-may-promote-hybrid-animals-video/#yvMmRpeyKrL1M86B.99 (accessed 26 September 2013).

33 Paul Virilio, *Grey Ecology* (New York: Atropos Press, 2011), p. 35.

7 Art of Politics

1 Gaston Bachelard, *The Psychoanalysis of Fire* (Boston, MA: Beacon Press, 1964).
2 See Victoria C. Gardner Coates, Kenneth Lapatin and Jon L. Seydl, *The Last Days of Pompeii: Decadence, Apocalypse, Resurrection* (Los Angeles, CA: J. Paul Getty Museum, 2012).
3 Interview with Peter Sloterdijk by Stephan Schmidt-Wulffen, in Jean Baudrillard, Hans-Georg Gadamer et al., *Art & Philosophy* (Milan: Giancarlo Politi Editore, 1991), pp. 117–18.
4 Friedrich Nietzsche, *The Gay Science* (New York: Vintage Books, 1974), p. 301.
5 Stephen Barker, *Autoaesthetics: Strategies of the Self after Nietzsche* (Atlantic Highlands, NJ: Humanities Press, 1992), p. 5.
6 Michel Foucault, 'On the Genealogy of Ethics'. In *The Essential Works of Michel Foucault, vol. 1: Ethics: Subjectivity and Truth*, ed. Paul Rabinow (New York: The New Press, 1997).
7 Simon Critchley, *The Faith of the Faithless: Experiments in Political Theology* (London: Verso, 2012).
8 Todd May, 'The Meaningfulness of Lives', *The New York Times*, Opinionator, 11 September 2011. Available at http://opinionator.blogs.nytimes.com/2011/09/11/the-meaning fulness-of-lives/?ref=opinion
9 Peter Sloterdijk, *Neither Sun Nor Death* (Cambridge, MA: MIT Press, 2011).
10 Gilles Deleuze, 'The Exhausted' in *Essays Critical and Clinical* (Minneapolis, MN: Minnesota University Press,1998), p. 162.
11 Deleuze, 'The Exhausted', p. 153.
12 Deleuze, 'The Exhausted', p. 163.
13 Evan Calder Williams, *Combined and Uneven Apocalypse* (Winchester and Washington: Zero Books, 2011).
14 Fredric Jameson, *The Geopolitical Aesthetic: Cinema and Space in the World System* (Bloomington, IN: Indiana University Press, 1992).
15 Gilles Deleuze, *Cinema 1: The Movement-Image* (London and New York: Continuum, 2005); Gilles Deleuze, *Cinema*

2: *The Time-Image* (London: Athlone Press, 1989); Julian Reid, 'A People of Seers: The Political Aesthetics of Postwar Cinema Revisited', *Cultural Politics* 7(2) (2011) 219–38.

16 Gilles Deleuze and Feliz Guattari, *A Thousand Plateaus: Capitalism and Schizophrenia* (London: Athlone Press, 1988).

17 Judith Butler, *Antigone's Claim: Kinship between Life & Death* (New York: Columbia University Press, 2000).

18 Bonnie Honig, 'Antigone's Laments, Creon's Grief: Mourning, Membership and the Politics of Exception', *Political Theory* 37(1) (2009) 5–43.

19 Honig, 'Antigone's Laments', p. 6.

20 Michel Foucault, *The Courage of the Truth* (trans. Graham Burchell) (New York: Palgrave Macmillan, 2011), p. 188.

21 William E. Connolly, *A World of Becoming* (Durham: Duke University Press, 2011), pp. 148–75.

22 Deleuze, *Cinema 2*, p. 222.

23 Deleuze, *Cinema 2*, pp. 222–3.

24 Foucault, *The Courage of the Truth*, p. 226.

25 In this sense, as Pucci notes: 'Recent critics generally agree that the oracle does not constitute a predestination, and that Oedipus has always been free'. Pietro Pucci, *Oedipus and the Fabrication of the Father: Oedipus Tyrannus in Modern Criticism and Philosophy* (Baltimore, MD: The Johns Hopkins University Press, 1992).

26 Marjorie W. Champlin, '*Oedipus Tyrannus* and the Problem of Knowledge', *The Classical Journal* 64(8) (1969), p. 339.

27 Mikhail Iampolski, *The Memory of Tiresias: Intertextuality and Film* (Berkeley, CA: University of California Press, 1998), p. 55.

28 Quoted in Iampolski, *The Memory of Tiresias*, p. 56.

29 Iampolski, *The Memory of Tiresias*, p. 235.

30 Phil Hoad, 'A Prophet shows us a multilingual future for cinema', *The Guardian*, film blog, 28 January 2010. Available at http://www.theguardian.com/film/filmblog/2010/jan/28/jacques-audiard-a-prophet

31 Jérôme Segal, 'Film festivals in the evolution of a common transnational identity', The 4th Annual Conference on 'Cultural Production in a Global Context: The Worldwide Film Industries', Grenoble Ecole de Management, Grenoble, France, 3–5 June 2010.

32 Hoad, 'A Prophet shows us a multilingual future for cinema'.
33 Jacques Derrida, *The Politics of Friendship* (London: Verso, 2006), p. 29.
34 Paulo Freire, *Pedagogy of the Oppressed* (Harmondsworth: Penguin, 1996).
35 Oscar Wilde, *De Profundis* (Ware, Hertfordshire: Wordsworth Classics, 1999).

Select Bibliography

Agamben, Giorgio, *Homo Sacer: Sovereign Power & Bare Life* (Stanford, CA: Stanford University Press, 1998).

Agamben, Giorgio, *The Kingdom and the Glory: For a Theological Genealogy of Economy and Government* (Stanford, CA: Stanford University Press, 2011).

Arthur, W. Brian, Steven Durlauf and David Lane (eds) *The Economy as an Evolving Complex System II* (Menlo Park, CA: Addison-Wesley, 1997).

Bachelard, Gaston, *The Psychoanalysis of Fire* (Boston, MA: Beacon Press, 1964).

Badiou, Alain, *Infinite Thought* (London: Continuum, 2005).

Badiou, Alain, *In Praise of Love* (London: Serpents Tail, 2012).

Barker, Stephen, *Autoaesthetics: Strategies of the Self after Nietzsche* (Atlantic Highlands, NJ: Humanities Press, 1992).

Barnett, Thomas P.M., *America and the World after Bush* (New York: Putnam, 2009).

Bauman, Zygmunt, *Modernity and the Holocaust* (Cambridge: Polity Press, 1991).

Bauman, Zygmunt, *Liquid Fear* (Cambridge: Polity Press, 2006).

Bauman, Zygmunt, *Liquid Times: Living in an Age of Uncertainty* (Cambridge: Polity, 2007).

Bauman, Zygmunt, *Collateral Damage: Social Inequalities in a Global Age* (Cambridge: Polity, 2011).

Beckett, Samuel, *Endgame* (London: Faber & Faber, 2009).

Benjamin, Walter, *Selected Writings: Volume 2 Part 2 – 1931–34* (Cambridge, MA: Harvard University Press, 2005).

Berlin, Isaiah, 'Two Concepts of Liberty'. In *Four Essays on Liberty* (Oxford: Oxford University Press, 1969).

Brassier, Ray, *Nihil Unbound: Enlightenment and Extinction* (New York: Palgrave Macmillan, 2007).

Buckle, Philip, 'Assessing Social Resilience'. In Douglas Patton and David Johnson, *Disaster Resilience: An Integrated Approach* (Springfield, IL: Charles C. Thomas, 2006).

Butler, Judith, *Antigone's Claim: Kinship between Life & Death* (New York: Columbia University Press, 2000).

Butler, Judith, *Precarious Life: The Powers of Mourning and Violence* (London and New York: Verso, 2006).

Butler, Judith, *Frames of War: When Is Life Grievable?* (London: Verso, 2009).

Caruth, Cathy (ed.), *Trauma: Exploration sin Memory* (Baltimore, MD: Johns Hopkins University Press, 1995).

Castells, Manuel, 'The Network Society: From Knowledge to Policy'. In Manuel Castells and Gustavo Cardoso (eds) *The Network Society: From Knowledge to Policy* (Washington, DC: Center for Transatlantic Relations, 2006).

Connolly, William E., *A World of Becoming* (Durham: Duke University Press, 2011).

Cooper, Melinda, *Life as Surplus: Biotechnology and Capitalism in the Neoliberal Era* (Seattle, WA: Washington University Press, 2008).

Critchley, Simon, *The Faith of the Faithless: Experiments in Political Theology* (London: Verso, 2012).

De Landa, Manuel, *1000 Years of Non-Linear History* (New York: Zone Books, 1997).

Deleuze, Gilles, *Cinema 2: The Time-Image* (London: Athlone Press, 1989).

Deleuze, Gilles, 'The Exhausted' in *Essays Critical and Clinical* (Minneapolis, MN: Minnesota University Press, 1998).

Deleuze, Gilles, *Desert Islands and Other Texts: 1953–1974* (New York: Semiotext(e), 2004).

Deleuze, Gilles, *Cinema 1: The Movement-Image* (London and New York: Continuum, 2005).

Deleuze, Gilles, *Nietzsche and Philosophy* (London: Continuum, 2006).

Deleuze, Gilles and Feliz Guattari, *A Thousand Plateaus: Capitalism and Schizophrenia* (London: Athlone Press, 1988).

Derrida, Jacques, *The Politics of Friendship* (London: Verso, 2006).

Dillon, Michael, *Politics of Security* (London and New York: Routledge, 1996).

Dillon, Michael and Julian Reid, *The Liberal Way of War: Killing to Make Life Live* (London: Routledge, 2009).

Duffield, Mark, *Development, Security and Unending War: Governing the World of Peoples* (Cambridge: Polity Press, 2007).

Edkins, Jenny, *Trauma; Memory, Trauma and World Politics: Reflections on the Relationship between Past and Present*, 2nd edn (Basingstoke: Palgrave Macmillan, 2010).

Esposito, Roberto, *Immunitas: The Protection and Negation of Life* (Cambridge: Polity, 2011).

Evans, Brad, *Liberal Terror* (Cambridge: Polity Press, 2013).

Evans, Brad and Mark Duffield, 'Bio-Spheric Security: How the Merger between Development, Security and the Environment [Desenex] is Retrenching Fortress Europe'. In P. Burgess and S. Gutwirth (eds) *A Threat Against Europe? Security, Migration and Integration* (Brussels: VUB Press, 2011).

Evans, Brad and Julian Reid, *Deleuze and Fascism: Security, War, Aesthetics* (London: Routledge, 2013).

Foucault, Michel, *The Order of Things: An Archaeology of Human Sciences* (New York: Pantheon, 1971).

Foucault, Michel, 'On the Genealogy of Ethics'. In *The Essential Works of Michel Foucault, vol. 1: Ethics: Subjectivity and Truth*, ed. Paul Rabinow (New York: The New Press, 1997).

Foucault, Michel, *Security, Territory, Population: Lectures at the Collège de France 1977–78* (Basingstoke and New York: Palgrave, 2007).

Foucault, Michel, *The Birth of Biopolitics: Lectures at the Collège de France 1978–1979* (Basingstoke and New York: Palgrave, 2008).

Foucault, Michel, *The Courage of the Truth* (trans. Graham Burchell) (New York: Palgrave Macmillan, 2011).

Freire, Paulo, *Pedagogy of the Oppressed* (Harmondsworth: Penguin, 1996).

Gardner Coates, Victoria C., Kenneth Lapatin and Jon L. Seydl, *The Last Days of Pompeii: Decadence, Apocalypse, Resurrection* (Los Angeles, CA: J. Paul Getty Museum, 2012).

Gavrilets, Sergey, *Fitness Landscapes and the Origin of Species* (Princeton, NJ: Princeton University Press, 2004).

Girard, René, *Violence and the Sacred* (London: Continuum, 2005).

Giroux, Henry A., *Stormy Weather: Katrina and the Politics of Disposability* (Boulder, CO: Paradigm, 2006).

Giroux, Henry A., *Twilight of the Social* (Boulder, CO: Paradigm, 2012).

Giroux, Henry A., *America's Education Deficit and the War on Youth* (Boulder, CO: Paradigm Publishers, 2013).

Graham, Stephen (ed.) *Disrupted Cities: When Infrastructure Fails* (Abingdon: Routledge, 2010).

Hall, John R., *Apocalypse: From Antiquity to the Empire of Modernity* (Cambridge: Polity Press, 2009).

Hansen, James, *Storms of my Grandchildren: The Truth about the Coming Climate Catastrophe and Our Last Chance to Save Humanity* (London: Bloomsbury, 2009).

Haraway, Donna, *Simians, Cyborgs and Women: The Reinvention of Nature* (New York: Routledge, 1991).

Hayles, N. Katherine, *How We Became Posthuman: Virtual Bodies in Cybernetics, Literature, and Informatics* (Chicago, IL: University of Chicago Press, 1999).

Heidegger, Martin, *The Question Concerning Technology and Other Essays* (New York: Harper & Row, 1977).

Holloway, John, *Change the World Without Taking Power: The Meaning of Revolution Today* (London: Pluto Press, 2005).

Iampolski, Mikhail, *The Memory of Tiresias: Intertextuality and Film* (Berkeley, CA: University of California Press, 1998).

Intergovernmental Panel on Climate Change (IPCC), *Managing the Risks of Extreme Events and Disasters to Advance Climate Change Adaptation* (Cambridge: Cambridge University Press, 2012).

Jameson, Fredric, *The Geopolitical Aesthetic: Cinema and Space in the World System* (Bloomington, IN: Indiana University Press, 1992).

Kauffman, Stuart A., *Investigations* (Oxford: Oxford University Press, 2000).

Kay, Lily E., *The Molecular Vision of Life: Caltech, The Rockefeller Foundation, and the Rise of New Biology* (Oxford: Oxford University Press, 1993).

Kay, Lily E., *Who Wrote the Book of Life?: A History of the Genetic Code* (Stanford, CA: Stanford University Press, 2000).

Kermode, Frank, *The Sense of an Ending: Studies in the Theory of Fiction*, 2nd edn (Oxford: Oxford University Press, 2003).

Klein, Naomi, *The Shock Doctrine: The Rise of Disaster Capitalism* (London: Allen Lane, 2007).

Krugman, Paul, *The Self-Organizing Economy* (Oxford: Basil Blackwell, 1996).

Laplanche, Jean and Jean-Bertrand Pontalis, *The Language of Psychoanalysis* (London: Karnac Books, 1988).

Levi, Primo, *The Drowned and the Saved* (New York: Random House, 1989).

Leys, Ruth, *Trauma: A Genealogy* (Chicago, IL: University of Chicago Press, 2000).

Lingis, Alphonso, *The Community of Those Who Have Nothing in Common* (Indianapolis, IN: Indianapolis University Press, 1994).

Martineau, Sheila, *Rewriting Resilience: A Critical Discourse Analysis of Childhood Resilience and the Politics of Teaching Resilience to 'Kids at Risk'* (Vancouver: University of British Columbia Press, 1999).

Michaels, Patrick J., *Meltdown: The Predictable Distortion of Global Warming by Scientists, Politicians, and the Media* (Washington, DC: Cato Institute, 2004).

Miccoli, Anthony, *Posthuman Suffering and the Technological Embrace* (Lanham, MD: Lexington Books, 2010).

Mondzain, Marie-José, *Image, Icon, Economy: The Byzantine Origins of the Contemporary Imaginary* (Stanford, CA: Stanford University Press, 2005).

Moore, Barrington, *Injustice: The Social Bases of Obedience and Revolt* (White Plains, NY: M.E. Sharpe, 1978).

Neiman, Susan, *Evil in Modern Thought: An Alternative History* (Princeton, NJ: Princeton University Press, 2002).

Neocleous, Mark, *Critique of Security* (Edinburgh, Edinburgh University Press, 2008).

Nicolis, Gregoire and Ilya Prigogine, *Exploring Complexity: An Introduction* (New York: W.H. Freeman, 1989).

Nietzsche, Friedrich, *The Will To Power* (New York: Vintage, 1968).

Nietzsche, Friedrich, *The Gay Science* (New York: Vintage Books, 1974).

Nietzsche, Friedrich, *On the Genealogy of Morals* (Indianapolis, IN: Hackett Publishing, 1998).

Nietzsche, Friedrich, 'Ecce Homo'. In K. Ansell-Pearson and D. Large (eds) *The Nietzsche Reader* (Oxford: Blackwell Publishers, 2006).

Nietzsche, Friedrich, *On Truth and Lies in a Nonmoral Sense* (Chicago, IL: Aristeus Books, 2012).

O'Brien, Robert, Anne Marie Goetz, Jan Aart Scholte and Marc Williams, *Contesting Global Governance: Multilateral Economic Institutions and Social Movements* (Cambridge: Cambridge University Press, 2000).

Peters, Tom, *Thriving on Chaos: Handbook for a Management Revolution* (New York: Knopf, 1987).

Prager, Jeffrey, *Presenting The Past: Psychoanalysis and the Sociology of Remembering* (Cambridge, MA: Harvard University Press, 1998).

Pucci, Pietro, *Oedipus and the Fabrication of the Father: Oedipus Tyrannus in Modern Criticism and Philosophy* (Baltimore, MD: The Johns Hopkins University Press, 1992).

Rancière, Jacques, *The Emancipated Spectator* (London: Verso, 2009).

Ravetto, Kriss, *The Unmaking of Fascist Aesthetics* (Minneapolis, MN: University of Minnesota Press, 2001).

Reid, Julian, *The Biopolitics of the War on Terror: Life Struggles, Liberal Modernity and the Defence of Logistical Societies* (Manchester: Manchester University Press, 2006).

Rosenau, James N., 'Citizenship in a Changing Global Order'. In James N. Rosenau and Ernst Otto Czempiel, *Governance Without Government: Order and Change in World Politics* (Cambridge: Cambridge University Press, 1992).

Rosenau, James N., 'Governance and Democracy in a Globalization World'. In Daniele Archibugi, David Held and Martin Kohler (eds) *Re-imagining Political Community: Studies in Cosmopolitan Democracy* (Stanford, CA: Stanford University Press, 1998).

Rosenau, James N., 'Information Technologies and the Skills, Networks and Structures that Sustain World Affairs'. In James N. Rosenau and J.P. Singh (eds) *Information*

Technologies and Global Politics: The Changing Scope of Power and Governance (Albany, NY: SUNY Press, 2002).

Rosenau, James N., *People Count! Networked Individuals in Global Politics* (Boulder, CO: Paradigm Press, 2008).

Rusin, Nicolai and Liia Flit, *Man Versus Climate* (Moscow: Peace Publishers, 1966).

Scarry, Elaine, *The Body in Pain: The Making and Unmaking of the World* (Oxford: Oxford University Press, 1995).

Siebert, Al, *The Resiliency Advantage: Master Change, Thrive under Pressure, Bounce Back from Setbacks* (San Francisco, CA: Berrett-Koehler, 2005).

Sloterdijk, Peter, *Thinker on Stage: Nietzsche's Materialism* (Minneapolis, MN: University of Minnesota Press, 1989).

Sloterdijk, Peter, *Spheres II: Globes* (New York: Semiotext(e), 2010).

Sloterdijk, Peter, *Neither Sun Nor Death* (Cambridge, MA: MIT Press, 2011).

Sloterdijk, Peter, *Rage and Time* (New York: Columbia University Press, 2012).

Sophocles, *Oedipus Rex* (Cambridge: Cambridge University Press, 2006).

Stern, Nicholas, *The Stern Review: The Economics of Climate Change* (Cambridge: Cambridge University Press, 2007).

Taubes, Jacob, *Occidental Eschatology* (Stanford, CA: Stanford University Press, 2009).

Taylor, Astra, *Examined Life* (New York: Zeitgeist Productions, 2008).

Thrift, Nigel, 'Peter Sloterdijk and the Philosopher's Stone'. In Stuart Elden (ed.) *Sloterdijk Now* (Cambridge: Polity Press, 2012).

United Nations Development Programme, United Nations Environment Programme, World Bank and World Resources Institute, *World Resources 2008: Roots of Resilience – Growing the Wealth of the Poor* (Washington, DC: World Resources Institute, 2008).

United Nations Environment Programme (UNEP), *Exploring the Links: Human Well-Being, Poverty and Ecosystem Services* (Nairobi: UN Publications, 2004).

United Nations Office for Disaster Risk Reduction (UN/ISDR), *Living with Risk: A Global Review of Disaster Reduction Initiatives* (Geneva: United Nations, 2004).

Virilio, Paul, *The Futurism of the Instant* (Cambridge: Polity Press, 2010).

Virilio, Paul, *Grey Ecology* (New York: Atropos Press, 2011).

Wang, Margaret C., Geneva D. Haertel and Herbert J. Walberg, 'Educational Resilience in Inner Cities'. In Margaret C. Wang and Edmund W. Gordon (eds) *Educational Resilience in Inner-City America: Challenges and Prospects* (Mahwah, NJ: Lawrence Erlbaum, 1994).

Weisman, Alan, *The World Without Us* (New York: Picador, 2007).

Wiener, Norbert, *The Human Use of Human Beings: Cybernetics and Society* (Boston, MA: Da Capo Press, 1954).

Wilde, Oscar, *De Profundis* (Ware, Hertfordshire: Wordsworth Classics, 1999).

Williams, Evan Calder, *Combined and Uneven Apocalypse* (Winchester and Washington: Zero Books, 2011).

World Commission on Environment and Development (WCED), *Our Common Future* (Oxford: Oxford University Press, 1987).

Žižek, Slavoj, *Living in the End Times* (London: Verso, 2011).

Index

.